DR FRANCIS PRYOR has spent over thirty years studying the prehistory of the Fens. A former presient of the Council for British Archaeology, he has excavated sites as diverse as Bronze Age farms, field systems and entire Iron Age villages. He appears frequently on the Channel 4 series *Time Team* and is the author of *Seahenge*, as well as the celebrated *Britain* series – *Britain BC*, *Britain AD* and *Britain in the Middle Ages*.

From the reviews of *The Birth of Modern Britain*:

'Hugely enjoyable … You will learn a lot from it – and one of the things is how much work has gone into unearthing all this stuff. You will certainly never look at the A5 in the same way again'
Daily Telegraph

'No one person has previously attempted such a journey into Britain's entire archaeological past, and this book brings the series to a successful – and refreshingly jargon-free – conclusion'
BBC History Magazine

'[Pryor's] enthusiasm for getting his hands dirty is infectious'
Sunday Times

'Much to admire … fascinating details'
Guardian

'Immensely fascinating case histories … wonderful pages on clay, pottery and bone china … heartening'
Daily Express

By the same author

SEAHENGE
BRITAIN BC
BRITAIN AD
BRITAIN IN THE MIDDLE AGES

THE BIRTH OF
MODERN BRITAIN

A Journey through Britain's Remarkable
Recent Archaeology,
1550 to the Present

FRANCIS PRYOR

Harper
Press

Harper*Press*
An imprint of HarperCollins*Publishers*
77–85 Fulham Palace Road
Hammersmith
London W6 8JB

This Harper*Press* paperback edition published 2012

1

First published by Harper*Press* in 2011

A catalogue record for this book
is available from the British Library

ISBN 978-0-00-729911-9

Diagrams by Rex Nicholls

Typeset in Minion with Photina display by
G&M Designs Limited, Raunds, Northamptonshire

Printed and bound in Great Britain by
Clays Ltd, St Ives plc

MIX
Paper from
responsible sources

FSC™ C007454

For my step-mother, Barbara Jean Pryor,
for her quiet support and encouragement.

CONTENTS

PLATES

Unless otherwise stated, all photographs are © Francis Pryor

Model farm, Holkham Park, Norfolk

A view across the lake towards the Pantheon (1754) at Stourhead, Wiltshire

The restored grotto at Painshill, Surrey

A view along the first turnpike road (1663) in the village of Caxton, Cambridgeshire

The cast-iron Waterloo Bridge which carries the great Holyhead Road across the Afon Conwy at Betws-y-Coed

A paired toll house and weighbridge house on either side of the A5 at Ty Isaf

Milestone No. 73

Sunburst gates at the southern end of the Menai Strait suspension bridge

The brickwork façade of the southern entrance to the Blisworth Tunnel, Northamptonshire

A view along the bed of the tramway that led from the valley up to the navvy camp on Risehill, North Yorkshire

Grooves left by drill-holes to pack an explosive charge

Bridge over the A43, where it is crossed by the M1 at Junction 15, near Northampton

The River Porter in Whitely Woods, Sheffield

York Gate

The Paragon

A view of the Forth Rail Bridge

A view of housing in Swindon, Wiltshire

A tipping-cistern toilet block at Hungate, York

The basement floor of so-called 'cellar houses'

The Stanley Mills, near Perth, from the River Tay

TEXT ILLUSTRATIONS AND MAPS

While every effort has been made to trace the owners of copyright material reproduced herein, the publishers would like to apologise for any omissions and would be pleased to incorporate missing acknowledgements in future editions.

ACKNOWLEDGEMENTS

FROM THE MOMENT I began this four-volume archaeological history of Britain I knew that, when I ventured outside my own field of expertise in later prehistory, I would have to rely on the cooperation and goodwill of many colleagues. But instead of encountering silence or, worse, resentment, I was astonished by the way medievalist scholars took me under their wing and made the task of writing *Britain AD* and *Britain in the Middle Ages* such a pleasure. For the present work I have had to draw on the knowledge of many post-medievalists and yet I have still to detect any impatience with my ceaseless enquiries. Two people who have had to bear the brunt of my curiosity are Drs Marilyn Palmer and Audrey Horning, both colleagues of mine in the School of Archaeology and Ancient History at the University of Leicester. They gave me informal seminars, sometimes even without the benefit of lunch, which helped me turn my face in what I hope has proved the right direction. Thank you both: my gratitude knows no bounds.

Michael Douglas, series editor at *Time Team*, shares my interest in the archaeology of more recent periods and played a major part in arranging the excavation of the Risehill navvy camp, North Yorkshire, and the Norman Cross prisoner-of-war Depot, Peterborough. While in Yorkshire, Bill Bevan was a great source of references and advice. At Norman Cross, Ben Robinson, the Peterborough City Archaeologist, was as ever amiable and authoritative, and Dr Henry Chapman, the *Time Team* surveyor, helped me acquire plans of the Norman Cross Depot site in advance of the full publication, which was scheduled to appear after my own manuscript's deadline. Dr Mike Nevell has been a splendid guide to the world of industrial archaeology. Neil (now Sir Neil) Cossons and David Crossley were a great help when I was first getting interested in industrial archaeology and we all sat on the Ancient Monuments Advisory Committee of English Heritage. Happy days! Another more than helpful friend, who goes back a long time xvi · THE BIRTH OF MODERN BRITAIN

with me, is David Cranstone. David started life as a prehistorian with me at Fengate and is now a leading authority on industrial archaeology in general and salt mines in particular. He kindly gave me several useful hints and references.

At HarperCollins I am grateful to Martin Redfern, who took on Richard Johnson's mantle, and to Ben Buchan, whose editorial comments have greatly strengthened this book. I am also deeply indebted to Rex Nicholls who drew the line drawings and to the book's designer. Special thanks too to Sophie Goulden, Ben Buchan, Richard Collins and Geraldine Beare.

I am also grateful to family members who provided me with unexpected information on various topics: Roderick Luis (Crimean War huts) and Nigel Smith (navvies in the North Pennines). Nigel, a bookseller by profession, found me articles and out-of-print books and his elder sister, my wife Maisie, organised my photographic expeditions and managed to sort out the mystery of the two Causey Arches – an example, incidentally, of how the internet can waste time and lead one astray. Heaven alone knows how she has put up with my moods during this four-book marathon. Finally, and despite the best efforts of all of the above, any errors that remain are mine alone.

DATES AND PERIODS

Period	Dates	Main Events	Notes
Early modern	1550–1750		Sometimes referred to as post-medieval
Modern	1750–present		
Tudor	1485–1603	Dissolution of the Monasteries (1536–8)	(in England)
Stuart	1603–1714	English Civil War (1642–51); Glorious Revolution (1688)	(in England)
Georgian	1714–1837	Act of Union with Scotland (1707); Great Reform Act (1832)	
Victorian	1837–1901	Irish Famine (1845–51); Repeal of Corn Laws (1846); Crimean War (1853–6); Boer War (1899–1902)*	
Edwardian	1901–14	Edward VII (1901–10)	
Early twentieth century	1900–39	First World War (1914–18); Wall Street Crash (1929)	
Later twentieth century	1939–2000	Second World War (1939–45); Cold War (1946–89)	
Post-war	1945–60	Attlee government (1945–51)	
European	1973–present	Britain enters the EEC (1973); Thatcher government (1979–90)	

* Strictly speaking this should refer to the Second Boer War. The First Boer War (1880–81) was more a skirmish, which the Boers won.

Introduction

Archaeology and Modern Times

BEFORE I GET involved with the 'meat' of the book I'd first like to say a few words on the nature of modern historical archaeology in Britain, which is probably the fastest growing branch of the subject. When I started my professional life my team worked with the Peterborough New Town Development Corporation clearing land for factory building. That was back in the early 1970s, long before television programmes like *Time Team* had managed to convince the public at large that there was such a thing as British archaeology. Too often we would arrive at a site and announce that we'd come to survey and excavate, only to be greeted with incredulous stares and humorous comments to the effect that surely we would be better employed in Egypt, Greece or Italy. Then, when I had shown the builders (and anyone else who happened to be hanging around on site) the air photographs with the ring-ditch evidence for Bronze Age barrows and explained that these were as old as Stonehenge – which in turn was much older than the Parthenon or King Tutankhamun – the scoffing would cease and most of my audience would become our enthusiastic supporters. Sometimes their enthusiasm was such that it was hard to get much work done.

But just suppose for one moment that we had arrived on site and announced that we were planning to survey and excavate the ramshackle nineteenth- and early twentieth-century farm buildings that were then such a common feature of the city's eastern fringes. In actual fact, those buildings were rather important, as the Fens, which were drained in the seventeenth century, were once a major producer of food for Britain's rapidly expanding urban populations. But I very much doubt whether we would have found it quite so straightforward to silence the scoffing, because even in the better-informed times we currently live in, many people suppose that the terms 'archaeology' and 'modern' are mutually exclusive.

It's not unreasonable to assume that a fair amount of time needs to pass before archaeological research becomes possible, let alone desirable, or informative. But, actually, this view is wrong because archaeology is not just about excavation; it's an approach to the past that can be equally relevant when applied to something as young as a month, or as old as a millennium. Just imagine, for example, that an entire townscape is bombed flat, as happened in Coventry or in large parts of east London. In those cases archaeology is almost the only way to resurrect in any meaningful way what enemy aeroplanes destroyed. Under such circumstances, old pictures and sketches can, of course, be useful, but accurate measurements, made then and there on the ground, will be needed if reconstruction is to be attempted. In postwar years town centre developers did as much damage to Britain's historic towns and cities as Nazi aircraft, and almost as quickly. Today this would not happen, but in the fifties and sixties pre-development surveys rarely took place. So such peacetime destruction was often horribly complete.

The simple distinction between archaeology (dirt) and history (documents), although never so clear cut, begins to break down in post-medieval times when documents of every conceivable sort become near-ubiquitous: everything from newspapers to till-roll receipts. And much of this material can find its way into the archaeological record by way of local private archives that can survive for years in abandoned offices and dusty attics. Sometimes, however, archaeologists can reveal new documentary sources that the conventional wisdom believed had long been destroyed. It was the professional and amateur archaeologists working as part of the Council for British Archaeology's Defence of Britain Project who discovered the paperwork drawn up in 1940 that ordered and duly paid for the building of the many concrete and brick pillboxes and other defences that can still be found in their thousands in unexpected nooks and crannies across Britain.

The Defence of Britain project shows how very important it is to keep archaeological research and survey up to date, because when it took place (1995–2002) huge numbers of Second World War defences were being destroyed as 'eyesores' – their historical importance notwithstanding. Some 20,000 records of military installations were made during those seven years and the most important of these were then given legal protection as Scheduled Ancient Monuments.[1] Without that project it would have been impossible to have drawn up a list of sites worthy of such protection. The same has since been achieved for Cold War sites. Would that something similar had been done before Dr Beeching wielded the axe that amputated the limbs of a once great railway network, whose Victorian stations, bridges and signal boxes now stand mouldering, while local people, stuck in traffic jams, have cause to regret their passing. The past is no less important just because it is recent. The real danger is that we take it for granted, like those wartime structures, because then we won't realise that it has gone until it's too late.

Of course, it's very easy to take things for granted. Everyone today, even the most rich and powerful people in the land, has to cope with repetition: the daily drive to work or the royal flight; the walk to and from the station; regular trips to the parents-in-law, etc, etc. Each time we take a familiar journey we inevitably attach less and less value to the buildings and places we pass by. Whether we like it or not, familiarity does indeed breed indifference, if not actual contempt. Most people would agree that it is impossible to retain one's enthusiasm for a building at quite the same level as when one first encountered it. But it doesn't always have to be like this. In my experience archaeology can help keep one's surroundings fresh and lively, simply by seeking out the links that tie the different parts of a particular place together.

Let's take the case of a provincial town or city where we have a railway station built in the late 1860s, followed by relatively humble housing developments nearby in the early 1870s. By the 1880s streets of somewhat grander, mostly middle-class, villas start to appear, at which point, too, a large red-brick mock-Gothic church was also constructed. In the mid-twentieth century the area became less fashionable as the middle classes moved to new suburbs on the fringes of town. The church was then converted to a sound-recording studio and a new mosque was built on land that had once been railway marshalling yards. I won't go on, but it's the tales of development, setback and change, only slightly hidden away in the layout of our towns and villages, that still have the power to excite me. But for how long will it be possible to reconstruct such stories from dry bricks and mortar? Increasingly the deep foundations of modern developments devour all before them, leaving nothing in their wake for future archaeologists to puzzle over, admire and enjoy.

So those of us with an eye for such things are already looking around at our surroundings, wondering what will come under threat next. And here we are faced with the dilemma that must confront anyone whose job is to predict such things, because almost by definition people in the future will decide that we got it wrong: that it was a mistake to Schedule* multi-storey car parks when it was shopping malls that were then rapidly redeveloped and promptly vanished.

So the answer is probably to cast the net wider and protect whole areas of towns or rural landscapes, rather than individual sites or buildings, if our attempts to second-guess posterity are to have any chance of success.[2] This is already being done in the so-called Conservation Areas and Historic Cores of certain historically important towns and cities; furthermore, designated Areas of Outstanding Natural Beauty can help to protect well-known tracts of rural landscape. But inevitably such designations must favour the chocolate-box view of landscape and townscape. I can't see anyone choosing to put forward the flat, treeless landscape where I have chosen to live, even though I personally regard it as life-enhancing and profoundly beautiful. The same could be said for many suburbs or industrial conurbations, which may well be recognised as important in two hundred years' time. The other problem, of course, is that such protection can then put a break (it's often termed 'planning blight') on commercial redevelopment and the area then starts to slip into economic decline – a process that can also be 'assisted' by those with vested interests.

My approach to archaeology has always been based around the landscape and by that I mean the physical setting for a particular site or monument. So it makes no sense to try to understand the mysteries of Stonehenge without thinking about why it was placed on Salisbury Plain, and why it is surrounded by hundreds of burial mounds and

---

* I use the terms Scheduled (for ancient sites) and Listed (for standing buildings) to denote that these places are protected by Act of Parliament.

other sacred places, some of which are actually much earlier than the famous Stones themselves. By the same token we can soon come to understand why Manchester and the towns of north-west England became an early centre of the textile trade when we know that this area had been producing woollen fabrics since the later Middle Ages, so was able to take advantage of, or 'add value' to, the rapidly developing trade in cotton between Liverpool and the southern United States. So if we are to understand the context of the nineteenth-century cotton industry in the North West, its economic setting should also include Louisiana and Georgia, and latterly the effects of the American Civil War on the supply of raw materials. Similarly, it would be impossible even to think about the hugely important ceramic industry of the area around Stoke-on-Trent without also considering where these millions of plates, mugs, teapots, cups and saucers were traded.

In prehistory stone axes and bronze implements could be traded over long distances – three to four hundred miles was not uncommon – but the amounts were still small. By the eighteenth and nineteenth centuries, trade had become global and the quantities involved were huge: thus pottery exports were measured in tons and improvements in ship capacity meant that distance had almost become irrelevant. So archaeology and those who practise it have had to develop new techniques and approaches if they are to throw genuinely new light on the complexities of the historic past. There is close collaboration, for example, between American archaeologists working on colonial-era settlements in Virginia and New England, and their colleagues in the English Midlands, where many of the exported goods were manufactured. One might perhaps expect that the flow of information was entirely from east to west, but in actual fact the American sites have produced results that have caused considerable surprise in Britain. Archaeology has a wonderful ability to prove the best-based predictions wrong.

There is, of course, always a danger when considering the archaeology of the recent past to become overwhelmed with detail. As a prehistorian I routinely recover a large proportion of the surviving debris from, say, a Bronze Age settlement. That might amount to 5,000 pieces of flint, maybe 200 potsherds and 10,000 bone fragments – half of which could prove identifiable. But today the amount of rubbish being produced by even a small-sized town can rapidly fill huge landfill sites. In such instances the best one can hope to do is to sample what is being discarded and for several years a team of archaeologists in Arizona did just that: in the Garbage Project they sampled what the city of Tucson was discarding day by day.[3] But, again, it's all very well to sample, but what really matters are the problems you are trying to resolve when you come to analyse the samples. That is undoubtedly why today historical archaeologists have grown increasingly aware that the questions they are posing must be closely tied down and tightly defined. It is no longer regarded as sufficient simply to study, say, steam engines for their own sake, because such myopic attention to detail will only tell us more and more about less and less. Instead, a historical archaeologist might try to understand the social impact of steam power: why did it become so significant and what were the effects its adoption had on the lives of people, not just in the factories where the engines were built, but in the towns and villages where the new, mass-produced goods it helped to produce were sold?

It has been said many times that archaeology is a very broad church and this is particularly true for the post-medieval period.[4] Some specialists have arrived in historical archaeology from their studies of the later Middle Ages; others, often excavators, have grown interested in those upper layers that in the past were given only passing attention on the way down to the supposedly more interesting ancient deposits closer to the bottom of the trench. Many have joined the ranks through more specialist research interests in, say, pottery, or churches. Some have come from outside archaeology altogether – and here I would include those many industrial archaeologists who have come to the subject through their concerns for old mines, factories, vehicles or machinery and the urgent need to protect and preserve them.

As time passes it would seem that the 'glue' that will bind these different strands together will be social. In other words, how did people in the past react to a particular stimulus, be it a new chapel, coal mine, crop rotation or steam engine? That, surely, is the key question. Because when all is said and done, chapels, mines, farming methods and machines are of little interest in themselves. Like, dare I say it, flint tools and Bronze Age weapons, they only come alive when they can be related to society and to people.

Earlier I mentioned the distinction between the sources of information drawn upon by archaeologists and historians, namely artefacts and documents. And here I must also admit that there has been a tendency among archaeologists to regard their information, perhaps because it is so very 'bottom-up' and derived from the ground, as somehow more reliable than written accounts, which we all know can be distorted in favour of a particular opinion. As a prehistorian I have the enormous luxury – actually it's a responsibility, too – of working with data whose analysis cannot be challenged by documentary sources, simply because writing didn't exist at the time. This makes it much harder to contest my conclusions, but that doesn't make them more reliable. So I still think it important to emphasise that it is just as easy to be misled by a spread of coal and clinker in what might once have been an engine room, as by the letters written by an eighteenth-century ironmaster to his bankers. There is nothing in the 'bottom-up' nature of archaeological observations that makes them necessarily more truthful than conventional historical sources. Both are different, that's all. It goes without saying that both, too, need to be treated with caution and care. I think one reason why historical archaeology is so exciting is the creative tension that appears at the moment, often late in the life of a project, when the written record is set against that from the ground. This is often when a new revelation suddenly becomes apparent.

One might suppose that the very abundant documentary records of the historical period mean that less attention need be paid, for example, to science. But in actual fact many written records don't address what people thought obvious at the time. So a factory manager doesn't describe all the details of a process when he purchases a new machine. He just goes ahead and orders one. This means that we must still employ some remarkably sophisticated techniques of scientific analysis if we are to understand what precisely was being manufactured and how it was done. Often, as we will see in Chapter 5 (when we examine the Moffat Upper Steam Forge, near Airdrie), this can be achieved through the careful analysis of material preserved on the floors of long-abandoned workshops. In my experience it's not always a straightforward matter to distinguish between these industrial deposits and the floors themselves. Again, the scientists in the laboratory can suggest which was what.[5]

By far and away the most productive approach to the historical past is collaborative: thorough excavation and survey combined with detailed documentary research. Certainly when it comes to the study of topics such as the trade in pottery or, indeed, in slaves, bills of lading, receipts and invoices can throw much-needed light on the thousands of potsherds and clay pipe stems found around the excavated sites of the period. I would go so far as to say that excavation without documentary research would almost certainly prove useless – or, worse, it could do serious damage to an important site.

Many people have heard about industrial archaeology and I quite frequently get asked about it. Most want to know what it is and when it got going. In fact, it has not been around for very long at all. The first widely accepted textbook on the subject traces it back to an article in the *Amateur Historian* for 1955.[6] The origins of industrial archaeology were diverse. They included a few academic historians and archaeologists with an interest in historical archaeology, but the majority were part-time enthusiasts, some of them active in, or recently retired from, engineering and industry, who were worried that so much evidence for the recent past was being needlessly destroyed by the rapid reconstruction of Britain in the early post-war decades. These enthusiasts covered a huge range of interests, ranging from railways to shipping, mining, road transport and heavy industry. In most instances their enthusiasm was centred on a particular site, usually, but not always, somewhere near where they lived or worked: towns like Coalbrookdale, even entire railways (such as the Great Western). Keen hard-working volunteers, often travelling long distances, helped to record and restore some of the most remote industrial monuments in Britain, such as the abandoned mines of Cornwall or Derbyshire. Inevitably, too, the emphasis tended to be on machines and mechanisms – where much of their expertise, often based on practical experience, lay. Far less attention was paid to the lives of the people who built, maintained and used these things. The machines also tended to be seen as objects in their own right, without, as we have seen, much attempt being made to reconstruct their social setting.

It's worth noting here that even the best known of the abandoned monuments to Britain's industrial past were slow to be protected under the Ancient Monuments Protection Act of 1882. Even the great iron bridge of Ironbridge, Shropshire, was not given statutory protection by Scheduling until 1934 and was only taken into Guardianship (i.e. public ownership, display and administration) as late as 1975. The following year the iron-making furnace at Coalbrookdale was at last Scheduled, almost exactly two hundred years after its final major rebuilding by the great ironmaster Abraham Darby in 1777. In retrospect the archaeological establishment was extraordinarily slow to protect the remains of the Industrial Revolution, and this despite one of the greatest acts of official Philistinism in the twentieth century.

The great Doric portico, universally known as the Euston Arch, was demolished in 1962 by the Transport Commission who believed it stood in the way of commercial success. I can remember standing beneath its towering columns and staring up at the classical entablature (not that I knew the word, of course) high above my head. And I can remember wondering why there wasn't a building directly behind it, as there was at, say, the British Museum. In my child's mind I couldn't grasp, any more than could the bureaucrats and politicians of the 1960s, that the great portico heralded the world's first main line between major cities. It was more than a mere symbol: it was a metaphor for what was to follow. And we tore it down.

There was massive public outcry at what is still seen as an act of wilful destruction, and this despite letters to the then Prime Minister, Harold Macmillan. The anger was not just that a fine building of 1835 was being unnecessarily destroyed, but it was a building that had come to symbolise the confidence of the Railway Age and ultimately Britain's role in the Industrial Revolution.[7] It was built by Philip Hardwick to be a triumphal entrance to the London to Birmingham railway and it was intended to impress – which undoubtedly it did.

The fight to prevent the powers that be from destroying the Euston Arch drew everyone involved in industrial archaeology together. Right across Britain, new societies were established involving academics, students, amateurs and professionals. As a result the support for this form of archaeology is probably more broadly based than any other branch of the subject. At first this diversity was seen by many in the academic world as a weakness. But today we generally view such things rather differently; indeed, industrial archaeology is becoming one of the more intellectually rigorous branches of the discipline, yet one which benefits greatly from the hands-on approach of its many part-time helpers. By now the bias in favour of machines over people has largely been addressed and quite soon the adjective 'industrial' will slip from general use.

Today industrial archaeology is seen as a branch of post-medieval archaeology which was the last of the major period societies to come into existence. The Prehistoric Society was the first (1935) and the Society for Medieval Archaeology appeared in the post-war years (1957). Just ten years after that (and five years after the destruction of the Euston Arch), in 1967, the Society for Post-Medieval Archaeology was founded. Its journal, *Post-Medieval Archaeology*, is still the bible for anyone with a serious interest in the period.

My own enthusiasm for industrial archaeology goes back some time and owes much to some remarkable people. Ever since I was a child and enjoyed making things with Meccano kits I have admired engineers. I suppose like most boys I grew up almost worshipping men like Brunel and Telford and I can well remember my maternal grand-mother, née Nora Parsons, telling me wonderful stories about our rela-tive Sir Charles Parsons as he steered his *Turbinia* (built in 1897), the first steam-turbine-powered vessel and then by far and away the fastest ship afloat, through the great dreadnoughts at the famous display of British naval might at Spithead. I loved the way he cocked a snook at the naval establishment who were then obliged to commission a turbine-powered vessel from his yard.

One of the first real live engineers to cross my path was a remark-able and very eccentric gentleman who was a distant relative, an old friend of the family and my godfather. He was a lovely man, but a hopeless godfather, at least as far as God was concerned. His name was Julian Turnbull. I first came across him when I was about ten. At the time he worked for the Iraq Petroleum Company, where he specialised in putting out desert oil rig fires, with explosives. Today he would be described as partially sighted and wore glasses with extraordinarily thick lenses. Even then I remember thinking that these must have inhibited his work in the blowing sands of Arabia.

He and his wife Dorothy lived in a tiny bungalow in Barnet and I recall my first visit to the shed at the bottom of his garden as clearly as my first step into the great nave of Ely Cathedral. It was impeccably organised, with spanners arranged in order of size, their outlines painted in black against a white background, doubtless to help his failing sight return them to their correct position. But the most remarkable feature of this quite small (maybe 15 x 8 feet) shed was his collection of screwdrivers, which in those days were all wooden-handled. It was vast and must have included hundreds – no, thousands – of examples which ranged from something shovel-sized, used by marine engineers, to a series of minute watchmakers' tools. The largest was about six foot long and next to it was one a bit smaller and a bit smaller, and so on and so on, until the hut walls had been encircled two or three times. I adored those screwdrivers.

In the middle of the hut was an old Atco lawnmower which Julian had converted to steam power, using the case of a wartime howitzer shell he had found in the desert as a boiler. All the pipes and pistons were lovingly lagged with carefully coiled string. I only saw it operate once on his tiny lawn. But once was more than enough. It belched prodigious quantities of coal smoke and sparks while its almost blind operator blundered around behind it, spending more time wrestling with its handlebars on the weed-choked flowerbeds than the lawn. After ten minutes of mayhem I asked him whether it gave a good cut. He said he had no idea about that, but the hot coals seemed to keep grass growth to a minimum for several weeks. So I suppose it did work after a fashion.

The second person was very different but no less inspiring. Today he is very well known as one of the founding fathers of industrial archaeology and has more recently spent time running the Science Museum and English Heritage. Sir Neil Cossons first crossed my path when he came to give a lecture at the Royal Ontario Museum in Toronto, some time in the early 1970s, when I was an assistant curator there. His talk was on the industrial archaeology of Ironbridge and Coalbrookdale, where he was director of the Museum and the Trust which ran it. I found it inspiring and the following year I couldn't wait until I had taken all our students from our dig at Fengate, on the outskirts of Peterborough, right across England to see what he and his team had achieved.

As we walked around Ironbridge I realised for the first time just how much archaeology could appeal to the general public, but only if it was well displayed – a lesson I have never forgotten. Later I got to know Neil rather better when we sat on English Heritage's Ancient Monuments Advisory Committee and I always made a point of seeking him out when we did field trips to industrial sites. This was because he had the rare gift of knowing where to find some obscure feature, nook or cranny which would bring the place vividly to life.

I've talked about Ironbridge, the Euston Arch and the origins of post-medieval archaeology and I suppose I ought to cover such major events in the history of industrial archaeology at some length in this book. But, on the other hand, this isn't a textbook. I'm concerned here not with the history of industrial archaeology, but with current research and the direction in which it is heading. Having said that, I am also attempting to provide a balanced account of the period for the general reader.

I must also come clean and confess that many readers of my earlier books have laughed out loud when I suggested to them that I have been in search of balance. And their response: 'Balance? You? You're a born partisan and could no more achieve balance than fly.' Which wasn't quite the reply I had expected, but is possibly true, nonetheless. So in this instance I will drop such pretence and follow my instincts, which are to see what the current generation of scholars finds interesting and exciting. I make no apologies for this approach, which will generally concentrate on recent research, because that's where the new developments are happening.

And while on the subject of bias, I should also add that I plan to pay more attention to those aspects of the period which have tended to be ignored. A classic case in point is the very start of what some historians have referred to as the Agricultural Revolution. For me this is when modern Britain really begins to emerge. I like to think I can identify with those independent farmers who, freed from old ties of feudalism, set about creating, possibly for the first time in British history, a true market-based economy. These were extraordinary times, in many respects far more interesting than the Open Field farms of the Middle Ages which are usually taught in preference at school. And while on the subject of revolutions, of course, what about the big one that everyone still talks about and takes thoroughly for granted?

When, in 1884, the great historian Arnold Toynbee published a book of his Oxford course under the title *Lectures on the Industrial Revolution in England*, he probably didn't realise that the phrase would immediately stick and remain current into the twenty-first century; indeed, by that time television documentaries would proclaim it as proven fact. Some people were even able to tie it down with precision. One of the best post-war historical accounts, by Professor T. S. Ashton, *The Industrial Revolution, 1760–1830*, published by Oxford University Press in 1948, compresses the period into a truly revolutionary seventy years – or roughly three (short) generations.[8]

Anyone who has any experience of life outside academia will immediately realise that the idea of such a short period of revolutionary change is manifestly absurd. The world – and especially the world of work – simply doesn't behave like that.[9] All change requires time and things never happen with a single bang: there are always mistakes, false starts and heroic failures such as Brunel's broad gauge for the Great Western Railway and John Logie Baird's mechanically based system of television transmission of 1926. But the idea of the 'Industrial Revolution' has certainly fixed itself firmly in the popular imagination and I doubt whether it will ever go away completely.

I think there are at least three reasons for this. First and foremost it plays very well in Britain where most of the early innovations were developed, if not (like the blast furnace) actually invented. Second, for the revolution to have happened there had to be heroes to push it forward and, of course, everyone likes to admire a hero. One thinks of James Watt or Abraham Darby; it's even better if these larger-than-life industrial pioneers were also highly enlightened men, like Robert Owen, Josiah Wedgwood or Titus Salt. Finally, the very idea of revolutionary change is exciting: we can gasp at the sheer pace of the events, wring our hands at the misery of the workforce and then thrill to the mastery of their monumental achievements, many of which are still out there in the landscape.

But for most of the post-war decades nobody working in the academic study of industrial archaeology has believed in a literal Industrial Revolution. Laying aside the impossible pace, revolutions are meant to sweep all before them, like so many aristocrats fleeing France at the onset of the Terror. Factories were supposed to have swept away small hand workshops, but in fact these persisted – and successfully – well into the twentieth century. We can also appreciate that the great heroes were actually ordinary individuals, many of whom didn't so much invent from scratch as modify a pre-existing machine, like James Watt who adapted Newcomen's engine to make the steam drive the piston in both directions, thereby more than doubling its power.[10] Similarly, as we will see shortly, great ironmasters such as the various Abraham Darbys used their commercial and marketing expertise to develop good ideas often produced by others working in their foundries. When we examine industrial Britain in the eighteenth and nineteenth centuries we see that it has many similarities with the contemporary world of the agricultural 'Improvers' such as Coke of Norfolk or Jethro Tull. Both history and the British propensity to admire heroes have been very kind to these men, many of whom were indeed great but probably less than heroic.

The final nail in the coffin of the rapid revolution idea has been the realisation that, far from starting in 1760, many of the industries of the period were already fully mature by then, with histories extending back over two centuries or even more, as we will see in Chapter 5 when we look at the early cutlery trade along the rivers of Sheffield, or the latest excavations in and around Ironbridge. In most instances, too, the pattern of trade and industry that developed in specific areas in early post-medieval times determined the shape of what was to happen in the era of massive expansion which began in the later eighteenth century. This was the time when infrastructure – canals, waggonways and roads – was improving rapidly. It also saw the introduction of new technologies such as coal-powered steam. Perhaps most important of all, social circumstances were changing in a way that first allowed and then actually facilitated the growth of industry. We must not forget that the era of industrial expansion was as much about social change as technology.

One might suppose that industrial archaeologists would strive to retain an idea with such popular appeal as the Industrial Revolution, but for many decades it has been only too clear that the process of industrialisation had been extended and in many instances can be traced back to the Middle Ages. One way round this dilemma has been to write of an extended or 'long' Industrial Revolution.[11] Another has been to subdivide the extended Revolution into sub-Revolutions, such as a 'chemical' followed by an 'extractive' Revolution. In Chapter 6 I will discuss the merits of various 'ceramic revolutions'. These were indeed fast, and revolutionary in their effects. But on the ceramic market alone. They never transformed people's lives. My own feeling is that these sub-Revolutions are really clutching at straws and are helping to perpetuate the use of a term that ought to be dropped, for the simple reason that it is both inaccurate and misleading.

Students of industrial archaeology study the physical remains of early factories and workshops. They make extensive use of documents – if they are available – but perhaps most important of all they closely examine the archaeological evidence for contemporary housing, for both workers and management. Increasingly today industrial archaeologists are concerned with the long roots of industrialisation and its social consequences.[12] The trend towards social perspectives has affected the scope of archaeologists who are now more concerned with the wider relationship between housing, factories and workshops; the effect has been to look at industries within the landscape: how and why they arose in a particular area and the influences they had on a given region's population and economy.[13]

The concept of landscape is particularly significant within industrial archaeology, because it can be used to decide why certain sources of power were originally selected – coal and water are obvious examples. Landscapes can also help to explain why workers' housing, for example, was located in certain areas, but social considerations always seem to have remained pre-eminent. For example, the switch from waterwheels to steam power in the late eighteenth and early nineteenth centuries often necessitated twenty-four-hour shift working to cover the additional costs of coal. This in turn meant that housing had to be positioned close by the factory or mill, whether or not the terrain was actually suited to such a change. Sometimes underlying social motives could be less apparent. For example, many of the great mill owners aspired to emulate the landed gentry (which they often achieved with notable success) and to do this they built their new homes to resemble the great country houses of the nobility. Their houses were placed relatively nearby (to enable them to keep an eye on the shop), but the positioning carefully avoided any visual reminders of the mills and back-to-back housing that actually generated their wealth. But all rules have exceptions, as we will see when we come to look at where the great industrialists Robert Owen and his much-underrated father-in-law placed their houses in the model town they created at New Lanark.

I have always had an interest in what one might term modern archaeology and found I had more time for it after I had completed work on the report of my excavations at Flag Fen, a process that occupied me, night and day, for some five years in the mid-1990s. When that was finished I decided I really had to get out more, see the world and 'get a life'. But I still had a deep and abiding interest in the past and the story behind the creation of modern Britain. So I found my attention was gradually shifting forwards in time. I was, however, completely astonished by the sheer diversity I encountered when I delved more deeply into the archaeology of modern times. It wasn't just about the obvious themes: the growth of industry or agriculture and the development of towns. I also found that students and researchers were approaching even these topics from unexpected directions, often with surprising results. This was one of the other reasons I decided it was impossible to present a 'balanced' view of the archaeology of post-medieval times and have opted instead to examine projects and ideas that give one a new slant or perspective, if not a 'sideways' look at the period. Although there are a few excellent history books that cast their nets wider,[14] too often such accounts approach early modern Britain from the viewpoint of the great and the good. Theirs is a story of major politicians, generals, bishops, kings, queens and princes. Mine, I hope, will be about everyone else.

Finally, I must say a few words about the way this book has been organised. Readers of the three other volumes of this four-part archaeological history of Britain will have grown used to a straightforward chronological layout. In fact, I'll be quite honest and admit that, for the sake of consistency, I tried to organise this book in the same way. But sadly it just didn't work. I found I was attempting an impossibly difficult juggling act with too many balls in the air at one time. Put another way, too much was happening too quickly across too many different areas of life to sustain a coherent narrative, especially when I switched themes, at which point, like a bad television documentary, I was forced to summarise or recapitulate 'the story so far'. Anyhow, after a few weeks I abandoned the unequal struggle and decided instead to follow a series of general themes, chapter by chapter. These topics will, however, be approached chronologically. Of course an author is never a good judge of such things, but, fingers crossed, I think it works rather better than I once dared to hope.

CHAPTER ONE

Market Forces: Fields, Farming and the Rural Economy

So FAR MY investigation of Britain's archaeological past has taken me almost two millennia this side of prehistory, my own area of expertise. I am now deep within unknown territory, what medieval adventurers might have described as *terra incognita*. With this in mind I trust readers will forgive me if I follow an old excavator's principle and work from the known to the unknown.

So I want to start our exploration of Britain in the post-medieval period in the farms and fields of the countryside. There, at least, I feel reasonably at home and not just because I was brought up in a small village, but because over the past thirty-odd years my wife Maisie and I have kept a small sheep farm which would regularly make a tiny profit, until, that is, 2001, when the market value of British livestock collapsed, rather like wheat prices after the Black Death. In our case the miscreants have been BSE/scrapie, foot-and-mouth (twice) and now the dreaded Bluetongue in all its grisly variants. More recently, and much to our surprise, things have picked up. This improvement followed directly on the bursting of the bankers' bubble in 2008, when the collapse of cheap credit forced an international reassessment of what matters in life. At last people have recognised that the era of cheap food was always unsustainable. Anyhow, my interest in sheep-farming has given me insights into, and much sympathy for, historic and ancient farmers. So let's start our journey where the food that nourishes human life originates: with farms, with farmers, and their families.

I would guess that over the years archaeologists have excavated hundreds, if not thousands, of prehistoric, Roman and medieval farms, farmyards and field systems. I myself have dug upwards of a dozen. But with one exception, which I will discuss shortly, I cannot think of a single post-medieval or modern farm that has been treated in this way.* This simple fact illustrates, if anything can, how different is the way that post-medieval archaeology is carried out. There are fewer excavations and instead far, far more effort goes into the accurate surveying of upstanding remains which are then painstakingly tied in with the documentary evidence. So that's how things are done and to some extent it makes complete sense, because why dig when you can measure and survey at a fraction of the cost?

It is all perfectly rational, but nevertheless the digger/excavator deep down inside me feels a bit uneasy: surely without entirely new and unexpected information from the ground there is always a danger that observations derived from surveys can somehow be made to 'fit' the documentary evidence? True, these two strands of research can together combine to reveal fascinating stories, but, speaking entirely for myself, I sometimes enjoy seeing theories – even my own – being turned rudely upside down. The inevitable rethink that follows can be wonderfully invigorating and is far cheaper than a bottle of Champagne. That's what makes the writing up of an excavation such fun: it becomes a prolonged process in which pennies drop with unexpected force, delight and frequency.

British archaeology has a distinguished history of long-term projects in which one or two slightly obsessive characters – and I'm happy to number myself among them – assemble a team of similarly slightly obsessive people who then work closely together, often lubricated with quantities of drink and coffee, to reveal the archaeological story of a particular place or region. In my various books on Britain's archaeology I have had good reason to thank these people whose work I have ransacked for ideas. Often these long-term projects can produce fascinating tales that develop gradually over the years and become suffused with a life and vigour all of their own. One of the very best of them is about the archaeology of the small Somerset parish of Shapwick. We first visited this village on the edge of the marshy Somerset Levels in *Britain in the Middle Ages*.[1] As I explained there, one of the slightly obsessive characters behind the Shapwick project is my

* More to the point, nor can Dr Audrey Horning (University of Leicester).

old friend Professor Mick Aston, better known to millions of viewers today as the grey-haired archaeologist in the stripy jumper on *Time Team*.

Although not religious himself, Mick will go to great lengths to help a church in difficulties and when, in the summer of 2007, I read in our local paper that the magnificent building in Long Sutton needed urgent repairs to its roof, I thought of Mick, and together we organised a public lecture, which was to launch the vicar's appeal for funds. The church is rather extraordinary. Like many around the Wash, it is very large and appears on the outside to be quite late – maybe fourteenth century – but when you enter be prepared for a surprise, because the interior is almost completely Norman, and Norman of a very high order. Mick got wildly excited and was convinced that the superb workmanship around us was Cluniac (a monastic order famous for its first-rate buildings). This book isn't about the Middle Ages (and I'll get to the point in a moment), but Mick's presence drew a huge crowd and the church was thronged with people. There were stalls selling local books and magazines, and the nearby village hall supplied a stream of people contentedly munching their way through vast Fenland cow pies. I was forcibly struck by the scene and realised that the church had suddenly become what it was in medieval times: the centre of a bustling community and not the exalted, pious and remote place that so many country churches have become since the liturgical reforms of Victorian times.

The following morning Mick appeared clasping what had to be the thickest paperback book I have ever seen. He thudded it down on my desk. It was, or rather is, a staggering 1,047 pages long and includes a CD-ROM of many hundreds more. Having written one or two thickish tomes myself, I know just how much effort it must have taken Mick, and his long-term collaborator, Chris Gerrard, to write and assemble such a Goliath. And now, a few weeks later, I have more or less digested its main findings and it is indeed an astonishing work of great scholarship. It is the account of a survey that took place over a decade, from 1989 to 1999, and involved the methodical field-walking and selected excavation of most of the parish of Shapwick.[2]

Field-walking, incidentally, is the process whereby a group of archaeologists walk slowly over a field, carefully following a grid. As they walk they put any finds they can see on the surface into bags which are marked with a grid reference. Strange as it may seem, this can be very hard work: on wet days heavy clay sticks to your boots and soon your shoulders start to ache because your head is permanently inclined towards the ground; by this stage, too, the constant dipping down to pick up finds gets to the muscles in your back and calves.

You might think that field-walking would best be done in the warmth of summer, but in fact it doesn't work like that. Obviously land put down to woodland, grass or permanent pasture can't be field-walked, but neither can ground that has been freshly ploughed or harrowed. Ideally, cultivated land should be left to the mercies of wind, rain and frost for at least three weeks before it is walked. That way, finds are washed clean and can readily be spotted on the surface. After a day's walking, the bags are taken somewhere dry where they are emptied, the finds washed and divided into various categories, such as bone, flint, tile, pottery, brick and clay tobacco pipe fragments (which are common on post-medieval sites of the seventeenth to nineteenth centuries).

One reason why post-medieval archaeology is so important is that it allows us better to understand what archaeologists sometimes refer to as 'formation processes'. In the past these tended to be assumed or were simply taken for granted, which was a shame, because in fact they are crucially important. So what are they? Perhaps the simplest way to think about them is to ponder the many possible ways that archaeological deposits were formed in the very first instance. Take an obvious example: when rubbish was swept under a reed mat or when coins slipped through holes in a tinker's pockets to land in the mud of a garden path. Some could have been formed through deliberate dumping (what today we would call 'fly-tipping'), or during religious offerings, sacrifices or perhaps in the course of a cataclysmic event, such as a fire, earthquake, hurricane, tsunami or the eruption of a great volcano.

Usually one can rule out certain options. Earthquakes and volcanic eruptions are generally infrequent in Britain, for example. But then it gets more complex. Dredging of the Thames to allow larger ships upstream in the late nineteenth and early twentieth centuries revealed huge quantities of Bronze Age weapons and human skulls. At the time it was assumed that these had been washed into the river from settlements along the shoreline. Somewhat later people preferred to think that much of this material had been lost when ancient travellers had attempted to ford the river. Today we tend to regard most of these river finds as being the result of deliberate religious offerings to the waters. In fact, there is precious little by way of hard and fast evidence to support any of these suggestions. As a general rule such explanations tend to depend on which theories are currently fashionable in academic circles – and nowadays ideas centring around religion and ritual are much in favour.

So let's suppose that we've emptied the contents of our field-walking bags onto a table. The first problem one has to address is simple: how did these hundreds (more usually thousands) of things find their way into, and onto, the ground? Now with very ancient prehistoric material it can be difficult to decide what surface finds actually represent. Soft, poorly fired pottery rarely survives attack by the humic acids in the ploughsoil, and bone succumbs quite quickly as well. So their absence does not mean that they were never there in the first place. As a result, all one is usually left with is flint. And it's usually impossible or very difficult to decide whether a scattering of flints originated from a permanent village, a camp or a temporary squat, where a handful of hunters stopped to prepare a few new arrowheads after breakfast.

Such conundrums can be easier to unravel in Roman and medieval times when the appearance of bricks, roof tiles and mortar can signal the existence of demolished buildings. But again, although Roman pottery is harder and tends to survive rather better in the soil, bone can soon vanish and iron rapidly rusts away to nothing. Only in post-medieval times does material survive so well in the topsoil that it becomes possible to decide with some certainty how, and indeed why, it originally became incorporated into the earth. And strangely, as Shapwick has shown so clearly, the manner in which some of this material seems to have found its way into the topsoil could be unexpected.

Viewed from an historical perspective, the end of the Middle Ages was traumatic, what with the Reformation, the rise of the Tudors and the Dissolution of the Monasteries. But although these were indeed

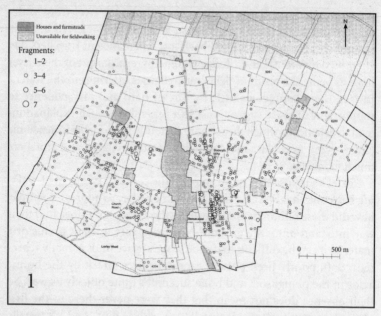

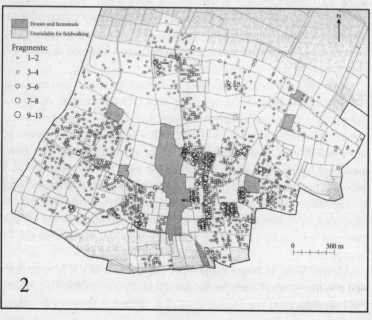

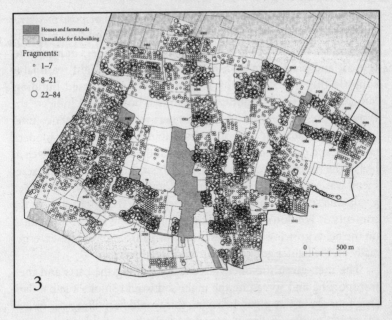

FIG 1   *Three maps of Shapwick, Somerset showing (1) the distribution of later medieval (twelfth–fifteenth centuries) and (2) post-medieval (sixteenth–eighteenth centuries) pottery; map 3 shows the distribution of unidentified brick and tile fragments. These maps clearly demonstrate that there was no break in settlement at the close of the Middle Ages.*

major events, we will see that their actual impact on the growth and development of Britain's rural and urban landscapes was surprisingly small. Of course specific sites – and here I am thinking most particularly of rural and urban monastic estates – were dramatically affected, but the general run of the landscape was not. It is becoming increasingly clear that many of the processes that became self-evident in the mid-sixteenth century had roots very much earlier, usually in the mid-fourteenth; this was the period which witnessed the first impacts of the successive waves of plague we generally refer to as the Black Death. We can see this continuity particularly clearly in the distribution of surface finds at Shapwick.

I have described how the range and robustness of post-medieval topsoil finds often provide clues as to how they found their way into the ground. Take an obvious example: if surface scatters of brick, tile, cement and plaster are discovered in a field, one might reasonably suppose this was the site of a demolished or collapsed building. Similarly, quantities of pottery and animal bone might indicate the erstwhile presence of rubbish tips. But here we immediately encounter problems, because the idea of useless rubbish is essentially a modern concept, and one which is already, thankfully, on the way out. Even as late as the nineteenth century much rubbish, including human excrement, was actually recycled and spread on the land where it provided a valuable source of nitrogen and other minerals. 'Night soil', as the contents of London's many millions of privies was called, was spread on the fields growing vegetables in Bedfordshire and Middlesex, especially on the lighter gravel soils around Heathrow.

The men given the unenviable task of filling the carts and then transporting and spreading the night soil would smoke a lethal dark shag tobacco in clay pipes, believing this would keep illness, as well as the stink, at bay. Today if you field-walk these fields you will be rewarded by the discovery of thousands of broken pipe fragments. So the discovery of pieces of pipe provides a good indication of how that particular soil might have originated. There are also other clues that allow us to make an informed guess about a deposit's formation process.

At Shapwick the concentration of small, unidentified brick and tile fragments did show some correspondence with the pottery distribution, but there were also other concentrations further away from the village, some of which could be associated with known demolished post-medieval buildings. Others seemed to have been dumped, most probably after a tile roof had been renewed or repaired. This distribution suggests that brick and tile was finding its way into the ground through a variety of quite different processes. But what about the quite clear replication of the brick/tile distribution with that of the pottery, especially to the immediate east of the village, where both seem to form a concentration in a broad strip, running north–south? We know that this strip was in existence in later medieval times and it is probably best explained as the detritus left, following the spreading of manure.

Today farmers tend to keep their farmyard manure and domestic rubbish separate, but I can remember farms in my childhood where the edible contents of the kitchen pail was fed to pigs and chickens while the stalks and bones were chucked away on the muck heap. Now the muck heap was not the foetid mess that townspeople might suppose. Its purpose was to allow muck to break down – today we would rather primly refer to this process as 'composting' – and become manure. This maturation usually took a year or less to complete. It's worth noting here that if muck is spread onto the fields too soon it has precisely the opposite effect to that intended: it breaks down in the arable ground and in the process removes nitrogen from the soil. And of course it is nitrogen that plants require if they are to grow vigorously.

In the past, household and other debris was placed on muck heaps, which archaeologists, for reasons best known to themselves, like to refer to as 'middens'. Middens also accumulated burnt wood (for the potash it contains), from which thousands of nails found their way into the soil. In regions where the subsoil was heavy or acidic, farmers would add broken bricks and mortar to help drainage and increase alkalinity. Pottery and glass sherds also helped clay soils to drain, so they were thrown onto the midden along with everything else. Then the process of hand-forking the manure into and out of carts helped break down the pieces of pottery, glass, brick and tile, which would explain the small size of so many of the sherds from that strip immediately east of Shapwick village.

So the distribution of finds from later medieval and post-medieval Shapwick proves beyond much doubt that the villagers continued to live in very much the same place and spread their manure in much the same way from at least the twelfth to the eighteenth centuries. After that time in Britain generally we see the gradual introduction of non-farmyard fertilisers, of which the best known is bird dung from the Peruvian coast, known as guano, but other soil improvers were also used, such as gypsum, chalk and lime.

It is now becoming clear that the farming and manuring pattern of later medieval times continued into the post-medieval period relatively unaltered, yet this was a period almost of turmoil in the world of local landowners. Glastonbury Abbey, always a prosperous foundation but possibly the richest monastic estate in England by this time, owned land and two manors at Shapwick which were taken over by private landlords after the abbey's dissolution in November 1539. This led to the enlargement of the mansion at Shapwick House sometime around 1620–40 when a long gallery was added to the medieval building. All this was happening, and yet the basic management of the landscape continued much as before. It is not, however, until the later eighteenth century that we see the village decline in size as the park around Shapwick House was greatly enlarged, a process sometimes referred to as emparkation. We know, for example, that seven houses near the great house were demolished between 1782 and 1787.[3] This process continued until the great park was completed in the 1850s, a process which even involved the relocation of the parish church!

At this point I should perhaps admit I've been a little unfair because I've started this chapter by jumping straight into the deep end of a pool of detail. I did that because I wanted to illustrate the complexities inherent in any attempt to understand how the rural landscape developed at this crucially important period at the very beginning of our story. But our tale is about to get more complicated. In many ways this reflects the reality of modern research into rural archaeology: many of the old certainties have had to be abandoned in the face of a growing mountain of evidence that what might once have been seen as clear national trends actually fail to apply at the local level. But this is nothing new, as we saw in the Middle Ages.

One of the great archaeological breakthroughs in the study of English medieval rural geography happened in the 1950s and 1960s with the recognition that many villages in the English Midlands had either been abandoned or had shrunk massively, usually from some time in the fourteenth century. When mapped out, these villages could be seen to form a Central Province which extended in a broadly continuous swathe from Somerset, through the Midlands, Lincolnshire, eastern Yorkshire and into County Durham and Northumberland.[4] The landscapes in this area featured villages that had been reorganised, or 'nucleated', by drawing outlying farms into a more focused central village, a process that happened in the centuries on either side of the Norman Conquest. The work of nucleation was carried out by local people, often encouraged by landlords and by other authorities, such as the Church and great monastic houses (as happened at Shapwick).

On both sides of this Central Province of 'planned', nucleated or 'organised' landscapes, the countryside was less formally structured, with dispersed settlements and smaller hamlets rather than nucleated villages. This landscape has been variously described as 'ancient' or 'woodland', but as both types are now known to have been very old indeed, I shall stick to the term 'woodland' as being slightly less misleading.[5] The distinction between the Central Province of nucleated and the provinces of woodland landscapes on either side can be seen in the distribution of known pre-Norman woods and even, to some extent at least, in that of Pagan Saxon (mainly fifth-century) burials.[6] So whatever allowed people of the Central Province to accept these changes, it must have been a social process with deeply embedded roots. Even more importantly for present purposes, the three provinces can clearly be distinguished when we plot the distribution of nineteenth-century parliamentary enclosures (about which more shortly). Today the landscape still reflects this tripartite split, with larger villages and more formal rectangular fields still largely confined to what had been the Central Province.

Farming in the woodland landscapes continued much as it had done in the Iron Age. It was based on individual holdings, which operated a mixed system of farming based around livestock and crops in those areas where lower levels of rainfall allowed them to be grown. The larger nucleated villages of the Central Province gave rise to the now famous collective Open Field farms of the Middle Ages where tenant farmers in the village shared their labour between their own holdings and those of the lord of the manor.[7] This was the basis of the feudal system, which never developed in Britain to quite the same extent as it did on the Continent. Farmwork itself took place in from two to four huge Open Fields where the individual holdings were organised in strips. Each year the individual Open Fields would grow specified crops or would lie fallow, to be fertilised by grazing livestock. The control of what was in effect a large collective farm lay in the hands of the manorial court, which in turn was overseen by the lord of the manor. This system of farming was particularly well adapted to the heavy clay lands of the Midlands, which require rapid ploughing by many teams of oxen in the spring when conditions are right. Get the timing wrong and you're left with a porridge-like field of mud.

When I learned about the manorial system at school I gained the impression that, once in place, it remained there, pretty much unaltered. This is perhaps where our views have changed the most. We now realise that it was a dynamic system that was modified from one area to another through time, depending not just on the local soil and climate, but on social factors, such as the wealth, power and influence of landlords. We have also discovered that the once clear distinction between the collective Open Field farms of the nucleated landscapes could not necessarily be distinguished from the individually owned farms of the woodland landscapes. In other words, there was Open Field farming in 'woodland' areas and vice versa.[8] So although the very broad distinction into the three provinces can still be said to hold true, it simply cannot (and must not) be used to predict what one might discover in a randomly selected tract of landscape.

These warnings become even more important from the fourteenth century, when the population was massively reduced following food shortages and the terrible impact of successive waves of plague that then continued right through to the seventeenth century. Although, as I have said, the feudal 'system' never really took a firm hold in Britain, even after the Norman Conquest, most of the ties and obligations that did exist began to slip when the rich and powerful could no longer rely on a large, docile and cheap workforce.[9] From the fourteenth century peasant farmers and working people realised they were no longer in a buyer's market, especially when it came to the negotiation of their land tenure and labour contracts. In the western 'woodland' regions this less restricted climate began to give rise to a new, dual, rural economy where the families of smaller farmers developed a second string to their bow, which was usually based around something to do with the land, such as spinning and weaving, or coal-mining in places such as the Forest of Dean where coal was readily accessible. These dual economies varied from region to region, but as we will see later they played a crucial role in the development and growth of industry in these areas.

So for practical purposes, we can see the Middle Ages in rural Britain drawing to a close from the mid-fourteenth century onwards, for which reason the following three hundred years have been described as an age of transition in which political and religious changes did not necessarily happen smoothly. But viewed in the longer term they did indeed happen, and what is more, the evidence they left behind can be traced both on and in the ground, for example in the way that people changed their attitudes towards rites of burial and memorial and even in more mundane aspects of life, such as their choice of domestic pottery.[10] The effects of these continuing processes of change, however, only became highly visible during the Reformation (c. 1480–1580), a period which saw the rise of Protestantism and the Dissolution of the Monasteries.

I think I can understand why the version of history taught at school paid so much attention to the Open Field farms of medieval Britain. It was, after all, a very different way of doing things and it also gave teachers a chance to discuss the social ties and obligations of feudalism, while at the same time it brought the Church, monasteries, great landowners and manorial courts into the story. I can well remember being struck by the mystery and romance of the times, supposing myself a wandering troubadour strumming a lute at the feet of beautiful maidens. Although on second thoughts, this makes me think I wasn't quite so young as I once imagined. Anyhow, the period that followed was, if anything, rather more fascinating, because it witnessed social and economic developments that are still affecting British life.

There can be no doubt that in many rural areas, especially in the old Central Province of the English Midlands, the post-medieval period got off to a shaky start. I'll have more to say about this later, but in essence the general population decline of the later fourteenth, fifteenth and earlier sixteenth centuries, which was ultimately brought about by successive waves of plague, left its mark on early modern towns and villages in the countryside. However, things were about to improve, slowly at first, but then with gathering rapidity.

At this point I must add a quick note about the process known as 'enclosure', which I will discuss in greater detail shortly. When we discuss the end of the Open Field system we find it replaced by enclosure. Used in this way the word refers to a change in landownership where several owners are replaced by one. I think many people still labour under the misapprehension that the manorial system and Open Field farming both came to an abrupt end some time between the

Battle of Bosworth (1485), which saw the effective end of the Wars of the Roses, and the Dissolution of the Monasteries, when a near-tyrant king effectively pulled the rug of power from under the feet of the Church. At least that is how things appeared. We now realise that both society and landscapes actually take rather longer to modify in so drastic a fashion. As I noted earlier, the seeds of change were planted in the mid-fourteenth century, but that was just the beginning. In many parts of Britain, especially in the Midlands and eastern parts of England, Open Field farms continued through the sixteenth century, but by its end nearly half had succumbed to enclosure. By 1700 three-quarters had been enclosed. So when statutory or parliamentary enclosure (see below, p. 38) began in earnest in the later eighteenth century only a quarter of the Open Fields required enclosure – and of course today we are left with just a single surviving Open Field parish, at Laxton, in Nottinghamshire.[11]

We have just seen that, although the dissolution of the great monastic house of Glastonbury had an immediate effect on landownership at Shapwick, the direct effect on patterns of farming was relatively slight. Only somewhat later, when the process of emparkation had got under way, did the longer-term results of the shift in landownership become evident in the landscape. In some places, however, the Dissolution had a sudden and dramatic effect. And nowhere was this more evident than in the Fens where a vast area of new land was drained, largely through the good offices of the Earls and then the Dukes of Bedford who had acquired money plus the vast estates of Thorney Abbey during the Dissolution; this provided the basis for the region's prosperity from the seventeenth to the nineteenth centuries.[12] We will see shortly that drainage, mostly to improve pasture, rather than to provide new arable land, was to become an important feature of the second phase of post-medieval farming improvements of the early and mid-eighteenth century.

During the fifteenth and sixteenth centuries we see a gradual move away from the Open Field system of farming towards a more complex set of regional patterns which better reflected local soil types, transport networks and what today we would call marketing opportunities. It was never simply a matter of finding the best soil to grow a particular crop. Take, for example, the vegetable farms around Sandy in Bedford.

Here, as any vegetable gardener could tell you, the Ouse Valley terrace gravels in their natural state are rather too light and well drained to grow the top-quality brassicas, such as the Brussels sprouts that are still such a noted speciality of the region; and it was only the addition of much manure and fertiliser, together with the ready availability of the vast market provided by a rapidly growing London population, that allowed the vegetable trade to develop successfully.

Plotting the development of early modern (1550–1750) farming has been a process which has owed much to economic historians and geographers, such as Joan Thirsk and Eric Kerridge, and without the basis of their pioneering research the recent work of more archaeologically orientated scholars, such as Susanna Wade Martins and Tom Williamson, would not have been possible. Today agricultural history is going through a very exciting period indeed. Thanks to people like Joan Thirsk we have long since abandoned some of the rather simplistic ideas – I almost said ideals – exemplified by terms such as the Agricultural Revolution and are now in the throes of creating a new history of rural Britain, based more on facts unearthed from survey and from detailed examination of sources such as estate records, than on over-arching concepts that sound good, but actually mean little. I shall return to the evidence for the timing of that supposed agricultural 'revolution' shortly.

In the later 1950s and 1960s Kerridge, followed in the seventies and eighties by Thirsk, together with other economic historians, began to produce maps that plotted the extent of early modern agricultural specialisation in England. These maps were actually plotting complexity, so they themselves can be daunting to read. But I make no apologies for that. I don't think it's necessary to grapple with precise details of individual regions, unless, of course, one has a specific interest, but the overall picture is nonetheless important, so I have reproduced Thirsk's simplified general plan here. This map was based on two more complex maps, the first of which showed English agricultural regions in the century and a half from the start of the sixteenth century (actually from 1500 to 1640); the second illustrated how the situation developed in the following century or so, from 1640 to 1750.[13]

The two detailed maps are, however, important because they illustrate well the growing complexity of the post-medieval farming

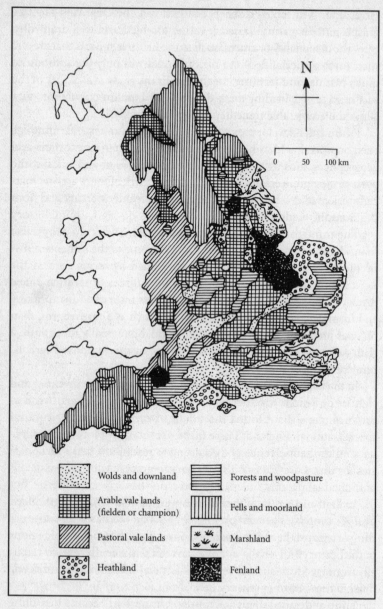

FIG 2 *Map showing the farming regions of early modern England (1500–1750).*

Wolds and downland

Arable vale lands
(fielden or champion)

Pastoral vale lands

Heathland

Forests and woodpasture

Fells and moorland

Marshland

Fenland

landscape. Both show a sharp distinction between mixed farming (arable and pasture) and pasture farming, which in turn is subdivided into woodland pasture and open pasture. All three main categories are then further subdivided into different varieties of mixed, woodland and open pasture farming. In the earlier map there is still a broad swathe of mixed farming that extends if not quite from Somerset, then from the south, through the Midlands, Lincolnshire, most of east Yorkshire and up to County Durham and Northumberland. Although this zone has altered somewhat from the Central Province of the earlier Middle Ages it is still broadly recognisable, despite now extending into parts of Norfolk, Kent and Essex. By the time we get to the second map, the areas of mixed farming have slipped south and east, largely departing from the medieval pattern.

The principal difference between the two maps is the far greater complexity of the second, later, one. Take just two regions. Post-medieval innovations are perhaps most marked in my own area, the Fens, which are shown in the earlier map (and indeed in the simplified one reproduced here) as a single region, given over to open pastoral farming involving stock-fattening with horse-breeding, dairying, fishing and fowling. After 1640, and the first phase of widespread, though still incomplete drainage, the earlier style of farming has been confined to a narrow area of marshland around the Wash, whereas the bulk of Fenland now comprises two broad areas, one to the north of silty soils that are devoted to stock- and pig-keeping, fattening, and corn-growing, while to the south the more peaty land is still mainly used for grazing and, of course, no cereals are grown. Incidentally, somewhat later, in the earlier nineteenth century, following the introduction of steam pumps, we see a further near-complete transformation of this particular landscape.

In Kent and Sussex, although the distinctive oval shape of Wealden geology continues to exert an influence (as indeed it does to this day), the varieties of farming become very much more complex in the period covered by the later map. This in part reflects the arrival of entirely new ideas, such as the introduction of fruit orchards and hop fields. The point to emphasise here is that early modern farming was a dynamic and increasingly specialised business which was becoming ever more dependent on the growth of towns and cities. Nowhere was this more important than around the two principal capitals of Edinburgh and London, which by the end of the Middle Ages had come to dominate the region and countryside around them. The areas peripheral to the large towns and cities not only provided food and raw materials for the growing urban population, but perhaps as significantly, they also provided a constantly renewing pool of labour, especially following the recurrent waves of plague that bedevilled many of the larger cities in later medieval and early post-medieval times.

We are still in the realms of general economic history and I want soon to come down to earth and see how individual farms and fields were adapted as economic conditions changed around them. But first we must briefly examine the idea of the 'Agricultural Revolution' which is traditionally thought to have happened between 1760 and 1830. A slightly longer view (1700–1850) would allow the main events to have happened in three stages, the first stage being completed sometime around 1750–70. These initial developments involved the introduction of new crops, especially root crops such as turnips, which we now know were pioneered not in Britain, but in the Low Countries, in the sixteenth and seventeenth centuries.[14]

As early as 1600 growing Dutch influence had seen the introduction of cabbages, cauliflowers, turnips, carrots, parsnips and peas to market gardens around London. Turnips were introduced to East Anglia from Holland in the mid-sixteenth century and they then formed an important element in the famous Norfolk four-course (crop) rotation of wheat, turnips, barley, clover and/or grasses.[15] The Norfolk four-course rotation required the land to lie fallow for less time (if the land had become too depleted the final crop of clover and/or grass could be extended for an additional season). This cycle of crops produced more grazing and fodder in the form of turnips which in turn resulted in more and fatter livestock and, perhaps just as important, more manure to be spread on the fields. I also believe it must have given livestock farmers greater security and peace of mind.

As I have discovered to my cost, in seasons when late winter rains continue into March and April it can be unwise to turn young animals out onto muddy fields and waterlogged pasture. As any livestock farmer knows to his cost, fast-grown grass is deficient in minerals and both ewes and lambs can soon develop 'grassland staggers'. So you house them for longer, but the next thing you discover is that the hay and straw they have been happily consuming over winter simply lack the nourishment that growing lambs so desperately need and soon they start to look thin, lanky and bony. They also lack vigour and don't rush about in that wildly enthusiastic, but completely mad and point-less fashion that can make them so endearing. In such situations today one buys in (expensive) supplements usually in the form of 'cake', but as farmers in the eighteenth and nineteenth centuries knew only too well, the sprouting heads of growing parsnips and the roots themselves were almost equally nutritious – and a lot cheaper.

Perhaps the most significant reform that enabled changes to happen in the British countryside was the concept of enclosure. Having said that, we shouldn't go overboard in our enthusiasm. For a start, huge areas of the later medieval landscape had never come into collec-tive ownership and large estates, both private and owned by ecclesiasti-cal authorities, were already in existence in the Middle Ages. As we saw at Shapwick, the latter could readily be transferred to private owner-ship. Many of the small farms of the two later medieval woodland provinces began to rationalise their holding first in later medieval times and with increasing rapidity from the sixteenth century. This was enclosure, but not carried out by individual Acts of Parliament, as was to happen much later. It has been termed 'enclosure by agreement' and it also involved the dismantling of Open Field farms and the taking in of common land.

Although we should record that in many instances the 'agreement' was imposed by a rich landowner and his lawyers (and this is particu-larly true in the case of the many large enclosures of Tudor times that were created to make vast, open sheep runs). The main era of enclo-sures by agreement was in the seventeenth and eighteenth centuries and today these landscapes can still be seen to cover large tracts of countryside in the west and south-west of England, especially in Devon and Cornwall.[16] As a general guide, early enclosures of this sort often preserve features of earlier landscapes in their layout, such as the gentle reversed S boundaries of abandoned Common Fields. That distinctive shape, incidentally, was a 'fossil' left by years and years of strip plough-ing, where the plough teams had restricted space to turn at each end, thereby leaving a slightly sinuous furrow.[17]

Modern landscapes that arose through early enclosure, or enclosure by agreement, and by means of parliamentary enclosure appear very different. Not only do the early enclosures incorporate previous features, such as those reversed S boundaries, but although they are generally square-ish or rectilinear, their fields certainly don't follow a rigid pattern and it is usually obvious that they arose as a series of distinct, one-off agreements. As such they tend to follow the shape and 'grain' of the topography rather better than the later (often parliamentary) enclosures which were accurately surveyed in. As a consequence, in these later enclosures dead straight lines and right angles predominate. Although many would disagree with me, I still like these later landscapes which I find have a charm all of their own – maybe it's because I grew up in them that I feel at ease there.

Parliamentary enclosure took place rather later in our story, generally in the late eighteenth and nineteenth centuries. Essentially it was a response to the increasing pace of enclosure by agreement in those areas of central and eastern England where the medieval Open Field system had left a complex legacy of sometimes quite large parishes with numerous smallholdings belonging to many tenant and owner-occupier farmers. In such complex situations agreement was often difficult or impossible. So the passing of individual Acts of Enclosure was seen as a way through these problems. In theory at least it was a fair and transparent system where the process of enclosure was overseen by a parliamentary commissioner who also saw to it that the land was surveyed and parcelled up by official surveyors. But there was much scope for potential abuse: for example, areas of common land and so-called 'wastes' (where nobody claimed actual ownership) had to be reapportioned among the landowners of the parish. And as so often happens, the actual results were rather different and by the end of the process the big estates had done very nicely thank you, while substantial landowners and rising yeoman farmers also generally increased the size of their holding; more importantly, these holdings were now arranged more rationally and could be farmed much more efficiently. But small farmers often ended up proportionately worse off than their larger neighbours.

The first Parliamentary Act of Enclosure was passed in 1604 and in the eighteenth century these rapidly became the dominant method of enclosure, with some four thousand Acts passed between 1750 and 1830, covering about a fifth of England's surface area.[18] The process continued through the nineteenth century. Apart from a contribution from the taxpayer, most of the cost of parliamentary enclosure was paid for by the larger landowners and this was probably why they tended to fare better than smallholders. It's not hard to work out why. If one bears in mind what one learned as a child about the ratio of surface to volume, the men with the smallest holdings had proportionately the longer boundaries. These then had to be re-fenced and re-hedged at their owners' expense. In many instances this was to prove too much so they sold out to their larger neighbours.[19]

In the English Midlands parliamentary enclosure must be considered successful, but that cannot be said for everywhere, even in England. In upland areas of northern England, for example, parliamentary enclosure often ignored topography and was sometimes frankly irrational. If anything, it made efficient farming more difficult.[20]

In Scotland enclosure was by agreement, or latterly by imposition of powerful landowners. In the Lowlands the process was well under way in the 1760s and 1770s and in the Highlands towards the end of the century, where they became known as the Highland Clearances; these enclosures often involved the clearance of entire rural populations to make way for sheep pasture and later for moorland game reserves. The Clearances continued late into the nineteenth century when huge numbers of people were either removed to new settlements often within the landowners' estates along the coastal plain, or were sent abroad, principally to Canada. To give an idea of the scale of the Clearances, some 40,000 people were removed from the Isle of Skye between 1840 and 1880.[21]

I think it would be a big mistake simply to think of the earlier postmedieval period in terms of big all-transforming movements, such as enclosure. Many poorer rural people lived outside the world of what one might term legalised land tenure. Theirs was an existence where possession was nine-tenths of the law and nowhere was this more evident than in the less prosperous parts of upland, non-Anglicised Wales. Because these holdings were, at best, quasi-legal, they have left little by way of a paper trail. So to track them down, my old friend Bob

Sylvester (who initially made his name by sorting out the medieval archaeology of the Norfolk Fens) has had to turn to archaeology.[22]

According to Bob, the traditional archaeological view of Wales was 'a single undifferentiated upland landmass, appended to the western side of England'.[23] Unfortunately, such attitudes made no allowances for the distinctive landscapes of Wales which often arose through the action of people and communities that were very different from those further east. One such distinctive feature has been termed 'encroachment'.[24] As the population of Wales began to grow from the later seventeenth century, and most particularly in the eighteenth and early nineteenth, impoverished landless people built themselves small houses and laid out smallholdings on the common land of the uplands, usually without the landowner (often the Crown) being aware. These people were often given moral and practical support by local parish councils who did not like seeing perfectly good land being left to stand idle. Sometimes landowners themselves encouraged such encroachment, especially if they were looking for labour to exploit coal and other mineral resources in these otherwise under-populated upland regions.

Informal settlements of this kind are fairly distinctive on the ground. They consist of a seemingly random scatter of small single-family households, within a couple of acres of land. Sometimes the more successful homesteads acquired the additional outbuildings of an upland farm and the various houses are usually served by a single, meandering lane. Encroachments are by no means confined to the uplands and can be found in valley floors, especially on land that was once poorly drained and uncontrolled, such as many of the tributary valleys of the Severn along the border country of Montgomeryshire and Shropshire.[25]

Despite local difficulties of the sort we have just discussed, the rationalisation of the rural landscape brought about by enclosure of all types meant that farmers and landowners were now able to take practical measures to improve their land. In most cases this involved under-drainage, which was particularly effective in the clay lands of East Anglia, where huge areas were drained in the first half of the nineteenth century. Under-drainage involved the cutting, by hand, of a series of parallel, deep, narrow trenches containing brushwood, gravel, stone or clay pipes, these then emptied into ditches along the field's edges, which in turn had to be deepened and improved. The work was often paid for by landowners.[26] The other major innovation which has left a distinct mark in the landscape, mostly of western Britain (although it was tried without the same success in drier East Anglia, too), was the extensive 'floating' of land through the construction of artificial water meadows in the years between 1600 and 1900.[27]

These projects involved the digging of numerous channels to carry water from a main cut, usually alongside a natural river, and from there into a series of subsidiary streams carefully positioned to distribute it evenly across the meadow. These flooded meadows could be extensive, covering many acres, and their construction also involved the erection of numerous sluice gates which had to be opened and closed in a specific order, depending on what was needed. In fact the actual business of operating and maintaining water meadows required labour, plus considerable skill and experience, which might help explain why they failed to thrive after the opulent period known as Victorian high farming (which I'll explain later) was brought to an end by the great agricultural depression of the 1870s.[28]

Ultimately water meadows were intended to extend the initial flush of spring and early summer grass, both through simple watering and by the laying down of a very thin layer of flood-clay (alluvium) which provided early season nourishment to the growing grass. Throughout the seventeenth and eighteenth centuries and well into the nineteenth, water meadows made the keeping of sheep and the growing of corn on the chalk downlands of Wessex and southern England such a profitable business. This is because the rather thin grass cover of the chalk downs doesn't really start growing in earnest until May, so the new water meadows on the richer soils of the valley bottoms meant that abundant grazing was now available in March and April, when stocks of hay were nearly exhausted. Almost as important, it also meant that the arable parts of the farm now had an even more plentiful supply of manure.[29]

There is now a general consensus that the concept of a short-lived and as such truly revolutionary period of agricultural 'improvement' is mistaken and instead we should be thinking of a more extended era of 'improvement', from, say, 1500 to 1850. And many, myself included, would reckon that such a length of time – some 350 years – was more evolutionary than revolutionary.[30] It's roughly the same length of time that separates the present from the execution of King Charles I. With all of this in mind, I prefer to refer to the period as the era of agricultural development – because it could be argued that, with hindsight, some of the so-called 'improvements' were actually nothing of the sort.[31]

Whatever one's definition of the period, the changes I have just been discussing are generally seen to have been the result of pioneering work carried out by enlightened, reform-minded, high-profile individuals, who are usually lumped together under the general heading of agricultural 'Improvers'. Jethro Tull, largely I suspect because of the 1970s rock band named after him, is the best known of these 'Improvers'. I remember being taught at school that he invented the seed drill, whereas in reality he urged its adoption and was a great believer in it. He didn't actually invent it. Other important 'Improvers' were the 1st Earl of Leicester, Thomas William Coke (1754–1842) of Holkham Hall, Norfolk (known at the time as 'Coke of Norfolk'), and the Whig Cabinet Minister Charles 'Turnip' Townshend (1674–1738) who helped to promote the Norfolk four-course rotation. We must not forget that the period also saw the introduction of important new breeds of livestock through the researches of men like Robert Bakewell (1725–95), of Dishley Grange, who farmed the heavy clay lands of Leicestershire.[32]

When one reads the correspondence of the different 'Improvers' it is hard not to be carried along by their sheer infectious enthusiasm. It is abundantly clear that they were convinced that their work was important for the general good of society. They were not in it either to create agricultural 'improvements' for their own sake, or just to make money (although that helped). The concept of 'improvement' had a philosophical basis firmly rooted in the eighteenth-century Enlightenment. It was seen as a part of the new rational ideal, the triumph of civilisation over nature. It's not for nothing that great agricultural 'Improvers', such as Coke of Norfolk, were also keen landscape gardeners. As with the new style of farming 'Neatness, symmetry and formal patterns, so typical of the eighteenth-century landscape garden, represented the divide between "culture" and "nature". Indeed, many landlords saw little difference between the laying out of parks around their houses and the new farmland beyond.'[33]

The 'Improvers' were undoubtedly remarkable men, but for various reasons to do with their social status at the time, or their enthusiasm for the promotion of a pet project (such as Tull and the seed drill), they have been treated more favourably by history than many of their humbler contemporaries. Modern research is, however, starting to redress this imbalance, largely thanks to detailed studies of individual estates and farms by historians such as Susanna Wade Martins, whose work is helping to transform our understanding of the period.

I hope readers will forgive me, but at this point I cannot help thinking how strange it is that certain remarkable people can drift in and out of one's life, barely leaving a ripple in their wake. Only later do you kick yourself for not seeking out their views at the time. It's rather like being the man who chose to argue the price of eggs with Sir Isaac Newton. In the case of Susanna Wade Martins, her husband Peter was the director of an Anglo-Saxon excavation I took part in, in 1970, at their home village in Norfolk. Susanna was around and about, but I knew her interests lay outside our dig and, afflicted by the myopia of youth, I failed to discover what she was researching at the time. A major lost opportunity, that.

Over the years, and perhaps more than anyone else, Susanna has thrown light on the lives of individual farmers; maybe this is in part because her academic work is deeply rooted in the experience that she and Peter have acquired running their own small farm. Indeed, as I have related elsewhere, we bought our first four sheep from them, back in the early 1980s.[34] Peter warned me that sheep could become addictive – and he was dead right.

Susanna sees the initial development of modern British farming as being the responsibility of 'yeoman farmers'. These men and their families emerged from the slow collapse of the feudal system and became very much more common in the sixteenth and seventeenth centuries. Yeomen were independent, small farmers who usually owned most, if not all of their own land. Later, they might enter into tenancy agreements with larger landowners, while retaining a core of land for themselves. In some instances they used the profits of their land to acquire estates and to better themselves in the greater worlds of politics and industry. A good example of a successful yeoman family were the Brookes of Coalbrookdale who did so much to develop the iron industry there in the later sixteenth century – but more on them in Chapter 5.

It was yeoman farmers who developed the system of 'up and down husbandry' in the later sixteenth and seventeenth centuries. This system involved a sort of long-term rotation where the land was cropped for arable – usually cereals – for, say, seven successive years, before it was returned to pasture to recover for a slightly longer period of up to a dozen years. This sort of farming was very productive and was adopted across most of the English Midlands. Interestingly, although the population of Britain was rising from 1670, grain prices actually fell year on year – which indicates, if anything can, the productivity of 'up and down husbandry'.[35]

Landowners only start to become generally interested in agricultural 'improvement' from round about 1750, following directly upon the demonstrable successes of what some have called the 'yeoman's revolution' of the seventeenth and earlier eighteenth centuries.[36] Prior to 1750, most landowners had invested any profits from their estates, not so much in farm improvements as in extra land or in additions to their stately homes. After that date they (and their agents), having seen what the yeoman farmers were able to achieve, decided also to invest time, money and ingenuity in improvements to their own farms.

By the mid-eighteenth century the attitude of most British landowners to their tenants had begun to change significantly. A national market was also beginning to emerge for farm produce. Prices for wheat rose steadily and then shot up when Britain declared war on France, in 1793. It now became a patriotic duty to 'improve'. These developments allowed landlords to increase their rents, and tenants to pay them. After 1750 both yeoman farmers and successful tenant farmers had prospered and were now in a position to negotiate new tenancy deals that stipulated realistic rents and encouraged landowners to invest capital in the new farm businesses.

From the mid-eighteenth century the old subservient relationship of tenant and landlord was gradually being replaced by partnerships where both parties profited from a shared enterprise. From as early as the Restoration (1660) independent yeoman farmers began to be replaced by a growing body of tenant farmers, and the more successful of these were able to take advantage of the wholesale reorganisation of estates that was happening through enclosure, which, as we have seen, was well under way when King Charles II resumed the throne.

To place these developments within context, the century from 1640 saw London's population increase by 70 per cent, and the growing metropolis was successfully fed by farms linked into the system of markets via a well-used specialised network of drove roads, which allowed sheep and cattle to be driven long distances from places as far afield as Scotland, down to specialised farms in East Anglia and the Home Counties, where they could be fattened for slaughter.[37] So the system worked and both landowners and their tenants prospered. But Susanna Wade Martins points out that the landowners were not looking for tenants motivated by Enlightenment ideals; instead they sought practical men who would be able to maximise income from their farms.[38] Social attitudes were changing.

This very broad-brush account of the first two centuries of post-medieval farming forms the background to the relatively few buildings of the period that still survive in the landscape. As we saw in the case of Shapwick, our best chances of learning about early modern times come from studying the final years of the Middle Ages. Rather strangely, perhaps, I cannot find studies that are specifically addressed towards rural sites and landscapes of the decades that followed the medieval period. It's almost as if nobody cares. More to the point, I suspect this void reflects one of the great historic divides in British archaeology, between the academic worlds of medievalists and post-medievalists or industrial archaeologists. In the past two decades, however, detailed regional research projects, although often geared towards specific periods and problems, no longer just ignore those topics that are not of immediate interest to them.[39] Along with a greater emphasis on entire landscapes rather than specific sites has come the realisation that continuity has more to teach than a narrow concentration on a particular period.

One of the best of these new regional studies has examined some twelve parishes in the heart of the Central Province on the Buckinghamshire–Northamptonshire border.[40] Recently the principal results of the Whittlewood Survey, as it is known, have been published and they show clearly that it can be very risky to make sweeping statements about rural settlement at the close of the Middle Ages. It would seem that while some villages, especially in those areas where the settlement pattern had been concentrated or 'nucleated', to use the correct term, were actually abandoned, others shrank, sometimes forming two sub-settlements within the same parish. This is not an uncommon pattern in lowland England. Indeed, the village where I grew up at Weston, in north Hertfordshire, had two clear centres, a smaller one around the Norman church and a larger, slightly later one around the village crossroads and the principal inn, the Red Lion, where I spent much of my youth.

Although on a larger scale than Shapwick, the Whittlewood Survey also combined detailed documentary research with field-walking and limited excavation and they were able to demonstrate the extent to which individual villages had changed their shape at the close of the Middle Ages. One example should illustrate the point.[41] Although most of the shrinkage that villages experienced during the later Middle Ages resulted in the random loss of houses, rather like gaps in a set of teeth, such a haphazard pattern was not universal, however, and it would seem that people were aware that communities needed to remain coherent, if not intact. This sometimes gave rise to village layouts where whole districts rather than single houses were abandoned.

The Whittlewood Survey showed that the centre of the village of Akeley in Buckinghamshire, along the existing Leckhampstead Road, had been abandoned quite early (by 1400). The survey was based on an enclosure map of 1794 which marked the houses of the main village around the medieval church and an outlying hamlet to the east of the by then long-abandoned Leckhampstead Road community. Plainly a map as late as 1794 cannot be taken as an accurate illustration of the later and post-medieval settlement pattern, so the survey also recorded the presence of houses that probably pre-dated 1700. In addition, they dug a series of very small test pits where the finds were carefully retrieved and sieved. These pits revealed a fascinating picture. They completely failed to discover sherds of Red Earthenware pottery, so characteristic of the sixteenth century and later, either around the abandoned Leckhampstead Road settlement, or in the fields between

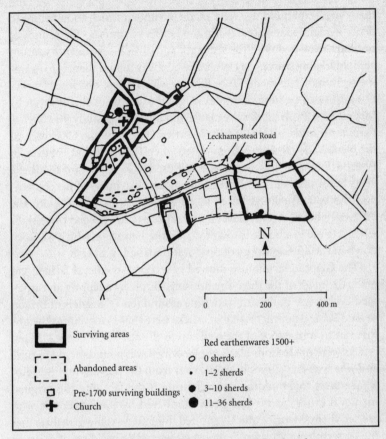

FIG 3   *A survey of the Buckinghamshire village of Akeley, based on an enclosure map of 1794. The distribution of pottery and of surviving buildings that pre-date 1700 clearly show that the centre of the original medieval village had been abandoned. Documentary sources suggest this happened very early, before 1400, but the new pattern continued largely unaltered into the sixteenth century.*

the two surviving communities, where, by contrast, such pottery was abundant. Clearly both these settlements thrived in the sixteenth century.

Although the population declined in the later Middle Ages, the housing stock was deteriorating. This partly reflected the fact that many medieval buildings were made of timber, which soon begins to decay if maintenance ceases for any length of time. So the houses of ordinary rural people of the sixteenth and earliest seventeenth century are remarkably scarce. Very often the best way to find them is to examine seemingly late medieval buildings, which often, on closer inspection, prove to be more complex. A good example of this is given by Maurice Barley in his very readable and pioneering study *The English Farmhouse and Cottage* (1961).[42] Maurice used to be the Chairman of the Nene Valley Research Committee when I excavated at Fengate, in Peterborough, during the 1970s, and I used to look forward to his site visits keenly. He was excellent company and like many of his contemporaries was equally at home in an excavation or working out the different phases of a medieval house. He certainly needed these skills when it came to a house in Glapton, Nottinghamshire, which was torn down in the senseless orgy of post-war destruction in 1958.

The Glapton farmhouse showed how a post-medieval farmer had made the most of the then dire housing supply by adapting an earlier, medieval, cruck-built barn sometime around 1600.[43] Readers of *Britain in the Middle Ages* will recall that crucks were those long, curved beams that ran from the foot of the walls up to the apex of the roof.[44] Many crucks were made from black poplar which was abundant at the time and which always curves its trunk away from the prevailing winds. But what makes this building so fascinating is the fact that the original medieval cruck beams had been numbered by the carpenters who erected them. Maurice quickly spotted this and was able to deduce that the eastern bay had been demolished when the building of the new conversion began.

So our anonymous Nottinghamshire farmer – who knows? Possibly an early yeoman – had spotted the Glapton barn as being ripe for conversion. The original building was of three bays and he still required half of it (i.e. 1½ bays) as a barn, for storage. He converted the remaining half-bay into a small farmhouse which he extended well beyond the old barn, mostly to the east – just as one sees so often today when Victorian barns are converted into houses, or second homes. The new timber-framed house was laid out in a way that was not strictly speaking medieval, but would nonetheless have been familiar to someone from the Middle Ages: there was a hall and parlour facing each other on either side of a cross-passage which led to service rooms (dairy, kitchen and buttery) behind the parlour. The house continued to be modified in various small ways for the rest of its long, but sadly finite, life.

If, as the Glapton barn/house showed, physical evidence for the rise of the first yeoman farmer families can be hard to track down, the success of their descendants has left a distinctive mark on the land- scape, in the form of some fine seventeenth-century houses. These houses indeed proclaim the message 'We have done well in life', but without the over-the-top ostentation and tasteless vulgarity of the much later 'financial crisis' profiteers. The latter eyesores are aggressive and lack any charm whatsoever, whereas their seventeenth-century antecedents reflect the fact that their builders were still rooted in the real world of cattle and sheep, ploughs and ploughmen. I suppose in the final analysis the surviving yeoman farmhouses of Britain can justify their prominent place in the countryside, because they were based on genuine risk and on real, non-paper products that actually fed the rapidly growing population.

The century after 1720 witnessed the rise of a new type of carefully laid out and planned farm whose architecture reflected the classical ideals of the great landowners of the time. These buildings are often Italianate in style, reflecting Palladian grace just as much as the need to house cattle or store turnips. What a great shame it is that modern farmers have completely abandoned any attempt to give their crudely functional buildings any architectural merit at all. It's as if they felt obliged to proclaim that their structures were erected to do the job cheaply and efficiently and to hell with the look of the landscape. They could learn much from later eighteenth-century architects such as Daniel Garrett or Samuel Wyatt whose elegant Italianate farm build- ings still function as they were originally intended. Some of his best- known creations can be seen around the estate of 'Coke of Norfolk', at Holkham Hall.[45]

Many of the elegant Italianate buildings of eighteenth-century model farms were still successfully in use during the next major phase of British farming, sometimes known as Victorian high farming, which began around 1830 and lasted until the great agricultural depression of the 1870s. This was a period of unparalleled prosperity which saw the

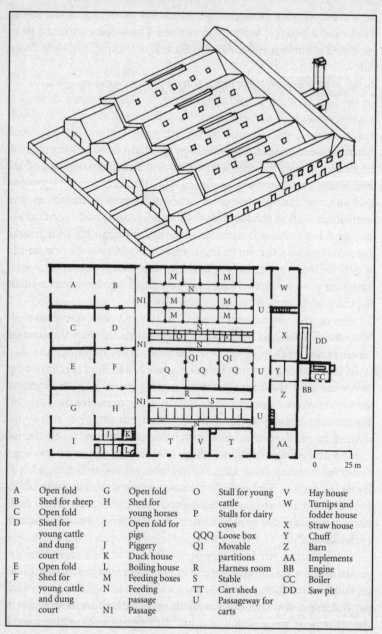

A	Open fold	G	Open fold	O	Stall for young	V	Hay house
B	Shed for sheep	H	Shed for		cattle	W	Turnips and
C	Open fold		young horses	P	Stalls for dairy		fodder house
D	Shed for	I	Open fold for		cows	X	Straw house
	young cattle		pigs	QQQ	Loose box	Y	Chuff
	and dung	J	Piggery	Q1	Movable	Z	Barn
	court	K	Duck house		partitions	AA	Implements
E	Open fold	L	Boiling house	R	Harness room	BB	Engine
F	Shed for	M	Feeding boxes	S	Stable	CC	Boiler
	young cattle	N	Feeding	TT	Cart sheds	DD	Saw pit
	and dung		passage	U	Passageway for		
	court	N1	Passage		carts		

FIG 4 *The prosperous era known as Victorian high farming lasted for much of the nineteenth century, from 1830 to 1870. It saw an increasing number of close partnerships between landlords and tenants, where the latter acted as efficient managers and the former provided capital. The resulting farms could sometimes resemble large factories. The farm buildings shown here are from a design by J. B. Denton of 1879, and were erected at Thornington, near Kilham, Northumberland, around 1880.*

construction not just of well-planned and laid-out new farms, but of farms which, even by today's standards, would be regarded as industrial. Designs for farms of this sort can be seen in contemporary pages of the sort of journals that progressive landowners read, such as that of the Royal Agricultural Society of England, where the range of buildings by J. B. Denton, illustrated here, first appeared.[46] Today nearly every medium-sized farm in Britain can probably boast a few buildings of this era, but those belonging to large estates where capital-rich landowners were able to choose competent tenants and together form mutually beneficial partnerships, are particularly well endowed and have left us a rich legacy of fine farm buildings. I shall have more to say about the development of farms and farming on large rural estates in the next chapter.

In lowland England, if not in Wales and Scotland, it is probably true to say that the big and medium-sized farms of the nineteenth century have had a disproportionately large influence on the shape of the modern landscape. Recently archaeologists have quite rightly focused attention on these places, which for some reason were largely ignored in the 1970s and 1980s. However, there is also a much older tradition of recording so-called 'vernacular architecture' which I will define for present purposes as buildings built by people rather than trained architects often using traditional designs and materials. I say 'often', because sometimes buildings that are vernacular in spirit can be fashioned from mass-produced components, such as some converted barracks in Shropshire or the 'Tin Tabernacle' in Northamptonshire, which I discuss in Chapter 7.[47] There used to be hot debate about what buildings were truly vernacular and which were not. But it was a fruitless debate and today we are less concerned about what is or isn't 'truly' vernacular and now include many threatened nineteenth- and twentieth-century buildings, such as prefabricated temporary school buildings and cinemas.[48]

Much of the earlier surviving post-medieval rural architecture of Scotland and Wales is vernacular and a surprising amount survives in England, despite, or in some instances because of, the era of high farming.[49] Many farming families are quite conservative and were reluctant to demolish earlier buildings, which they often 'improved' by adding huge and usually unsympathetic new wings and ranges. My own great-grandfather more than doubled the size of his modest Queen Anne house in Hertfordshire, a few windows of which now appear to squint out from behind a massive red-brick late Victorian pile. Indoors, and with sufficient time to spare, you can just work out the shape of the earlier building.

The post-medieval centuries witnessed the creation of the diverse rural landscapes that we all inhabit. True, there is evidence within those landscapes of much earlier times, but this is often hidden away, as humps and bumps, or sinuous field boundaries. Most of the 'furniture' of the countryside, the fences, gates and the drystone walls that surround our fields, were erected in the past two centuries – and if not, you can be certain that they have been extensively repaired in that time. Similarly, although there are indeed a few surviving ancient hedges (although sadly we no longer believe that these can be aged simply by counting their component species[50]) these will have been laid, interplanted and today trimmed back by mechanised flail-cutters countless times in the last hundred years.

Anyone with even a passing knowledge of the British countryside will be aware that the eastern side of the country has a drier climate, which is why the landscape here is given over to arable and mixed livestock and arable farming. To the west the more moist, Atlantic climate tends to favour pasture. This broad distinction was first mapped by the farm economist James Caird in 1852 and it applies with even greater force today, when grazing livestock are almost completely absent across huge areas of east Yorkshire, Nottinghamshire, Lincolnshire and East Anglia.[51] If livestock are absent I also fear for the knowledge and traditions that were once a part of animal husbandry. The much-parodied grasping 'barley baron' whose eyes are only focused on the 'bottom line' and whose vision requires him to grub up all trees and hedgerows to create vast prairie-like fields, was, until very recently, not a complete figure of fun. Although most farmers used the availability of EEC grants responsibly, such men indeed existed and their depredations can still be seen, especially in parts of eastern England.

Indeed, anyone blessed with good eyesight could appreciate the devastation that was caused to the landscape of lowland Britain from about 1950 to 1990 when some 400,000 kilometres of hedgerow were destroyed.[52] As I noted, much of this was perpetrated in the name of agricultural progress (I almost mistakenly said 'improvement') and often with huge injections of taxpayers' money. The trouble is that any taxpayers with interests other than increased agricultural efficiency were simply ignored. With the single exception of Scheduled Ancient Monuments (i.e. sites protected by law), no regard was taken of any archaeological remains that might be damaged by the new methods of power-farming. After some thirty years of unrestrained destruction, during which the vast majority of lowland sites and monuments were either destroyed or severely damaged, the powers that be reluctantly acknowledged that the plough was a threat to what little remains of our past.[53]

Let's finish this chapter by taking the long view. There can be little doubt that there were far larger changes to Britain's rural landscapes than those that began in and then followed the Second World War. The arrival of farming itself in the Neolithic, around 4500 BC, is an obvious example. The development of the first fields in the earlier Bronze Age, from about 2000 BC, is another. In historic times further eras of change included the later Saxon period (in, say, the three centuries after AD 800), when we saw the rise of the Open Field system and the nucleation of dispersed settlements into more compact villages.[54] Finally, and as we have just seen in this chapter, the disruption to rural life caused by successive waves of plague in the two centuries following the Black Death of 1348 was to prove of great importance, as it led directly to the regionalisation of the countryside that was such a prominent feature of the early modern period.

The rural transformations of prehistory and history, however, happened slowly, usually as part of more widespread changes in northern Europe (although the development of fields in Bronze Age Britain does still seem to have been a largely insular development).[55] And when I say 'slowly', I mean over at least two, and more usually three or four centuries. In the case of the Neolithic adoption of farming, the process took a full millennium. But the changes that the British government decided to push through, in order to meet the threat to food supplies posed by the Nazis across the Channel, happened very rapidly indeed. Something broadly similar took place in the Roman period when southern Britain became, in effect, the western Empire's 'bread basket', providing huge quantities of wheat for the Roman army. But unlike the rural reforms of the Second World War, the Roman changes were reversed in the late fourth and fifth centuries, when the troops were withdrawn – and large areas of the countryside reverted to grassland.[56]

The rapid movement out of pasture and into cereals and other crops that happened between 1939 and 1945 seems to have had a permanent effect. Recent research has drawn attention to the wartime changes to British farming which were intended to feed the populace, despite Hitler's U-boat Atlantic blockade.[57] Those reforms were urgently needed but they helped turn farmers and landowners from countrymen to businessmen, and everything that followed – especially the grant-driven over-production inspired by Brussels – was made possible by what happened then.

The wartime changes to the farming economy and landscape of Britain do help explain why subsequent developments, largely funded by EEC grant-aid in the form of the Common Agricultural Policy, or CAP, had such different effects on either side of the Channel. The small – tiny by British standards – landholdings of the French countryside were largely sustained by the injection of CAP cash – as, indeed, the legislation had intended from the very outset. But in Britain the far larger landowners and farmers, who had developed their businesses during the war, duly accepted the CAP handouts and used the money to further increase the size, and therefore the profitability, of their operations. They now had the capital to buy up smaller, generally less efficient operations, with the result that commercial farms in Britain grew rapidly in size throughout the seventies and eighties. Meanwhile in France, CAP money continued to support what was in effect a peasant-farming economy.

So ultimately, when I'm out field-walking and I angrily ponder the dark line left in the soil by a recently destroyed hedgerow, I first blame Nazis and then Eurocrats. I suppose it's much easier than blaming myself, and millions like me, who allowed such terrible things to happen to the countryside of lowland Britain in the last three decades of the twentieth century.

If torn-out hedgerows are a prominent feature of the rural land-scape bequeathed to us by the later twentieth century, then so-called 'agri-mansions' must be another. These large houses, built by success-ful farmers, contractors and farm managers, feature all the trappings of the more affluent outer suburbs, from swimming pools to gazebos and barbecues able to grill a medium-sized elephant. Large four-wheel-drives may be seen on their appropriately vast paved forecourts. These places were not built to conceal wealth. Far from it. They are latter-day symbols of power and prosperity: expressions in brick and stone of individual success and personal wealth. And as such, of course, they are nothing new.

CHAPTER TWO

'Polite Landscapes': Prestige, Control and Authority in Rural Britain

IF THERE IS ONE aspect of Britain that is widely celebrated abroad it must surely be the literally astonishing beauty of its parks and country houses. I use the word 'literally' because I've long been addicted to house and church visiting and I still come across scenes in parks and gardens that make me gasp in astonishment. I will never forget, for example, a visit to Stourhead in Wiltshire, once the home of perhaps Britain's greatest early archaeologist/antiquary, Sir Richard Colt Hoare. The park around Stourhead was designed by his ancestor Henry Hoare II and has remained open to visitors since the 1740s.[1] The carefully laid-out walk around the great artificial lake takes one past a succession of beautifully positioned temples, vistas and grottoes.

As a keen gardener myself, I am convinced that the main reason why the layout of the grounds at Stourhead work so well is that Hoare created them gradually, by degrees. Unlike most garden designers today, he did not start with a blank piece of paper and then impose his design on the landscape. Instead, the design *is* the landscape, only subtly, and sometimes not so subtly, modified to fit its creator's long-term vision. For me, Stourhead, together with Stowe (Buckinghamshire), Painshill (Surrey) and the water gardens at Studley Royal (North Yorkshire) are some of the greatest achievements of British art and design. One reason for their success is the discipline acquired by accepting the confines of their respective landscapes; I think this is why such gardens are infinitely superior to the stage-design set pieces one encounters today at events like the Chelsea Flower Show.

I well remember the hot autumn day when my wife Maisie and I first visited Stourhead. We had almost finished the descent from the last of the great garden buildings, the Temple of Apollo, and as we walked down the path we were both thinking similar thoughts, along the lines of a cool drink and a large sandwich. We approached the houses of Stourton, the estate village that successive owners of Stourhead had subtly altered to make more attractive, when my gaze was suddenly taken by a glint off the water to my left. I had forgotten all about the lake in my eagerness to find lunch and almost missed one of the greatest man-made views in the British landscape, over to the Palladian bridge and across the lake towards the Pantheon. I was so captivated by the scene before me that I then spent the next half-hour wrestling with cameras and tripod, attempting to take the perfect photograph. Meanwhile, lucky Maisie was grabbing something to eat before the pub closed for the afternoon.

Of course that view at Stourhead was no accident and was always meant to be the visitor's final *coup de théâtre*. After more than two and a half centuries it had lost none of its power or magic. A succession of inspired individuals have contributed to the growth and development of the British landscaped park, which is still regarded by many as the nation's greatest contribution to world art, so I would like to make it clear from the very outset that in this chapter I shall not attempt even a superficial history of its development, as others are far better qualified to do that than I.[2] Instead, I want to look at what archaeology can reveal about what was happening around the periphery of the great houses, parks and gardens; at how the estates and houses that went with them were built and run; and how private individuals and public authorities together organised life for the ordinary inhabitants of rural Britain.

But first, a few words on garden history and archaeology which over the past thirty or so years have become sub-disciplines in their own right.[3] One of their spin-offs has been the movement to restore old or overgrown parks and gardens to something approaching their former glories. This in turn has led people to research into more abstract subjects, like Georgian aesthetics and attitudes to landscape, because you cannot attempt sympathetic restoration without appreciating the subtleties of what the original gardeners and landscape designers were trying to achieve.[4] There have been a number of major excavation projects like those by Brian Dix, at Hampton Court Palace, or the great ruined Jacobean house at Kirby Hall, Northamptonshire, which have subsequently been followed by the restoration of entire formal gardens.[5] Garden archaeology has established itself as a sub-discipline in its own right. These highly specialised digs make extensive use of historical documents, and a variety of clever procedures, such as the meticulous plotting of the many rusted nails used to join the edging boards of long-lost flowerbeds.

As a general rule, many of the features revealed by garden archae-ologists can be very slight. Although they are from a much earlier period, I'm put in mind of the shallow trenches dug for the elaborate box hedges at the palatial Fishbourne Roman villa in Sussex.[6] Very similar traces have been found at the two sites just mentioned, Hampton Court and Kirby Hall. In many instances even these slight remains can be detected without putting a spade in the ground, through the use of various geophysical surveys.

Put simply, geophysics involves the use of highly sophisticated machines which are wheeled, dragged or lifted across the ground, and in the process record certain aspects of what lies beneath the surface.[7] Resistivity meters measure minute fluctuations in the soil's ability to conduct an electrical charge; magnetometers can detect tiny changes in the local magnetic field. Both techniques can reveal buried wells, post holes, ditches and walls.

Recently an entirely new generation of machines has come into being. Known as GPR, or ground penetrating radar, these instru-ments detect the way that radio waves are distorted and reflected back to a receiver on the surface. GPR plots a succession of buried layers and can penetrate deep into the ground. A particularly useful geophysical technique to industrial archaeologists is known by the rather unlovely name of magnetic susceptibility sampling, or 'Mag Sus' for short. Mag Sus can detect areas of magnetic enhancement caused by burning and can provide a fairly accurate indication of the temperatures involved – so it can readily distinguish, for example, between a bonfire and a furnace. More to the point, its results are instantaneous.

The rapid development of fast, lightweight, portable computers has revolutionised geophysics. When I began in archaeology in the early 1970s, I would routinely have to wait a week or a fortnight for my survey reports. Today it's usual to have finished results in an hour or two. Indeed, when filming for *Time Team*, our resident geophysicist, Dr John Gater, has been known to produce an accurate printout in minutes.

Although, of course, they are deeply wonderful (and France, for example, is full of them), I have to say I don't find strictly formal gardens very attractive, largely, I suppose, because I can imagine myself spending weeks and weeks meticulously trimming pyramids of box hedging and quietly going mad in the process. My own favourite restored garden is the one at Painshill in Surrey, which was originally laid out by Charles Hamilton between 1738 and 1773.[8] As at Stourhead, visitors perambulate around a great lake and are treated to a series of contrived views which include the usual colonnaded temples and a magnificent Turkish tent, successfully and imaginatively re-created in fibreglass. Perhaps the greatest feat of restoration at Painshill involved the rebuilding of a fanciful watery grotto, complete with side chambers, waterfalls and glittering crystal spar stalactites.

Today it is true to say that gardens are places of beauty and pleasure, but they have largely ceased to be instruments of political advancement and even intrigue. While most gardens were indeed permanent fixtures, some were created for a specific purpose, often the visit of a monarch and his or her court, and were always intended to be temporary – rather like the show gardens at Chelsea. Much controversy has recently been caused by the reconstruction at Kenilworth Castle in Warwickshire of such a temporary garden, created by Robert Dudley, Earl of Essex, to impress Elizabeth I when she made a two-week visit there for nineteen days, between 9 and 27 July 1575. Dudley, of course, is famous for being the Queen's favourite and we can only imagine what might have been his true motives for creating such a magnificent showpiece, which cost English Heritage the eye-watering sum of £2,100,000 to reconstruct, largely on the basis of a sketch and a single, albeit detailed, eyewitness letter.[9]

The garden is now permanently open to the public and it does give visitors a good impression of the lengths that people were prepared to go to impress the Tudor court, although doubts remain as to the so-called 'eyewitness' letter, which may have been a contemporary spoof or satire on Dudley's pretensions. But even if it was, one could argue that the garden it depicts might have been the sort of creation that would have been inspired by such a royal visit. On the other hand, there is some archaeological evidence to support it, such as the discovery by Brian Dix of fragments of a fountain similar to the one described in the letter. Taking all things together, I tend to accept that the garden was indeed constructed and I find the controversy, which has already generated at least one television documentary, fascinating. The modern re-creation was constructed just before the financial crisis and only six months later, in less profligate times, it now appears an excess. Doubtless the original garden impressed Her Majesty, but if I had been one of the impoverished tenants of the Dudley estate I might well have been rather less enthusiastic.

I have stated that I have no intention of attempting a history of designed landscapes, but it is worth pointing out that many books that approach the subject from an art historical background tend to ignore the complexity of what actually happened out there in the real world. Today garden fashions come and go with bewildering rapidity: a few years ago everyone was covering their lawns with pergolas and wooden decking, then they painted their garden furniture blue, and now one cannot step into even the smallest back garden without running the risk of toppling into a water feature. Much the same could be said about the past except that then taste was not dictated by television makeover programmes. Of course there were highly influential people, such as 'Capability' Brown or Humphrey Repton, whose general influence was widespread but there were also other, often complementary traditions, too.

Recently the landscape archaeologist and historian Tom Williamson has called for a more regional approach to garden archaeology. There is a natural tendency to sing the praises of a particular, often grand garden and to make it sound as if it stood in magnificent isolation, whereas in reality it was often surrounded by parks and horticultural creations of comparable quality. Tom has eloquently pointed out that the estates and homes of less grand, local landowners helped create regional traditions with a unique style all of their own.[10] It wasn't just that earlier traditions remained popular with many people, but sometimes innovations, which the textbooks would have one believe were universally and rapidly adopted, actually failed to find acceptance in

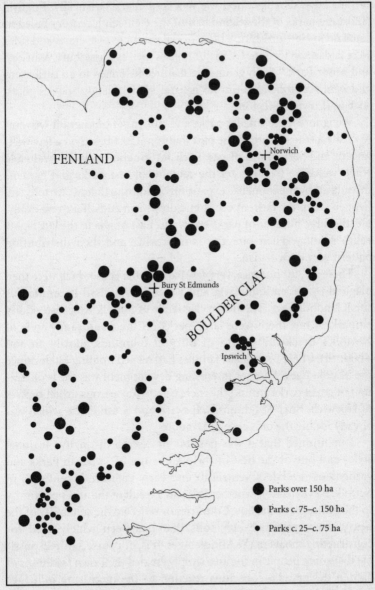

FIG 5   A map showing the distribution of landscape parks in East Anglia in the late eighteenth century.

certain areas. For instance, the new and characteristically 'English' landscape parks of the second half of the eighteenth century failed to catch on in Hertfordshire, where formal plantings of avenues and rides were laid out in the 1760s at major houses such as Cassiobury, Ashridge and Moor Park.[11] Such geometric features belonged to an earlier era and went very much against the 'natural' spirit of landscape designers, such as Brown or Repton.

We ignore these smaller parks and gardens at our peril if we want to create a true picture of the past that is not just based on a few well-known and very grand places. Such information will be invaluable when we come to interpret the remains of lost parks and gardens threatened by the immense expansion of housing that we are told will happen when the current economic downturn ends. Take one example: the large number of parks created in East Anglia in the late eighteenth century. Their quantity is impressive and their distribution pattern very informative.

There are, for instance, very few parks in the Fens, which were then plagued by endemic malaria and were characterised by numerous small landholdings. The heavy clay lands of Suffolk were also poorly emparked, but there were large parks on the poor, sandy soils of Norfolk's Breckland (north of Bury St Edmunds, mostly around Thetford), where prominent families had owned hunting estates since the Middle Ages. Another interesting development was the proliferation of small parks around the increasingly prosperous urban centres of Norwich, Bury St Edmunds, Ipswich and south Essex, which was already feeling the influence of London.

I mentioned that it was possible to discern distinctive regional styles and one of the best of these is the use of canals in parks and gardens of the late seventeenth and early eighteenth centuries in Suffolk. It is debatable whether this was a result of the area's proximity to the influence of the Low Countries or reflected the suitability of the heavy, water-retentive clay soils that had been widely used for constructing moats in the Middle Ages. It is, of course, entirely possible that some people in the area simply created their own traditions of garden design as a conscious reaction to the increasing influence exerted by London fashions and popular designers like 'Capability' Brown, which many independent local landowners resented.[12]

We tend to think that the great parks and gardens were the product of the seventeenth- and eighteenth-century Enlightenment, with perhaps a few Tudor excesses such as Hampton Court, Hatfield and Burghley Houses to point the way forward. In reality, however, members of the upper echelons of medieval society were showing off their power and influence by constructing staged and elaborate approaches to their castles, and by fashioning their own landscaped parks.[13] A particularly fine example is to be found on the approaches to the now ruined castle at Castle Acre, in Norfolk. This involved the redirection of a Roman road in the mid-twelfth century, by way of a newly founded Cluniac priory. Even when driving these narrow rural lanes today, this circuitous diversion, which was only done to impress visitors with the family's piety, still feels distinctly odd.[14]

By the same token, we also tend to see 'agri-business' and industrial farming as rather unpleasant and ultimately unnecessary creations of the later twentieth century, but, again, the reality is rather different. The rapid growth of Britain's population throughout the nineteenth century meant that the additional mouths had somehow to be fed and although imports could (and did) help to meet the shortage, in pre-refrigeration times the majority of food, especially of milk and meat, had to be produced at home. And here the well-laid-out model farms of the large rural estates were to play a crucially important role.

We will see in Chapter 5 that the monuments to Britain's industrial past have been cared for and cherished since the subject of industrial archaeology first emerged from the shadows back in the 1960s. But their rural equivalents have only very recently received anything like their fair share of recognition – and almost too late, because numerous farm buildings of the eighteenth and nineteenth centuries are now becoming rather tatty and even derelict, simply because farmers in the twenty-first century are finding the money for their maintenance harder and harder to come by.[15] A proportion has been saved for posterity by conversion to office or light industrial use, but sadly these remain a minority. The rest are quietly slipping into neglect and disrepair.

The great landed estates that were such a feature of the countryside from the seventeenth to the earlier to mid-twentieth centuries have, of course, left us superb country houses, parks and gardens.[16] But these were essentially the cherries on the top of the cake. They were the obvious symbols of power and success, but much of the money needed to build and maintain such grand edifices came from the land surrounding them, which therefore needed to be efficiently farmed. And make no mistake: some of the estates could be very large indeed: the Census of 1871 shows that estates of the Duke of Bedford in his home county comprised a staggering 35,589 acres (14,408 hectares).[17]

By any criteria these estates were major businesses and they needed to be well run. They also had a huge influence on the development of the countryside and of rural communities – a role that has recently been recognised by historical archaeologists.[18] But this was also the period when educated people had learned the lessons of the Enlightenment. They were not simply concerned with making money, but needed to establish and maintain their place in society, while at the same time demonstrating their good taste. It was a period, too, when growing urban industries could provide alternative sources of employment for rural people. So for these and other reasons, the eighteenth and nineteenth centuries saw the construction of a series of model farms, the majority of which (as we saw in the previous chapter) were built as partnership ventures between entrepreneurial tenants and their estate landlords.

The slide into disrepair of so many estate farms has happened quite slowly, and bodies such as English Heritage have been able to anticipate events by carrying out surveys of model farms which have given rise to specific reviews and an excellent overall synthesis by the leading authority on the subject, Susanna Wade Martins.[19] I have to say that, although I was aware of changes in the design of modern and early modern farm buildings, I was not able to discern any obvious pattern, apart from a general progression from small to large and also from decorative – even whimsical – to the more businesslike and severely functional buildings of Victorian high farming.

I mention whimsicality because sometimes farms occurred within sight of a carefully arranged view from a landscaped park, in which case they needed to be camouflaged to resemble a suitably romantic Gothic pile.[20] Susanna gives several examples of these, one of which, illustrated in the pages of the Gentleman's and Farmer's Architect for 1762, actually includes corner towers that appear to have been reduced by artillery fire.[21] My own favourite is the disguise of a range of farm buildings overlooking the great park at Stowe, Buckinghamshire, which have been made to resemble the turrets and battlements of a not very convincing medieval castle, which looks particularly odd – rather like a brick-built film set – when viewed from the modern road, which passes by on the 'wrong' side.

The evolving patterns of farmyard layout are important as they illustrate the changing attitudes and outlook of the great landowners, and those who served and advised them. Sometimes, but not always, these shifts in emphasis mirror developments in the design of the great parks and gardens they helped to finance. More often than not, however, they reflect wider changes in the worlds of politics, trade or economics and latterly, too, of agricultural science. The recent survey of model farms by English Heritage has revealed that four broad phases can be discerned, beginning with the philosophy of 'Improvement' whose underlying principles could be defined as beauty, utility and profit. This phase, which I've discussed in Chapter 1, lasted from 1660 until 1790 and was followed by one of 'Patriotic Improvement' (1790– 1840). During these years farming and profitable estate management were seen as patriotic duties at a time when Britain was often at war with France, and food prices generally remained firm. George III set an example to all by employing the well-known land agent Nathaniel Kent to manage the farms and other resources of Windsor Great Park profitably.

The third phase (1840–75) was characterised by 'Practice with Science' and coincides with the time of Victorian high farming. The final phase, 'Retrenchment', from 1875 to 1939, saw estates hit by the collapse of prices and the farming depression of the 1870s. This was a result of many factors, including the import of cheaper food, especially grain, shipped in bulk from overseas. It could also be seen as a much-delayed after-effect of Peel's repeal of the protectionist Corn Laws of 1846.

In the 1850s and 1860s, British farming was able to cope with the freed-up market, but the large-scale importation of grain, made possible by the introduction of larger ocean-going vessels from the 1870s, caused major problems. After that, British farming entered a prolonged recession which continued, with a few relatively minor ups and downs, until the Great Depression of the 1930s, followed by the Second World War, when many of the great estates started to disintegrate – a process that was hastened in the post-war years by the introduction of death duties and other taxes on inherited wealth.

This brief history of the development of later post-medieval estates could readily have been derived from historical sources alone, but what makes the recent survey of model farms so important is the large number of buildings that were measured and photographed right across England. The owners and workers were also able to provide the surveyors with information on how the different spaces were actually used within living memory. The result is a hugely important body of information which will undoubtedly form the basis of many studies in the future. But to give an idea of its general scope, they have provided English Heritage with brief county-by-county summaries of the principal estates, their best surviving farms and a glimpse of their histories.[22] It makes fascinating reading as it stands, but the information behind it has also been used to construct four plans of typical farm layouts between 1750 and 1900, which I have reproduced here.[23]

All farm buildings, whether on large lowland estates or on small upland family farms, were constructed to provide shelter for livestock and to keep stored crops dry. They could also be used for threshing and other crop-processing tasks, and for the preparation of fodder (e.g. hay and straw) or feed (e.g. grain or turnips) for livestock. Other uses, such as specialised milking parlours, became increasingly popular later, especially in farms near large cities. One additional important function of a post-medieval farmyard was the converting of chemically 'hot' raw animal dung to benign, nutrient-rich manure for spreading on fields. This is a biological process that involves the storage of the material in a muck heap, or midden, in well-drained conditions, with or without a roof.

The earliest estate farms (1750–1800) were based on a courtyard plan with the house on one side and the barn opposite. On either side of the yard were stables and animal sheds with a muck heap at the centre of the yard. In this layout the house was an integral part of the farmyard as nearly all the labour, including threshing, was carried out by hand. In the next period (1800–40) the house has been completely detached from the yard, which has now become E-shaped, with a main

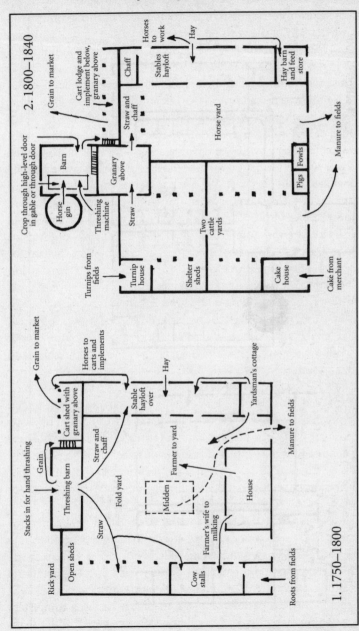

FIG 6   The layout of typical model or estate farms in England around 1750–1800 (left) and 1800–1840 (right).

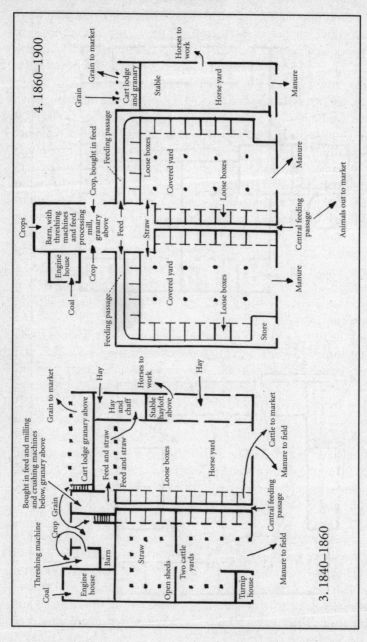

FIG 7 The layout of typical model or estate farms in England around 1840–1860 (left) and 1860–1900 (right).

two-storey threshing barn at right angles to the long range, from which sprang three parallel ranges (the arms of the 'E'), where the horses and livestock were housed and fed. By this period many tasks were now mechanised, the power being provided either by horses or water. On many farms you can still spot the circular walls that surrounded a horse 'gin', where a horse or horses pulled or pushed a long arm, rather like a treadmill.

The plan of earlier Victorian estate farms (1840–60) remained essentially E-shaped, but now the layout had become increasingly industrial, with the functions of the barn moved closer to the livestock accommodation. By this time, too, imported feeds were becoming more important and machinery previously used to thresh home-produced corn was now used to process the new feeds. The fattening of livestock was also becoming better understood and animals were separated into individual stalls or smaller groups to prevent undue competition. Some of these stalls were serviced by way of a central feeding passage. These better designed and more compact yards were often roofed over to keep the middens dry, thereby speeding up and improving manure production.

In the final decade of Victorian high farming the builders of model farms turned their attention to livestock units when the earlier plan with a central barn at right angles to the other ranges reappeared, but this time the building functioned more as a feed-processing factory than a barn. In the late nineteenth century (1860–1900) all livestock was housed in stalls that were conveniently accessed by feeding passages. By this time labour was becoming more expensive and routine tasks such as feeding and mucking out were made as straight-forward as possible, with feed in some instances being moved on trol-leys and tramlines. The two central covered yards continued to be used for the maturation of muck into manure.

I can well recall sitting down to watch television on freezing winter nights when I was working at the Royal Ontario Museum, in Toronto, in the 1970s. Inevitably I sometimes felt rather homesick, which is probably why I watched repeats of all the episodes of *Upstairs, Downstairs*, a British TV series then being shown in Canada. I still think it was a fabulous series, beautifully researched and acted, and quite rightly hugely popular in Britain and North America. What I didn't realise at the time was how remarkably archaeological the approach of the programme makers was, because they showed precisely how a great house was serviced and operated; this is not something one can generally read about in novels of the period, which tended to focus on the goings-on of the great and the good 'upstairs'.

Television costume dramas have played an important part in the way that country houses are now shown to the public, with greater attention at long last being paid to the servants' hall, the cellars, the kitchens and the butler's pantry – not to mention the stables, carriage house and scullery. I for one would far rather look at a nineteenth-century kitchen range than a display case stuffed with Meissen porcelain – or, indeed, some luckless volunteer dressed up rather awkwardly as a Georgian ladies' maid or a footman. I find that the practical things of daily life, such as tools and implements, especially if they still retain the patina and scars of repeated use, have a power to re-create the past, something that fine objects often lack.

The service ranges of large country houses were where the work took place. Often they were of comparable size to the space occupied by the family itself. It was not uncommon to find that several entire storeys, or sometimes complete wings, were occupied by the domestic servants and there was a network of stairs and passages that allowed them to go about their daily duties without bumping into anyone from the employer's family. In larger houses the world 'below stairs' was indeed a world – and, as *Upstairs, Downstairs* showed so well, it was often as vigorous and exciting as that in the great drawing rooms 'upstairs'.

If we examine the shapes and layout of these domestic ranges they can tell us a great deal about the social changes that were taking place in early modern times, especially if the excavations are on a reasonably large scale. A few small slit trenches might establish construction dates and that sort of thing, but one needs an entire range to be stripped and excavated if one is to understand how it was used. Happily, this is exactly what has happened in a fine Jacobean (formerly) country house now surrounded by the streets and dwellings of modern Birmingham. I had been aware for some time of the presence of a great house as one drove towards the city centre on that long stretch of raised road south of the M6, but, to be honest, I had dismissed it as something Victorian – which I'm now aware was an error on my part. But I've been back there since and taken a closer look, and to my surprise I was completely wrong. Aston Hall really is rather special: a large three-storey Jacobean house with prominent turrets and banks of chimneys, elevated on a natural terrace and still dominating the landscape, which, as I've said, consists mainly of modern urban buildings. The notable exception is the village of Aston's medieval parish church nearby, and a small park, which manages to retain a reminder of the area's once rural surroundings.

Today Aston Hall is run by Birmingham City Council Museums and Galleries and in 2009 it reopened after a £13 million programme of repair and refurbishment, which included extensive excavation.[24] As the digs were a part of a major project they took place on a suitably large scale. Anything else and the results would inevitably have proved less conclusive and, of course, far less exciting.

The house itself was built between 1618 and 1635 by Sir John Holte, probably to the designs of John Thorpe, and it represents a clear statement of the new relationship between master and servant that had developed in post-medieval times.[25] Had Aston Hall been built in the early fifteenth century the kitchens, pantries and other domestic rooms would have been inside the main buildings, together with servants' accommodation which was not kept particularly separate from that of the owner's family. Although the family would have dined at a separate high table, when eating on public occasions few efforts were made in the Middle Ages to separate the lives of the domestic staff from those they were serving. All of that changed quite rapidly in the later sixteenth and seventeenth centuries, when new houses were designed to keep the activities of resident domestic staff separate from the daily lives of the owner's family.

In new houses of the seventeenth century, domestic staff would have been housed in their own quarters in either a basement or a separate wing and additional sleeping space would have been provided in the (often rather draughty) attics. For the first time, these various rooms would have been linked by their own network of stairs and passages which meant that the owner's family need never contact a servant unless, that is, he or she wanted to. Similarly, although the kitchens remained in the main house (but very much within the domestic area), the rooms where other household activities took place, such as the brewhouse, stores, washing rooms, bakehouse and dairy were removed either to separate wings, or (as at Aston Hall) an altogether separate Service Range.

The Service Range at Aston was very carefully positioned at the foot of a slope some twenty-five metres from the main house, and largely concealed by a tall brick wall. It is interesting that Dugdale's 1656 view of the house uses perspective to give the impression that the Stable Range is even more removed and it entirely conceals the Service Range. Indeed, guests at the great house need never have been aware that the Service Range even existed. The main house and its North Wing formed one side of the domestic Stable Court, which was open to the west but enclosed to north and east by the Service and Stable Ranges. Inside the North Wing were the kitchen, the wine and beer cellars, scullery and servants' sleeping quarters on the upper floor. This arrangement meant that no guest or member of the owner's family need ever have to look out onto the Stable Court.

In anthropological terms the increasing separation of 'those upstairs' from 'them downstairs' might be seen as hierarchical, but the developing social hierarchies did not stop there. Below stairs, and fully recognised by the owner's family, we see an emerging ranked society in which senior household servants, such as the butler, who waited directly on the owner, the cook and housekeeper and others were accommodated within the domestic apartments of the main house, which at Aston Hall were in the North Wing. Junior servants would have to find their sleeping spaces in the Service Range or attics.

I must have read thousands of excavation reports and a high proportion of them have been almost unendurably dull. This sad situation has arisen because over the past twenty or so years, ever since changes in planning law made it compulsory for developers to pay for archaeological examination of sites they were about to destroy, large numbers of quite insignificant excavations have had to take place – and then reports be written up. In theory – and in practice, too – these small projects add to our sum of knowledge about a given region and in time they start to produce coherent stories. But it is not a rapid

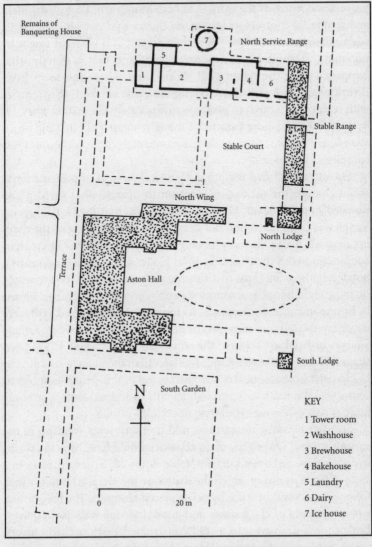

FIG 8 *A general plan of Aston Hall, Birmingham (built 1618–35), showing the location of standing buildings (shaded) and walls exposed by excavation in the North Service Range. The main approach to the house would have been from the east, between the two lodges. Behind the house was a landscaped terrace, with the principal gardens to the south.*

process and much of the work is, at best, humdrum. That is why most archaeological contractors leap at the chance of doing larger projects, where the element of new research is greater and where it might be possible to write a good, original report. And that is exactly what happened after the Aston Hall excavations, where the team from Birmingham University have combined evidence from the trenches with historical research to produce an absolutely fascinating story. I'll be quite honest: before I started, I thought a paper about a dig on an abandoned service range would make extremely dry reading, but I was completely mistaken.

Having established the broad historical context of post-medieval social change, the excavators went on to discuss what the dig had revealed in more detail. The first surprise was that the North Service Range was in all likelihood not designed by the architect of the main house at all. Instead it was probably built by the builders' foreman in conjunction with the client, Sir John Holte. Although by no means a botch job, there are signs that this building was put up more cheaply than the main house. It accommodated the ground, rather than altered it. In one instance, for example, a chimney and reinforced wall were never completed and were positioned elsewhere, but leaving telltale courses of brickwork where the work had been started. It has been suggested that the Service Range was later than the main house, but the bricks used were identical in size and typical of the earlier seventeenth century, so if it was later it was only slightly so and was almost certainly built as part of the main building operations of 1618–35.

So what have the excavations told us about what went on in the various rooms? One of the main activities would have been the washing of clothes, bed linen, curtains, table cloths etc. This took place in a suite of three rooms of which the main one was the washhouse which followed medieval practice by being placed alongside the brewhouse, where a supply of clean water and good drainage was also required. Both rooms drained into a well-constructed brick-arched culvert, which ran across the Service Range diagonally, below the brewhouse floor. Hot water for the washhouse probably came from a range in the brewhouse next door and heated coppers were probably not added until the eighteenth century, when two were installed in the north-east corner. Washing would have been very hard work, carried out entirely by hand. The laundry was where the ironing and finishing was carried out. We know from an inventory of 1654 that a laundry existed but we don't have its location; the laundry shown on the plan (Fig. 8) was an eighteenth-century addition. Similarly we don't know precisely where the drying room would have been, but it seems likely that it was upstairs on the first floor, probably above the washhouse.

The brewhouse and bakehouse were positioned next to each other, but separated by an original seventeenth-century partition wall. The positioning of the brewing and baking rooms next to each other probably reflects the fact that both processes needed yeast. Both needed heat, too, and although much of the evidence at Aston had been removed when the site was cleared of recyclable building materials after demolition of the buildings around the Stable Court in the 1860s, the hearths in the brew- and bakehouses were different in pattern, which clearly indicated that the two rooms were used for separate purposes. The brick-built oven in the bakehouse was probably built back-to-back with the open hearth of the brewhouse next door, although we cannot be absolutely certain about this. Grain was stored in the room over the bakehouse, which we know from an eighteenth-century inventory contained a special mill for sieving flour. This was probably where the dough was initially prepared, although in winter it would be taken downstairs to rise in the warmer room.

The large open hearth of the brewhouse had to be big enough to accommodate the two large coppers that appear in the eighteenth-century inventory. Malt for brewing was probably germinated and dried elsewhere (the process requires much space), but was stored in the room above the brewhouse. The brewhouse relied on gravity to feed the unfermented beer, known as wort, from the coppers into cooling vats and thence into the fermentation vessels. We don't know the precise size of the two coppers but we can guess from the size of the brewhouse and the hearth that they must have been large, each holding between 85 and 400 gallons (386–1,818 litres). Having spent two years of my life working in a brewery I know only too well that the malty smell when the coppers are boiling the mash can be quite overpowering. It even sticks to one's clothes at the end of the day, which is doubtless why the ventilation of the brewhouse was carefully arranged to avoid the washhouse nearby.

The dairy was carefully positioned to avoid excessive winter cold or summer heat, sheltered from cold winds by other buildings, but with a northern aspect and no windows on its southern side. One unexpected discovery was an original seventeenth-century (enlarged in the nineteenth century) cellar below the dairy, which would have been used to store cheese, butter, milk and cream. At the western end of the range was a tower or turret room whose purpose remains uncertain, although it was used in the nineteenth century as a lavatory, which was placed over an earlier culvert below. Ice became important for making the sorbets and ice creams which became fashionable in smart circles in the eighteenth century. Incidentally, the first use of the term 'ice cream' was at the feast of St George at Windsor, in May 1671, and the earliest recorded English ice-cream recipe was created in 1718.[26] The Aston ice house dates to the eighteenth century. It was placed appropriately on the cold (north) side of the North Range and was circular, but was built with a single, rather than the more usual cavity, wall.

When I was a boy we used to go to my mother's family's house in Co. Carlow, in the Republic of Ireland, for our holidays. In fact it wasn't so much a house as a small castle, complete with battlements, a deep well and a dungeon. It originally dated to the aftermath of the sixteenth-century Desmond Wars of Co. Wexford, was completed in 1620 and has been in the family ever since. It had even come under siege in the English Civil War of the mid-seventeenth century when the well became haunted by the ghost of an unfortunate housemaid who fell down it one night. It was wonderfully Anglo-Irish, more than a little rundown and in some ways very eccentric, with a theatre, still in use, converted from a farm building which was brightly decorated with my mother's somewhat whimsical pre-war paintings of (I think) cavorting nymphs and shepherds. You can read about similar such places in the wonderful novels of Molly Keane, whose family lived in another country house just a few miles away.

I used to go for long solitary walks through the massively overgrown gardens that ran down to the river and there, lurking in the undergrowth, I found a tin shed over a concrete-lined tail race. Below the shed, in exactly the same fashion as Viking-period water wheels of Scotland and Northern Ireland, was a horizontally mounted turbine, whose shaft drove a generator in the shed above it. The power was then conducted to the castle by wires mounted on small telegraph poles and I can just remember, probably in the late forties or very early fifties, the lights coming on and shining with the strange, soft, amber-coloured light of 120-volt DC power. They even had a few single-bar DC heaters which were incredibly dangerous, because the constant polarity of DC (as opposed to the alternating polarity of AC) attracts rather than repels, if, that is, you have the misfortune to make direct contact with it. And I can recall being terrified by very Irish tales of electrocuted housemaids finding themselves curling helplessly around heaters and receiving horrible burns before dying a lingering death. For what it's worth, I believe that original generator is now safely in the Science Museum in Dublin, but the tin shed and tail race are still *in situ*, quietly rusting in the persistent, warm mists created by the River Derry.

That anecdote illustrates what one might term the preservative power of country houses, where space is rarely a problem and where in the past the expenses of demolition or removal could be avoided simply by closing a few doors, or planting half a dozen rambler roses. My colleague at Leicester University, Professor Marilyn Palmer, has written eloquently on the subject and is leading a one-woman campaign aimed at the various heritage organisations, such as the National Trust, to make them realise that Britain's country houses still contain a surprisingly rich resource of defunct technology.[27] Her message has now, I am delighted to say, struck home. They do make a welcome change from the ubiquitous shelves of showy porcelain.

It should come as no surprise that some country houses have in effect become time capsules. Many of their owners, when the houses were first built in the late eighteenth and nineteenth centuries, could afford to install the very latest in water supply and sanitation, but then the prosperity brought about by of the era of Victorian high farming came to a sudden and resounding halt with the agricultural depression of the 1870s. This was followed by the Great War, the Great Depression and then the post-war changes in taxation that were intended to reduce and redistribute inherited wealth. So many of the families who actually had to live in these great piles also had to cope with poor-to-non-existent heating, lighting and other facilities that the urban and suburban population were by now taking for granted. Marilyn Palmer records a wonderful quotation that sums up the situation very well: 'on the whole, hospitals, prisons and lunatic asylums were centrally heated and lit by gas long before country houses'.[28] The great house at Calke Abbey in Derbyshire, for example, did not acquire electricity until 1962 and the eccentric, reclusive character of the Harpur-Crewe family, who lived there until 1981, has been captured by the conservators of the National Trust who have given visitors a wonderfully evocative display of what the place would have looked like in its final, and very run-down, days.

We are becoming perhaps too accustomed to seeing country houses and their gardens re-created or 're-imagined' to look as they might have appeared in their prime. At the risk of sounding curmudgeonly I have to say I don't like these restorations, no matter how much time and money has been spent in trying to make them authentic. For me, the effect is not authentic so much as 'authentick'. It's phoney, simply because you cannot re-create the totality of the past. If you put a twenty-first-century young woman in a Victorian maid's dress she will always look modern – because that is what she is. If anything, it's even worse if professional actors are employed. And besides, I find these efforts invariably destroy or overwrite the pictures in my head, which, like those on the radio, are better than anything placed before me on stage, in country house, or on screen. They may not be perfect but they are, as the saying goes, 'mine own'.

So I was more than delighted when I came across Sir Vauncey Harpur-Crewe's bedroom at Calke Abbey. Far from being tarted up, this room had been left in the state it was in, when first found, in 1985. The walls were cluttered with hunting trophies and sundry photographs of ancestors, together with paintings of seascapes and naval scenes. Further faded Victorian pictures were on the floor, leaning against the damp-stained blue wallpaper. The bed was covered in stuffed and mounted foxes' and deer's heads. At the foot of the rusty iron bedstead there was a wooden towel rail, several more stacked pictures, a battered doll's house, an empty wooden box of 'Hudson's Dry Soap' and a cheap, white-painted chair whose wickerwork seat had broken and collapsed. There was no carpet on the rough wooden floor, nor were there any lights or power points. The only thing missing from this remarkable display was the smell, which I could imagine, but would rather not describe in words.

TOP: Model farm, Holkham Park, Norfolk. Holkham was the estate of the prominent eighteenth-century agricultural 'Improver', Coke of Norfolk, the 1st Earl of Leicester. These buildings are by the architect G. A. Dean, who worked for the estate during the 1850s, a prosperous era known as Victorian high farming. The Italianate style was widely adopted not just on many rural estates, but on the railways that were then being built on a very large scale. The range shown here, for example, quite closely resembles many of the station buildings at King's Cross, in London.

ABOVE: A view across the lake towards the Pantheon (1754) at Stourhead, Wiltshire, with the Palladian bridge (1762) in the foreground. The artificial lake (c. 1754) and its surroundings were laid out by Henry Hoare II, and most of the buildings were designed for him by Henry Flitcroft.

RIGHT: The restored grotto at Painshill, Surrey. The garden was laid out by Charles Hamilton between 1738 and 1773 and featured an artificial lakeside grotto complete with sculptures in niches, waterfalls and side chambers. The vast cost of the grotto was a major reason why Hamilton was forced to sell his estate in 1773. The glistening walls are made from satin spar and calcite fixed to a hidden wooden framework.

ABOVE: A view along the first turnpike road (1663) in the village of Caxton, Cambridgeshire. During the Middle Ages the Old North Road became an important arterial route to the north and the turnpike trust was established to pay for its maintenance, which was proving too much for the parish authorities. This view shows two former roadside inns: in the foreground is the seven-bay, eighteenth-century George Inn; beyond is the white-painted sixteenth-century Crown Inn. Both these inns illustrate well the prosperity the turnpike brought with it. The George Inn was converted to a large private residence with a fine new front door and the Crown was completely re-fronted in Georgian times.

BELOW: The cast-iron Waterloo Bridge which carries the great Holyhead Road across the Afon Conwy at Betws-y-Coed. The elaborate inscription, THIS ARCH WAS CONSTRUCTED IN THE SAME YEAR THE BATTLE OF WATERLOO WAS FOUGHT, was an astute political move by Thomas Telford to appease the government, which had funded the Holyhead Road. In fact, although the components had been completed in 1815, the year of Waterloo, the actual erection took place the following year. It soon became popular with tourists as a symbol of British engineering prowess.

ABOVE: A paired toll house (right) and weighbridge house (left) on either side of the A5 at Ty Isaf, some 3.5 km due west of Llangollen, Denbighshire. These, like most of the roadside structures of Telford's Holyhead Road, are to standard designs. The toll gates between the two buildings would probably have been of sunburst design, with matching turnstiles for pedestrians.

RIGHT: Milestone No. 73. This original standard Telford milestone, of dressed Carboniferous limestone with inserted cast-iron plate, has been reset into the modern revetment wall of the lay-by near the Ty Isaf toll house, near Llangollen. It is one of eighty-three milestones, all of which have now been replaced or re-created. They were set at mile intervals from Holyhead and also show the distance to local towns, in miles (M) and furlongs (F).

HOLY-
HEAD
73
CORWEN
6M-2F
LLANGOLLEN
3M-6F

LEFT: Telford's Holyhead Road included some distinctive ancillary structures such as these fine iron sunburst gates to the side of the bridgemaster's house at the southern end of the Menai Strait suspension bridge. Gates like this would have been used at most toll points. Today some survive as reused farm gates, which have often been repaired by welding. Note that this original gate is riveted. A toll house, plus gates, has been rebuilt at the Blists Hill Open Air Museum, Telford, where the principal Telford archive is housed.

ABOVE: The unpretentious brickwork façade of the southern entrance to the Blisworth Tunnel, Northamptonshire. The tunnel passes through the limestone ridge on the southern side of the Nene Valley and marked an important stage in the development of the Grand Junction Canal on its completion in 1805, after three years of difficult construction. An earlier attempt to take the canal through Blisworth Hill in 1793–6 had failed, probably due to flooding. The Grand Junction linked London and the Thames Valley with Oxford, Leicester and the Black Country.

BELOW: A view along the bed of the tramway that led from the valley up to the navvy camp on Risehill, a part of the Settle–Carlisle Railway, in North Yorkshire. The tramway wagons were hauled by a stationary steam engine located just behind the camera. To the right is one of two huge heaps of rocks that were winched up the air shaft from the tunnel far below the ground. Each of these rocks was cut or blasted by hand.

RIGHT: Grooves left by the drill holes used to pack an explosive charge can still be seen on many of the larger rocks.

BELOW: Bridge over the A43, where it is crossed by the M1 at Junction 15, near Northampton. This is part of the earliest stretch of the M1, mostly built in 1959 and opened to traffic the following year. The bridges, which were designed by Sir Owen Williams and Partners, were of six standard types, the larger of which, such as this, were colonnaded, heavy and permanent in appearance. In this respect Williams's work recalls the concrete structures of the pre-war German *Autobahnen*, rather than the lighter, more graceful styles of the 1960s.

ABOVE: The River Porter in Whitely Woods, Sheffield. The rivers of Sheffield were lined with water-powered workshops for the production of cutlery and edge tools. Most of these mills were built in the seventeenth and eighteenth centuries. This view from the river is looking down a 'head goit', a channel or tail race feeding into a millpond (out of view, to the left). Note how the mill builders had made use of the harder rock that formed the riverbed to provided a natural base for the angled dam (left) that diverted water into the head goit. Some mills along the River Porter continued in use until the 1930s.

BELOW: York Gate was the elaborate watergate built for George Villiers, 1st Duke of Buckingham, for his new London residence, York House, which he acquired from the Archbishop of York in 1624. Today York Gate stands at some considerable distance from the north shore of the river it once served, following the construction in 1862 of the Northern Low Level Sewer. Sir Joseph Bazalgette, the engineer behind London's sewer system, built the Victoria Embankment to consolidate and protect the new sewer from erosion by the Thames.

BELOW: Four of the seven blocks of double houses comprising The Paragon, a crescent on the edge of Blackheath, south-east London. These elegant houses were designed by the local architect and developer Michael Searles and built between 1796 and 1807. They represent the first (and most upmarket) stage of the development that saw Blackheath village change from a rich but essentially rural area into a series of residential estates for people working in London. Most of the area had been developed by 1840; for the remainder of the nineteenth-century development in the area mostly involved infilling between plots and rebuilding of older properties.

TOP: A view of the Forth Rail Bridge from the head of the North Queensferry town pier (right) where the ferry berthed prior to the opening of the Forth Road Bridge (in 1964). The small hexagonal lighthouse with the copper roof was constructed around 1810 as part of John Rennie's improvements to the ferry facilities. The magnificent cantilever railway bridge was the largest ever built and the first with a steel superstructure. It opened in 1890 and was designed by Sir John Fowler and Sir Benjamin Baker.

ABOVE: Back-to-back housing was not necessarily squalid, nor confined to the industrial north alone. This view of housing provided by the Great Western Railway in Swindon, Wiltshire, shows the alley running between Reading Street (left) and Oxford Street (right), from the arched entranceway corridor off East Street. Both streets were built in the same operation between 1846 and 1847. The great engineer Isambard Kingdom Brunel would have closely supervised, if not drawn up himself, the design of these houses.

LEFT: A tipping-cistern toilet block at Hungate, York. Water from sinks and bath tubs accumulated in the cistern (bottom of picture) which automatically tipped when full, discharging a rush of water which washed away waste from beneath the toilet downpipes, one of which is still in position (two others in stalls beyond have been removed). Tipping-cisterns were introduced in the mid-nineteenth century and some, such as these, remained in use into the 1930s. In hot weather, and when water was scarce, they failed to work properly and solid waste would accumulate, this becoming a potential source of disease.

ABOVE: A view of the basement floor of so-called 'cellar houses' which the early textile manufacturer Sir Richard Arkwright provided for the workforce of Shude Mill, Manchester, at the time of its opening in 1781. The house seen here was part of a terrace along Angel Street. Each house was entered from the rear by way of a paved yard, which can be seen in the foreground. The cellar room where the two archaeologists are working had a fireplace and a brick floor and was used for eating and cooking. By the 1830s single rooms like this were being used to accommodate entire families.

BELOW: Terrace housing at Caithness Row, New Lanark. These houses were built by David Dale, Robert Owen's father-in-law, in the 1790s to house an influx of Highland workers. This was the time of the infamous Clearances and the first Highlanders to work at New Lanark were on a ship to North Carolina from the Isle of Skye, which was forced to berth at Greenock by storms in 1791; other workers from the Highlands came from further north, hence the name of the terrace.

BELOW: A view of the Stanley Mills, near Perth, from the River Tay. This complex of textile mills had a chequered history, despite a good supply of water which was brought to the site through tunnels. After powering the mill wheels the water returned to the river through the square outfall visible in the foreground, left. The nearest building is the Bell Mill, built by Richard Arkwright in 1787; beyond are the Mid Mill (built in the 1820s) and the taller East Mill, which first opened in the 1790s and was rebuilt in the 1820s, after it burnt down in 1799.

ABOVE: Robert Owen is often believed to have created the settlement around the mills at New Lanark, but nearly all the housing was built in the 1790s by his father-in-law, David Dale, including the fine classically-inspired New Buildings tenement block seen here, with the steep wooded sides of the Clyde Valley behind. Robert Owen's house, with two distinctive dormer windows, can be seen in the foreground, left.

BELOW: A view along the washing rakes at the North of England Lead Mining Museum, at Killhope, Co. Durham. Ponies, walking along the planked path (left), towed tubs of ore, or 'bouse', from the mine behind the camera. This was tipped into the stalls of the Bousesteads where the ore was barrowed the short distance to the washing floor where children reduced impurities by washing and screening. The lower railway then took it to the water-powered crushing mill which is just visible, to the right.

BELOW: Spar boxes were an important folk-art tradition in Weardale in the final two decades of the nineteenth century. They began life as display cases made by miners to display their collections of mineral crystals from the North Pennine lead mines. Some of the later examples showed the crystals against a scene from daily life, such as this view of a lead mine by William Ridley of Allenheads, who was himself a working miner; his spar box has carrying handles at opposite ends, which suggest it was routinely carried around the area for display.

That display of Sir Vauncey's bedroom was in theory about the house as it was revealed in 1985, but for me it spoke volumes not just about social attitudes in Victorian and Edwardian England, but also about the downside, the limitations and personal restrictions that were the inevitable accompaniment of inherited wealth and status. To return to our 'upstairs, downstairs' theme, the poorly paid servants who lived below stairs had in many important respects more freedom than their supposed superiors upstairs. And this was particularly true of minor members of the great families, who were often slavishly dependent on the charity of their more prominent relatives.

We still lack a coherent set of records about the technology employed at country houses and we will need these if we are ever going to write useful accounts of how the people who lived and worked in them adapted to the gradual arrival of the modern world. It could be argued that this is of slight importance, given how few families actually lived in such grand style; but it's not about the 'upstairs' families alone: we are interested as well in the lives of the servants, agents and tenants who also lived, visited or worked in the great houses. Country houses were, after all, an important – if not *the* important – component of many rural societies and, if nothing else, such narratives might tell us something about the daily lives of ordinary country folk, about whom we still know precious little.

Our knowledge of the workings of country houses reflects the traditional bias of the many guidebooks towards the great state rooms and pictures; yet we still know little about the early installation of gas or electricity. Similarly, we know how water was supplied, for example, to the great lakes and fountains at places like Chatsworth, yet we know remarkably little about the supply of water to the houses themselves, or the removal of waste once water closets had been installed. These, incidentally, were patented by Joseph Bramah in 1778 and in less than twenty years he claimed to have made six thousand units.[29]

When one reads the blurb, both in leaflets and on the internet, about various country house gardens, the text is full of references to rockeries, rhododendrons, statues and summer houses, but never to drains, septic tanks or sewerage. Indeed, you would have to make special arrangements with the National Trust manager for permission to view the remarkable private sewerage works at Leopold Rothschild's country mansion at Ascott House, in Buckinghamshire. But it would be well worth the effort.

Ascott House was built in the late nineteenth century by the great sanitary engineer Thomas Crapper (1836–1910) of Chelsea, south-west London. If Crapper did not originate the water closet, as is so often claimed, he did invent some important plumbing sundries, including the ballcock. Interestingly, another false attribution has been attached to his name, which is entirely coincidental and has nothing to do with the word 'crap' (as in to defecate), whose origins, so my dictionary tells me, lie securely in Middle English when the term was used to refer to waste and detritus of various sorts. Rothschild chose wisely, because Crapper held several royal warrants and is famous for installing thirty water closets, plus cedar-wood seats, at Sandringham House, Norfolk, for Prince Edward (later Edward VII). I would love to see for myself if they are still there – and if they retain the patina and scars of repeated use that I mentioned earlier. Archaeology tells us that grand country houses have always been about display and prestige, a principle that applied to the smallest detail, including, it would seem, the plumbing.

A good archaeologist must rely heavily on contributions from other disciplines. As a prehistorian, for example, I often find myself reading anthropological papers, as the pages of *Britain BC* make clear. Those who study the archaeology of Roman Britain are in constant contact with scholars of classical literature and medievalists work closely with historians. The archaeology of post-medieval Britain draws on many different resources, but among the most important are the researches of historical geographers, as we saw when, in the previous chapter, we discussed farming regions and the work of Joan Thirsk and her colleagues. Historical geographers have played a particularly important role in disentangling the complicated story of medieval villages and their origins, many of which, especially in northern England, were actually erected as part of a larger plan by the Normans.[30]

A broadly similar process, although motivated by very different reasons, also took place throughout Scotland, with the exception of the Northern and Western Isles and the Highlands of the North West.

These new planned villages were, however, very much later, most being erected between about 1730 and 1855 by a series of different landowners and for a variety of reasons. The factors behind the creation of these new settlements altered through time and from one landlord to another, and historical geographers have devised classifications that attempt to explain the entire phenomenon of planned villages. There had to be, so the reasoning ran, certain unifying elements that drew everything together.

The planned villages of Scotland are numerically important. We know for a fact that more than five hundred villages were founded there between 1730 and 1855. And that has to be explained. But my concerns here are not about the details of the explanations, so much as their origins and application. So next I want briefly to consider the classification of the planned villages and then two views on their dating. After that I'll turn to a modern study which challenges both the classification and the dating.[31]

Scottish planned villages were considered to fall into four main categories: first, villages associated with agriculture and rural estates (such as Ruthwell, Gasstown); second, villages associated with manufacture (Gatehouse of Fleet, New Langholm); third, with fishing or coastal trade (Port Logan, Powfoot); and fourth, with spas and tourist centres (Glencaple, Moffat). These categories are self-explanatory except, perhaps, for the spas which in Scotland developed around hydrotherapy (a form of water cure or health spa), from the 1840s until the early twentieth century, which in many instances became very profitable enterprises, with substantial buildings which survive to this day, often, as at Peebles, located towards the outskirts of towns.[32]

Two quite separate chronological schemes for Scottish planned villages, one proposed in 1948, the other thirty years later, have some features more or less in common, including the timing and duration of the principal phases, which we can summarise as follows: from 1745 to 1770 villages were established to accommodate tradesmen and labourers when earlier small farming townships (known as fermtouns), whose roots lay in the Middle Ages, were enclosed by larger landowners and their workforce dispersed.[33] The next phase (1770–1800) was the peak period for creating new villages, which were centred around farming, fishing and manufacture, especially around watermills. From

1800 to 1820 the emphasis shifted to the Highlands and the changes of land use that followed, from the clearance of settlements from upland sheep pastures and the resettlement of displaced people, often in planned villages along the coast. Finally, from 1820 to 1855 we see the establishment of numerous small communities in the Highlands, mostly along the coast and beside roads and the new railways; these were occupied by labourers and weavers, many of whom journeyed to work in the nearest town. After 1840 the pace of new village foundation slowed down sharply.

My immediate reaction on reading the two chronological schemes was that in broad terms they made sense and fitted in well with what we know about Scottish rural history. I was rather less happy with the functional explanation which to my eye seemed altogether too simple and clear-cut. My rather naïve misgivings were, it seems, in part borne out by a recent detailed study of eighty-one known planned villages in south-west Scotland, which also revealed some rather more serious flaws in the two typological schemes.

For a start, the planned villages in Dumfries and Galloway started earlier and finished sooner than in the general schemes. The first village, Lockerbie, was actually founded in 1730. The vast majority (fifty-seven of the eighty-one – 70 per cent) were established between 1770 and 1810 – a rather extended main phase – but very few were created after 1820. A close study of individual parish records shows that it was indeed possible to attribute a general functional classification to the various villages, but instead of just four categories, ten were needed. None of these ten could be shown to have occurred in a single period, other than the 'bulge' in village plantation that happened between 1770 and 1810. In other words, the regional reality was vastly more complex than the generalised picture might suggest.

Laying aside points of detail to do with chronology and classification, the study of villages in south-western Scotland has shown that the main drawback of earlier thoughts on the subject was their rigidity. They assumed that villages were classifiable entities in their own right, whereas in reality they were collections of living people, and when they came together in the new settlements the results were often unpredictable, with economies going their own way and in different directions. Some villages came to be more dominant, and, as time passed, they

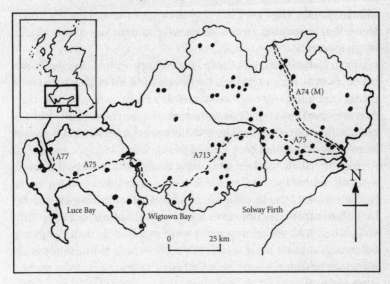

FIG 9   *A map showing the location of eighty-one planned villages erected between c. 1730 and 1855 in south-west Scotland (Dumfries and Galloway). Note that the line of the A74(M) follows that of a military road built between 1763 and 1864.*

often became specialised, whereas others discovered that the way to survive and prosper was to become more diverse. The main danger of the earlier schemes, which were based on a village's function, was that they presented a static, almost formulaic, view of rural Scotland, which failed to capture or represent the dynamism of the real thing. The lesson from this is that if we want to understand the truths behind historical communities, we must treat them like our friends: i.e. with respect and with an eye both to their past and to their other relationships. They must never be isolated, nor be taken out of context – even if it does produce a tidy, academically pleasing story.

Archaeologists are increasingly taking what one might term a 'social perspective' to the problems of interpretation that confront them. So we ask 'What was it about the way people lived their lives that motivated them to do certain things?' In many instances we come up with unexpected answers. Very often, for example, the rich and powerful were not motivated by what one might term a tabloid view of human nature. They were not driven by greed or the love of luxury alone. Rather, they were more concerned about the way they were seen by their peers.

Their contemporaries were the people they wanted to impress, and the best way to achieve this was to provide outward evidence that their estates were being well run. Sometimes this might involve the construction of elegant farm buildings. Sometimes it gave rise to neatly laid-out estate villages. In other instances visitors or travellers would note how huge areas of land had been cleared to run sheep, as happened in East Anglia and the Midlands in late medieval and early modern times, and in Scotland in the late eighteenth and nineteenth centuries. In the former case the broader social effects were positive or neutral, in the latter they were not only disastrous, but not particularly profitable either. And yet many estates were involved in these Highland Clearances – so we must seek other motives, and the need for landowners to be seen as 'modern' and 'efficient' seems, so far, to be the best explanation.[34]

But it was not just the rich and powerful whose lives were motivated by social concerns. Ordinary people were social beings, too. They were not helpless puppets to be exploited and manipulated willy-nilly by the employers, as another, essentially tabloid, view of the past might have us believe. As time passed and wealth became less polarised, larger numbers of people, in both town and country, were able to affect the surroundings in which they lived and worked. Later in this book we will examine how the people lived, whose labour, technical and management skills drove the rapid development of industry. It's not just about housing and domestic conditions; it's also about community, communication, social relationships, leisure, worship and those aspects of life that make us all human.

In the Middle Ages rural communities were held together by the ties of feudalism, backed up by the Church. As a general rule the population was less mobile; rural folk stayed in the country, townspeople in towns. From the later fourteenth century, however, life in the countryside for most people became less rigidly confined. The workforce was freed up as the nation was depleted by successive waves of plague. No longer was the labour market biased in favour of employers. During the fifteenth and sixteenth centuries many rural working people moved to the greater freedom of towns and cities, away from the feudal ties of their village of birth.

These were some of the bottom-up processes that led to a breaking down of the town/country divide that had been such a prominent feature of the Middle Ages. During the seventeenth and eighteenth centuries the arrival in rural areas of new landowners, a number of whom had made their fortunes in banking, trade or industry, further undermined the distinction. The families controlling many of the great estates discussed in this chapter would also have spent time doing a London 'season' in the winter, not to mention visits to Bath and other fashionable spas. And, of course, they would have taken many of their servants and professional advisers with them for longer or shorter visits. The point is that these movements were built into the social calendar and even if people themselves didn't make the journey, the latest news, fashion and gossip from the big cities would soon be the general topic of conversation in every rural town and village.

The various processes involved in breaking down the barriers between town and country are still under way, but they rapidly gathered pace with the improvements in infrastructure that began as early as the sixteenth and seventeenth centuries. The point to make is that these improvements did not happen 'out of the blue', as it were. They were a part of general changes, social, technological and industrial, that had been taking place since the later Middle Ages. And that is doubtless why people and communities were able to adapt the way they lived their lives. They learned how to cope with a new world in which change was to gather pace with increasing rapidity. And it's a process, of course, that has never stopped. With the enhancement first of roads, then canals and finally railways, the once separate realms of rural and urban Britain were starting to come of age.

CHAPTER THREE

The Rise of the Civil Engineer: Roads, Canals and Railways

IF THIS IS WHERE you've started reading this book, I'm guessing that you are probably male and possibly aged somewhere between fourteen and eighteen. Even if I'm right, please don't stop. Read on. I mention this because if you do happen to be a young man of that age, I would hope you're in the process of deciding that this chapter, of all the others, might be worth a closer look. And I think you'd be right: it undoubtedly has some very interesting bits, with lots of fascinating stuff about feats of engineering, building railways, bridges and so on.

For what it's worth, I, too, was given history books by doting relatives keen to foster what they thought might be my growing interest in history – and some of them (the books, that is) were so dry they came fairly close to killing any emerging enthusiasm. My parents realised that as a child I had developed a fascination with dinosaurs, which they thought could be nurtured into an interest in geology. And they were quite right: eventually it evolved into something of an all-consuming passion for archaeology. But, in common with many other youngsters, I also had another side, and from about twelve to fourteen my every waking moment was spent either with my model railway layout or gluing the various tiny bits of Airfix plastic aeroplane kits together. I was fascinated by machines and engineering.

My early teenage imagination could be set on fire by trains, cars, ships and aeroplanes, and by the creations of the great engineers – the bridges, canals and tunnels – that went with them. I spent happy hours at Hitchin and Cambridge railway stations noting down locomotive numbers (quite why I have never understood). I'd have my father's huge pair of wartime Zeiss binoculars (family legend has it they were 'liberated' from a German officer in 1944), that weighed a ton, slung round my neck, the better to scrutinise their often indistinct tar- and oil-soaked registrations. In the 1950s even famous steam locomotives were hot and dirty beasts, and like animals they gave off an alluring smell, which, of course, made them far more exciting than their gleaming hi-tech equivalents of today. It was all great fun and marvellous fuel for the imagination.

Tuppence (two old pence) bought me a platform ticket and a whole day of entertainment. After a good day on the platform at Hitchin I would later boast to friends who did not have the good fortune to live near the East Coast Main Line how I had once seen no fewer than six of Sir Nigel Gresley's streamlined A4 Pacifics (the fastest steam engines of all). I vividly recall one of these superb thoroughbreds actually pulling a goods train! All this 'fieldwork', as I would now see it, would be backed up by hours spent poring over books that described every conceivable steam engine in exhaustive detail. Strangely, these books never discussed the trucks and carriages that the great beasts hauled, largely, I suppose, because carriages and their furnishings were probably seen as a bit 'girly'. Anyhow, the steam engine books were illustrated with rather grainy black and white photographs of locomotives belching smoke, while straining up a formidable slope – often the infamous Shap incline on the West Coast Main Line. Then, in my late teens, twenties and thirties I set aside such childish things entirely and devoted myself to archaeology and attempts to explain human behaviour in the distant past. So it would seem that the intellectual side of the youthful Francis Pryor had triumphed over the incipient technical nerd. Or had it?

To tell the truth my nerdy side – and I suspect this is true of most male colleagues, and probably of men in general – had with great cleverness transformed itself and acquired a new identity, an interest in technology that was acceptable to academics and the middle classes alike. In the 1970s computers were very much the coming thing and were seen as OK. Few people thought them nerdy. But now that I am in my sixties, I find myself rebelling against this pseudo-intellectual prejudice. Why should an interest in machines, mechanisms and technology be considered a bit sad? After all, the machines were made and designed by human beings for the benefit of people who also operated them, usually well, oft-times badly – and sometimes bravely.

When, around 1844, J. M. W. Turner painted *Rain, Steam and Speed*, an extraordinary image of a steam train seeming to be flying across the Thames over Maidenhead Bridge, he was working near the climax of the railway-building boom. But was he having a rare nerdy moment? I think not. His visionary imagination, in common with that of many other people, was celebrating the dawn of a new heroic age. He was captivated by the excitement of mankind's first attempts to harness forces beyond mere humans: the energy locked up in the physics and chemistry of water and fossil fuel. So if this is the first chapter you're reading, may I say you're more than welcome; there is nothing wrong with enjoying technology, with letting machines fuel your imagination, just as they did for Britain's greatest painter.

Now the traditional way of approaching the development of Britain's infrastructure is to be strictly chronological: to start with roads, followed by canals and then finally, in a blaze of patriotic fervour, railways. Much as I would like to break with convention, this approach does make sense, so I shall follow it here, but I would like to emphasise from the outset that the sequence should not be viewed as a simple development from low-tech, via medium-, to hi-tech. After all, roads can be used by pedestrians as well as by cars, and the complexity of their construction must reflect this. We also tend to see roads as unglamorous, familiar and workaday. This is because they are everywhere and most of us make use of them several times in the course of a few hours. But in recent years archaeology has shown that the roads of early modern Britain were not the potholed and muddy monstrosities that still blight the pages of certain history books.

British roads used to be seen as a cause of something approaching historical embarrassment. It would seem that we, the British, could not get them right. To make matters worse, the skeleton of our current system, which, incidentally, has been closely followed by the motorways, was neither built nor laid out by the British, but by the Romans, mostly in the first and second centuries AD. When the Romans departed, so the story goes, the feckless Brits abandoned their magnificent roads because they feared hordes of marauding Anglo-Saxon invaders would use them to travel deep into their land. So they positioned their settlements away from the roads and positively encouraged their neglect. This bleak (and very misleading) view of Britain's infrastructure continues into the Middle Ages when everyone seems to have spent their days paddling around in deep mud as they tried to journey from A to B. In post-medieval times nothing really improves until the late seventeenth and eighteenth centuries, when the first turnpikes were constructed, but even these were expensive, were laid out piecemeal and were only used by those with money to pay the tolls. So it was Britain's hopeless road network that provided the incentives to build first canals, then railways. That at least is one way of looking at it.

The big problem for those who take this bleak long-term view of Britain's roads is the simple fact that an economy cannot develop without an effective infrastructure and the British economy continued to grow steadily, even in the Dark Ages and Saxon times. We now know that Britain had an effective network of prehistoric lanes, tracks and roads, but that this layout differed from that of today, because Roman *Londinium*, which formed the hub of their system, had yet to come into existence. So prehistoric roads formed a true network rather than the radiating system we have now grown used to. Far from being avoided in post-Roman times, Roman roads continued in use and became an essential part of the growing economy of later Saxon Britain. The same Roman roads were also the basis of the medieval system and many were substantially repaired and improved, especially in towns and cities. But it was not until the construction of the first turnpike toll road in 1663 – and even that made use of a Roman road – that things began to change for the better. Last, of course, we have the motorways, which most people today love to loathe, but which I predict will one day be viewed much as we now see the railways – as an economic and social blessing.

So if the roads of post-medieval times were not so useless after all, why did people feel it necessary to construct a network of canals and railways? The answer is that even the best early roads were never an effective, low-cost means of transporting heavy goods in bulk. Horses and wagons can be quite effective on flat ground, but present them with even a slight slope and they soon grind to an exhausted halt. By the later seventeenth century British industry needed coal and iron in ever-increasing quantities and it was the necessity of transporting such commodities efficiently that gave rise to the canals and the too often neglected horse-drawn railways of the eighteenth century. Heavy goods came first, people second.

The usual view of Britain's infrastructural development is both evolutionary and progressive. We tend to emphasise the 'big' movements that were often inspired or encouraged by central government: for example, the turnpikes and canals of the eighteenth century, or the first great railway boom of the 1840s. Such a view can ignore or neglect the informal and the unofficial, especially if these are in distant, out-of-the-way places, far removed from Edinburgh or London. Perhaps two of the most significant are the drovers' roads and the waggonways, or horse-drawn railways. Being unofficial, these networks of transport and communication are very amenable to archaeological survey and investigation, and – like Roman roads – many still await discovery and exploration.

I find the archaeology of roads both fascinating and at the same time a challenge. The point is that, although roads seem permanently to be 'up', in the sense that men in hard hats and reflective jackets find endless opportunities to dig holes in them, these holes are not archaeological trenches and, anyhow, it is very doubtful whether many major roads would reveal their distant past in the stratigraphy of their foundation layers, simply because their modern, heavy, load-bearing foundations would have obliterated earlier remains. As a consequence the archaeology of post-medieval roads has made use of rather less direct methods. Maps and historical documents, such as rights of way, have played a major role, as of course has aerial photography; nonetheless, it is still possible to adopt more hands-on, or less remote, approaches. One of the most interesting has been pioneered by the ecologist Stephen Martin who has spent his retirement studying the ecology and vegetation of roadside verges, which he memorably describes as 'the Long Meadow'.[1]

We used to believe that a close study of surviving vegetation could reveal surprisingly precise information about the age of a particular feature in the landscape. Hedges were the prime example, and it was thought that a formula which involved the counting of species in a given length of hedge could reveal the century in which it was planted. It was an excellent idea and it sort of worked, but recent research has shown that such precision is actually impossible and that it is far safer just to conclude that most species-rich hedges are old, whereas those with one predominant plant, say, hawthorn, are likely to be more recent.[2] So a somewhat mechanistic formula has been replaced by common sense.

Martin's study of road verges doesn't set out to establish when a road was built. Instead, he uses the plants along its verges to reconstruct a picture of that road's history. And he has revealed some remarkable insights. My first surprise was the sheer size and extent of road verges, which together comprise almost 1.5 per cent of Britain's surface area – the equivalent of a medium-sized county such as Berkshire. I knew from my own observations that roadsides often conserved plants from old gardens and long-vanished woodlands, and I also knew that the banks along ancient sunken roads could be far more florally rich than the arable countryside around them, but I had never appreciated the longevity of such effects.

Take, for example, Roman roads. One might suppose that the verges of surviving roads into Roman towns or legionary forts might contain plants used or introduced by the Romans, such as garlic, but the reality is actually rather more subtle. Paved roads, which the Romans introduced to Britain, are in effect stable in all weathers, provided, of course, that vehicles remain on the carriageway (which sadly is not always the case today, when the rear wheels of huge articulated trucks can cause massive ruts alongside narrow lanes). This stability also means that their verges are stable as well, and it is these stable verges that preserve vegetation that was in existence in the area shortly after the paving was first laid down. In ancient and medieval times much of Britain was covered by species-rich grassland habitats, which in chalky areas included the native perennial flax (*Linum perenne* subsp. *anglicum*). This now scarce plant is often found on the verges of Roman roads that are still in use and has become, in effect, an indicator species for Roman roads. The same general principles can also be used to illuminate the histories of later roads.

While roadsides have preserved native grassland plants they have also provided a welcoming habitat for the many new species introduced to Britain by man, which now outnumber native species by 1,402 to 1,396.[3] For various reasons, roadsides have become favourite habitats for neophytes, as the introduced species are known, often being spread there in the twentieth century by lorries carrying bulk loads of imported host or vector seeds, such as grain for flour or brewing, soya or oilseed. Many of the verges of roads leading to and from ports are home to neophytes that entered the country in ships' ballast. Today these processes are being speeded up by climate change.

Stephen Martin used the term 'Long Meadow' to refer back to the use of wide verges as summer grazing, especially in dry seasons when grass became scarce. As I write, it is still common to see tractors out and about cutting the verges of the long, straight Fenland roads around our house. When the hay is turned and baled, drivers passing by need to be alert and I can foresee a day when the health and safety gestapo at County Hall decide that it will have to stop. Sadly, that will mean an end to the species-rich 'Golden Verginia',* which wily local farmers sell to wealthy hobby horse keepers for a small fortune.

The informal 'Long Meadow' system actually worked quite well: summer grazing prevented the grass from becoming rank and stale and in winter, when the livestock population was lower and many beasts were housed, the extra width of the verge allowed travellers to skirt around boggy patches. This certainly applied to the many drove roads which formed an important source of nutrients for the animals being driven along them. The traffic in driven livestock was large and the distances travelled were immense. We have seen, for example, how cattle were driven down from Scotland to specialised farms in Essex and Suffolk where they were intensively fattened up for sale in London.[4]

Drove roads have their origin in the earlier Middle Ages and had grown into an informal network whose traffic continued to expand throughout post-medieval times and well into the nineteenth century, when eventually the railways were to provide a cheaper and much faster means of transport. I have a personal interest in drove roads because I live on one of the many droves of Fenland, next door to an old drover's pub, the Gate Hangs High (probably a reference to a sluice gate), which still traded in the 1950s. The gate which formed its sign was suspended in a nearby chestnut tree.† A few drovers' pubs still

---

* For younger readers this is a terrible pun on a once common tobacco for rolling cigarettes.

† The sign can now be seen in the Museum at Elgood's Brewery, North Brink, Wisbech, Cambs.

survive. I know of others alongside Fenland droves and have come across them in rural areas, especially in the Home Counties, closer to London. They often have names (and signs) that a drover might recognise, such as the Bull's Head or the Barley Mow. Sometimes their attached paddocks also survive, if only as a car park. These small meadows were essential for their livelihood. Livestock was kept overnight in these secure fields, while their drovers ate, drank and slept indoors. Names which reflect these temporary grazing charges, such as Halfpenny Lane, can still be used to plot the location of long-vanished inns.[5] During daytime smaller flocks and herds could be grazed for free along the drove verges which often widened out as inns were approached.

Scottish beef was highly esteemed in Regency and Georgian London. Because of its climate and topography the farming economy of Scotland has long been based around pastoralism and livestock. Unlike plants, farm animals can move around and this makes them the ideal targets for thieves.

But animals were not only moved by rustlers. Any livestock farmer knows the importance of constantly renewing blood lines with more vigorous strains from outside. As I write such renewal is the claimed justification for the crazy practice of importing cattle from areas of continental Europe where the deadly disease Bluetongue has become established. Markets are where farmers buy in the prize-winning bulls and rams which they hope will improve their blood lines.

In Scotland the network of drove roads probably has its roots deep in prehistory and I suspect that for three or four millennia much of the traffic was at best semi-legal. Records show that this seems to have been the case in later medieval times and into the sixteenth and seventeenth centuries.[6] From these informal roots there arose a comprehensive and highly effective livestock distribution network which grew in importance after 1707 and the Union of the Two Crowns, which brought about greater stability and opened up important new markets south of the border. Both the internal Scottish market system and trade in livestock with England increased rapidly throughout the eighteenth century and continued to thrive well into the nineteenth, when the network was at its peak.[7] The Scottish system operated through collecting points on the edges of the great upland grazing

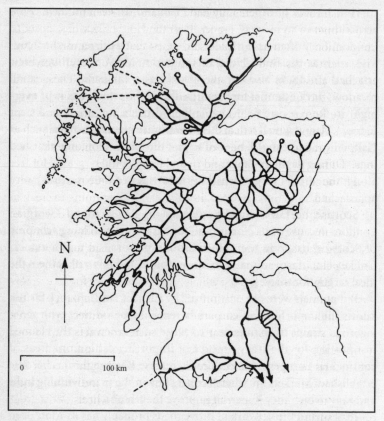

FIG 10 *A map of the drove roads of Scotland. This informal network of routes for driving cattle and sheep arose in medieval and earlier times, but became firmly established in the seventeenth and eighteenth centuries. They took animals from upland grazing (open circles) to lowland farms and on to markets in towns and cities of central and lowland Scotland. From the early eighteenth century many head of cattle were then exported to specialised farms in England where they were fattened for market, principally in London.*

areas and conducted livestock down to lower pastures and thence to markets in the larger towns and cities. It was from the larger lowland marts that drovers/entrepreneurs took their newly acquired herds south of the border for the long drive to more southerly English farms where they were fattened up for London.

British roads have generally had a poor press. Even today they are seen as inferior to those of France, Germany and Italy, which popular imagination links to strong leaders like Napoleon, Hitler and Mussolini. The latter two also made the trains run on time. Wonderful. Anyhow, as I have already mentioned, the British system, like those across the Channel, did undoubtedly benefit greatly from those other 'strongmen', the Romans, whose routes still provide a substantial element of Britain's A and B class roads.[8] It was the Romans who established England's radial arrangement of routes out of London, one that was followed first by the railways and then the motorways.

Although the medieval road network was nowhere near as inadequate as it is sometimes painted, it was certainly beginning to creak in the sixteenth century, thanks to a rising population coupled with the need to move quantities of the heavier goods being produced by newly emerging and expanding industries.[9] Something had to be done, if nothing else just to maintain existing roads. This led to the passing of the first Highways Act of 1555, which remained in force for an extraordinary 280 years. This legislation stipulated that road upkeep was the responsibility of individual parishes whose authorities were given power to command equipment such as horses and carts, and labour from local people. As a system it worked after a fashion, until traffic began to rise in the seventeenth century. It was during this period that wheeled wagons began to replace pack horses and individual riders gave way to coaches and carriages – and, of course, wheels were harder on road surfaces than hooves.

Parishes with increasingly well-travelled roads, and sometimes more than one of them, simply couldn't cope with the duties imposed on them, so standards of upkeep slipped rapidly. This time the solution was not imposed from above. Turnpike trusts were formed by local politicians in different parishes along a popular route. They were supervised by local Justices and needed individual Acts of Parliament for their formation, but once in existence they had the power to raise money for road improvement and maintenance by charging fees at toll gates, or turnpikes, as they were known at the time. The term can refer specifically to a pedestrian turnstile (two wrought-iron examples survive on the Holyhead Road[10]), but it was also used to describe a larger barrier or gate that was opened on payment of a toll. The first Turnpike trust was

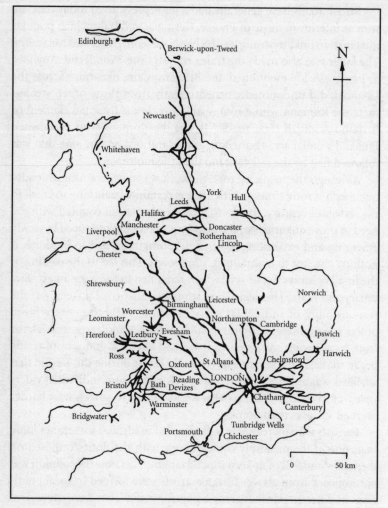

FIG 11   *The principal long-distance routes in England and Wales in the seventeenth century, prior to the turnpikes (above). The map (right) shows the turnpike network in 1750 at the end of the first great wave of road building.*

established in 1663 for a busy length of the old Roman road Ermine Street, through parts of Huntingdonshire, Cambridgeshire and Hertfordshire.[11] Today the road is known as the A10 and A1198.

At first the growth of new turnpike trusts was slow and focused around London, but it soon gathered pace, spread, and by 1750 there were 146 trusts which managed 3,400 miles (5,500 kilometres) of road. By 1772 a further 418 had been formed and the total mileage of turnpikes was now over 15,000 (24,000 kilometres). By the end of the century another 152 trusts were created. All early trusts took responsibility for existing routes, although sometimes this would involve the straightening out of bends and the avoidance of particularly steep hills, but after 1815 we see the construction of entirely new routes and of these by far the best known is the great Holyhead Road created by the Scotsman who, for me at least, still remains Britain's greatest engineering genius of all time. I refer to Thomas Telford (1757–1834).[12]

I won't go into the politics behind the construction of the road other than to say it was to do with Britain's recent political takeover of Ireland (the Act of Union of 1801) and the perceived need to keep Westminster in touch with Dublin, via Holyhead (Anglesey), where, incidentally, you can still catch the Irish ferry. The road was conceived by Telford from the outset as a unified whole and it includes a series of magnificent bridges among which are the world's first large suspension bridge (opened January 1826) across the Menai Strait, another fine suspension bridge across the River Conwy (opened July 1826) and the elaborately decorated single-arch, cast-iron Waterloo Bridge at Betws-y-Coed, which opened a year after the famous battle, in 1816.

Telford planned and built the great Holyhead Road much as Brunel and other railway engineers executed their great projects. The road ran from London to Holyhead and first (from 1815 to 1817) Telford surveyed the entire route in detail. The greatest engineering challenges were, however, provided by the 106 miles (170 kilometres) between Shrewsbury and Holyhead – a stretch that took from 1815 to 1830 to complete. As soon as one starts to look more closely it becomes apparent that the road through the Welsh mountains has many points in common with a railway line.

For a start, all the roadside 'furniture', the grit and ballast containers, the milestones, the turnpike and the weighbridge houses, were designed in a uniform style. Incidentally, although no turnpike weighbridges have survived intact we do know from the discovery of their mounting points (of which there were four) that they operated on the balance principle, rather like old-fashioned kitchen scales, except that the arm which carried the weights was greatly extended to increase leverage. Broadly similar weighbridges are known from very early railways and ironworks.[13] As well as the bridges, the new road includes numerous cuttings and carefully constructed embankments, because, as with a railway, Telford was keen to keep inclines as slight as possible with no gradients steeper than 1:30.

Today the road (now the A5) survives best in the eighty-three miles (138 kilometres) of its upland reaches, between Holyhead and Chirk on the Welsh side of the border, near Llangollen. Anyone with even a passing interest in early roads should drive slowly along these eighty-three hallowed miles, where there are numerous lay-bys into which one can scuttle to let impatient holidaymakers overtake. Try to choose a lay-by on an embankment, such as that near Nant Ffrancon in Snowdonia, and look down at the superb retaining wall that is still exactly as Telford left it.[14] Incidentally, the Nant Ffrancon Pass was the only place where Telford was forced to depart from his 1:30 gradient and even today the road is slightly narrower here than elsewhere – a response to the huge engineering problems he encountered. All eighty-three milestones have also been preserved or re-created and as one drives along one can still spot some fine toll houses and weighbridge buildings, although Telford was at pains to prevent unnecessary delays and so reduced the number of turnpike trusts along its route from the twenty-three he inherited to five.

Although the early turnpikes were indeed better at coping with large, wheeled vehicles, they were never intended to be used for shifting industrial quantities of iron or coal. And besides, the areas where iron and coal occurred naturally, such as north-east England or South Wales, featured steep hills, often dissected by numerous and sharply cut valleys. In these areas bulk raw materials were moved either by horse-drawn railways, or by canals. I'll discuss the former shortly, but the canals are important, if only because historically they have been seen as the forerunners of the steam railways of Victorian times. Canals were crucially important to our story because, like steam railways, they needed to be thoroughly planned and tightly engineered. Good advance surveying was essential and, of course, gradients needed to be kept to an absolute minimum. As someone who has spent many hours wrestling with the intricacies of surveyors' levels and theodolites, I can appreciate how hard it would have been to ensure, for example, that canals retained an even depth of water, sufficient to float a fully-laden narrow boat. Many of the engineering solutions to problems encountered on the steam railways – for example, embankments, tunnels and viaducts – were first developed for the canals.

We tend to think that everything of an early industrial nature was pioneered in Britain, but in fact good-quality canals were being built and operated on the Continent before the start of the eighteenth century and well before any were constructed in Britain.[15] The first purpose-built British commercial canal was built to serve a specific industry, coal, in an area where the inclines were not too steep and where water was available. More importantly, much of the land was owned by a single landowner, the Duke of Bridgewater, whose Worsley estate was just five miles from Manchester. The Duke speculated that if he constructed a canal then coal from his estate mines could be shipped to the growing mills of Manchester at much lower cost. In the event he was to be proved right, and his production costs dropped by a half. In 1759 he employed an eccentric itinerant millwright called James Brindley to build the first lengths of what would later be known as the Bridgewater Canal, from Worsley to Manchester. This was finished in 1765 and, during its completion, Brindley realised that his vocation was to be a canal builder, a task to which he devoted the rest of his life until his death in 1772.[16] Brindley was one of the first to grasp that if canals could be joined together into wider networks they would have an economic impact on more than a single industry. Later he saw to it that the Worsley to Manchester canal was extended, now as the Bridgewater Canal, to the Mersey at Runcorn, some 18 miles as the crow flies.[17] A few years later Brindley engineered the Grand Trunk Canal linking the rivers Trent and Mersey.

The establishment of a canal network comparable with that of the later railways was never fully completed, but given the problems they faced, the early canal engineers did remarkably well. Ultimately, of course, they were to be defeated by the arrival of the railways in the 1840s. Indeed, one of the last major canals, the Chard Canal (from Taunton to Chard), was completed in 1842, at precisely the same time as the great explosion of railway building was under way. Each canal had its own story but as a case study I'd like to take the Grand Junction Canal, which is fairly typical of the way the network grew. It was also positioned in an area that was strategically important for the development of the wider network. This is doubtless one of the reasons why the National Canal Museum was sited there.

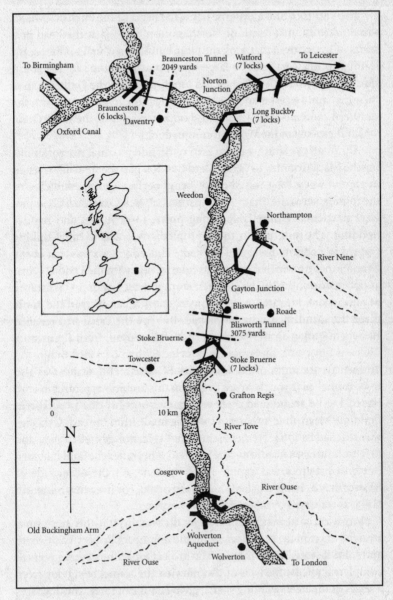

FIG 12 *A map of the Grand Union (earlier the Grand Junction) Canal, in Northamptonshire.*

The village of Stoke Bruerne lies at the heart of the English lowland canal network, just south of Northampton.[18] It sits at the head of a series of seven locks that took the Grand Junction Canal up the ascent leading to Blisworth Hill, a large outcrop of limestone on the south side of the Nene Valley. The Grand Junction linked the Oxford Canal, Birmingham, Leicester and the Nene Navigation, to the north, with the southern canal network leading to London, by way of the River Ouse, which it crossed at the Wolverton Aqueduct.

Although the south-eastern arm of Brindley's canal network linking the Black Country to Oxford and London had theoretically opened in 1790, it was a long way short of being perfect. Certain stretches of the route, such as the Thames Navigation between Oxford and London, were particularly unreliable, being prone to droughts and regular flooding. The solution to these problems was a new canal linking Oxford to London direct and the route chosen in 1792 was that of the Grand Junction which ran from its intersection with the Oxford Canal at Braunston (near Rugby) to Brentford, in west London – a distance of almost one hundred miles. Construction began in 1793 and some three thousand men were employed. By 1796 the canal had reached Blisworth, today on the outskirts of Northampton, from Braunston. This was quite an achievement as it included the 2,042-yard Braunston Tunnel. To the south of Blisworth was Blisworth Hill, which was also to be tunnelled through. Work began on this ambitious project in 1793, but had to be abandoned three years later, probably due to persistent flooding. Meanwhile, progress was being made from the east: Uxbridge was reached in 1794, Hemel Hempstead (Hertfordshire) in 1799 and Leighton Buzzard (Bedfordshire) in 1800. Thereafter the land flattened out and progress was rapid, Stoke Bruerne, on the other side of Blisworth Hill, being reached shortly after 1800. For five years Blisworth Hill was traversed by a horse-drawn tramway.

Work on a new tunnel through Blisworth Hill, this time on a straight alignment, as proposed by the engineers Robert Whitworth and John Rennie, began in 1802. The project took almost three years to complete and cost the lives of two navvies, the tunnel being dug from a series of nineteen working shafts, giving a total of forty working faces (allowing for a party at each of the two tunnel entrances). The engineer in charge, James Barnes, and a small team of workmen first drove a brick-lined drainage culvert well below the line of the actual canal tunnel. This removed the water that had forced the earlier tunnel to fail, and is still running to this day.

In January 1929 the five companies constituting the Grand Junction Canal were formed into a single organisation, the Grand Union Canal. An early move by the new company was to broaden the canal to take barges as well as narrow boats. Work began in 1931 and by the onset of war all the locks and bridges were widened except for seventeen in the Watford region, which remain narrow to this day. All work along the canal was called off between 1939 and 1945. After the war (in 1948) the canals were nationalised and commercial traffic continued to dominate the Grand Union until the 1960s, when leisure boats began to take over. In 1977 the Blisworth Tunnel was closed when it was found to be unsafe. It took several years to raise the money needed for its repair, and work on replacing most of the centre section with concrete-ring reinforcements began in September 1982. The tunnel eventually reopened in August 1984, but today the traffic passing through it is almost entirely non-industrial.

Earlier in this chapter I mentioned that movement of heavy loads, such as coal and iron, was the main stimulus behind the construction of the canals. But that is not to say that canals were the sole means of doing this. In the past we have tended to underestimate the role of horse-drawn railways, known as waggonways, which were not as primitive as their name suggests. In the coal-mining areas of north-east England, for instance, the terrain was far too steep for canals so a series of waggonways were constructed along the upland valleys that drained into larger river basins such as the Tyne and Tees, and ports, such as Newcastle, where the coal was then exported to London and other towns along the east coast. Generally speaking, waggonways were left simple, to keep costs to a minimum, but sometimes embankments and bridges had to be built. Indeed, the oldest surviving railway bridge in the world is the Causey Arch, near Stanley in Co. Durham, which was constructed between 1725 and 1726 and at the time was the longest (at thirty-two metres) single-span arch in Britain.[19]

A fascinating glimpse into the workings of a horse-drawn railway has been provided by the recent excavations at the Bersham Ironworks, near Wrexham in North Wales.[20] This remarkably unsung project has revealed the earliest excavated railway in the world, dating to the mid-eighteenth century. One might imagine that timber tracks would be rather crude and 'jerky', being built in straight lengths, but if the forty-metre length exposed by the dig is anything to go by, the wagons were hauled along a smooth, gentle curve, complete with a set of points that closely resemble those of the great Victorian railway age a century or so later. Standard gauges (the term used to describe the distance separating the two rails) were not a Victorian innovation, but have origins in the eighteenth century. In northern Britain, for example, the gauge was quite wide – between 4 and 5 feet – and the Bersham tracks, at 4 foot 1 inch, clearly belong in this tradition. Around Coalbrookdale mines were often accessed via horizontal passages, or adits. This meant that sometimes wagons could be taken right up to the coalface; so it made sense to keep the gauge as narrow as possible to penetrate the cramped passages of the mine. As a consequence the gauge of most West Midlands waggonways was about 3 foot 6 inches.

At the start of this chapter I described how trains and railways had excited me as a young teenager, and I have always retained a little of that fascination, especially if I catch the distinctive whiff of Yorkshire Steam Coal smoke – usually the sign of a railway preservation society somewhere nearby. I have also kept, and from time to time added to, a small collection of railway books. Now I have to admit that most of these are aimed at enthusiasts and would be considered by many as rather over-specialised, but there are occasional exceptions, one of which first caught and then held my attention.[21] It's about the construction and operation of the Settle–Carlisle Railway, but it doesn't focus on trains alone. The author was a geographer as well as an enthusiast and he successfully chronicled the impact of the new line on the local, mainly rural, economy.

The short (seventy-two miles) Settle–Carlisle Railway was the last main line to be built by traditional hand labour, in many respects just like the lines of the great railway boom of the 1840s. But first I want to discuss the reasons why this, the most mountainous and challenging of all British main lines, was ever constructed at all. The story behind the Settle–Carlisle Railway is an altogether odd one.

FIG 13   *The excavated traces of wooden railway (or 'waggonway') lines dating to about 1750, excavated at the Bersham Ironworks near Wrexham, in North Wales. This horse-drawn railway was built to bring coal and iron ore to the blast furnace and these tracks are probably the earliest evidence for a railway in the world.*

The origins of the line lie back in the early 1850s but it was not constructed for some twenty years, until the 1870s, and it opened to light traffic in 1876. Its principal purpose was to provide its builders, the Midland Railway Company, with their own route northwards to Scotland. The Midland, incidentally, was the latest of the major railway companies and its routes ran north from St Pancras station in London to the English Midlands, and the North West. The sole purpose of the Settle–Carlisle was to avoid the West Coast Main Line, which was owned and operated by their great rivals, the London and North Western Railway. So, largely for reasons of corporate vanity, the Board of the Midland Railway constructed what is today the highest and most spectacular of British main lines. With hindsight, it is now obvious that it never really paid off financially, yet it still exists today as a magnificent visitor attraction and commercial railway.

My own involvement with this remarkable railway began in the autumn of 2007 when Maisie and I set out on one of those hectic trips to take photographs for our current projects. At the time I was putting the finishing touches to *The Making of the British Landscape* and needed a picture of the infamous Ribblehead Viaduct. I say 'infamous' because, although a magnificent engineering achievement, it was completed at the cost of some two hundred lives, a high proportion of the victims being members of the navvies' families – their wives, part-ners and children. Many of these unfortunate souls met their untimely ends in the navvy camps provided by the railway contractors and a memorial to them – erected by the railway company and the navvies themselves – can still be seen in the little church at Chapel-le-Dale, high in the Yorkshire Dales. Of course there were accidents during the construction work – two men are known to have died when handling explosives – and in transporting plant and materials to the works, but one of the main causes of death at the navvies' camps was disease, especially smallpox, which occurred several times in various places. Drink also took a toll, sometimes indirectly. For example, one man was killed when he lay down for a sleep across the tramway line that serv-iced the camp at Risehill. He was hit by a runaway wagon. Another man at Risehill committed suicide in the latrines.[22]

I had just returned from that photographic excursion and was film-ing one of the late summer episodes of Channel 4's *Time Team*, when, over a pint, I told one of the researchers for the forthcoming (2008) series about my trip to Ribblehead. I mentioned the Scheduled navvy camps on Blea Moor Common overlooking the great viaduct, and also threw in that another twenty or so were known to exist along the Settle–Carlisle Railway. After we'd finished filming, I e-mailed the researcher my notes for the book and a few references to chase up. The next thing I knew was shortly after Christmas when the telephone rang. It was Michael Douglas, the editor of the 2008 series. Was I interested in being the archaeological director for an episode at Risehill Navvy Camp, high above the Risehill Tunnel, just a short distance down the line from Ribblehead? *Was I interested?* I almost bit his hand off.

In the weeks leading up to the three days of filming I had a fairly lengthy correspondence with Michael about the project, which he would personally be directing. I had told him about the area and its remoteness and he decided very sensibly to programme the excavation for high summer, when conditions were more likely to be favourable. But little did we know. As time passed, it became apparent from our conversations that the entire operation was proving a major challenge – rather like digging the tunnel in the first place. For a start, everything had to be brought up and into the area – and I mean *everything*: from paper, to food, to drinking water. When we arrived on site we were greeted by our own temporary village, with gently throbbing generators which included a temporary incident room (where the graphics computers were housed), dining hall, radio communications centre and sundry other tents I never managed to investigate. To get there we had to drive for over an hour from our hotel on the outskirts of Kirby Lonsdale, the nearest town of any size.

The Settle–Carlisle Railway was constructed in some five to six years after its commencement in 1869 and was notable for the huge numbers of navvies that took part. For its building, the line was divided up into five contracts and the Risehill Tunnel fell into contract two, from Dent Head to Smardale. The successful contractors for this length of track were Benton and Woodwiss, and their records show that some 36,000 men are known to have worked on their various bridges, tunnels and embankments.[23] Conditions high up on Risehill were dire. In 1872 an astonishing ninety-two inches of rain was recorded (the average for the area is about sixty-eight) and the contractors had to make some effort to provide improved accommodation or they would continue to lose labour.

Like all but the very deepest, the Risehill Tunnel was actually dug on several faces at once: at either end and from two brick-lined air shafts located about one-third and two-thirds of the distance along its three-quarter-mile route. Men lowered into these shafts worked in two directions, making six working parties in all. The rock was drilled and then blasted. After each explosion the navvies would clear the thousands of fragments and a few large blocks weighing up to a ton – or sometimes more – each. I still recall how nearly every one of the huge rocks of the spoil tips was still marked by the distinctive drill holes used to place the charges. In the case of the two parties working from the tunnel mouth and exit, the rubble was loaded onto wagons that were hauled out along the tracks. But for the men working below the two air shafts the rocks were winched up the shafts by steam-powered hoists and were then loaded onto a narrow-gauge railway, which took them along the top of the huge spoil heaps, where they were then tipped. These spoil heaps remain exactly as they were left in the 1870s: long fingers of rubble and massive rocks with absolutely flat tops. The wagons tipped their loads and the largest rocks came crashing down the steep slopes to splat into the peat of the boggy hillside, where they can be seen to this day.

If the excavation was only to be about massive blocks of rock it probably wouldn't matter much if the weather was to turn nasty, but I knew we had much more delicate tasks to perform, which is why I became distinctly apprehensive when the clouds began to gather in the mid-morning of the first day. By then our presenter, Tony Robinson, had finished his introductory piece-to-camera. By then, too, Phil Harding, our principal field archaeologist, John Gator (our geophysicist) and I had filmed a scene in which we decided on our initial tactical objectives. These included the excavation of at least one navvy hut.

I mentioned that there were two air shafts on the top of Risehill. Unfortunately, the land around Shaft 1 had been disturbed by recent quarrying, so that was where we placed our own campsite. Shaft 2 was very much better preserved and we could readily see where the railway builders had been, because in these areas the fragile mosses of the rain-fed bog had been replaced by the much coarser sedges, reeds and grasses that were able to thrive on the disturbed ground. It's a sobering thought, but it takes centuries for bogs to recover once they have been interfered with by man.

I am aware that to many people the digging of a navvy hut just 130 years old is very different from, say, the excavation of a Bronze Age house of 1300 BC, but in actual fact the problems that confront the archaeologist are very similar.[24] For a start we knew very little about navvy huts, as up until then very few had been fully excavated. By way of contrast, we do actually know a fair bit about Bronze Age houses, because dozens have been excavated – and to very high standards. So we decided to carry out the excavation of the Victorian hut with the same care we would normally bestow on a prehistoric house. That meant recording all the finds by metre square, which would prove no mean task as weather conditions deteriorated.

By great good fortune the Census of 1871 had included the Risehill navvy camps and we knew that the one by Shaft 2, which was the best preserved, had originally included four dormitory huts. Of course we couldn't take this account as gospel, as there are many reasons why the people who filled in the Census returns might have wanted to embellish or curtail the truth, but it did give us something to think about. In the end, our excavations actually showed the Census to have been correct – a result in itself. We also knew from further research into the building of the Settle–Carlisle Railway that the majority of navvies would actually have been housed at the bottom of the larger hills. So the camp on top of Risehill would probably have accommodated the specialist mechanics and tradesmen needed to maintain and operate the various steam engines for the cranes and winches used to operate the access tramway and the hoists on top of the air shafts.

On that first morning, while Tony was doing his piece-to-camera, several of us climbed up onto the main spoil heap and looked down on the land where the navvy camp had been. Down below us Emma, one of John Gator's team of geophysicists, was marching along a strict grid carrying a proton magnetometer which was plotting changes in the subsoil's magnetic properties. It's a technique that is particularly good at detecting buried hearths, ashes and fireplaces. This survey was to reveal where the four dormitory huts were positioned, although at the time we weren't altogether clear what it was that the geophysics were telling us. John was also quite certain that other areas had had their magnetic properties hugely enhanced by fire, and he correctly guessed that these might prove to be workshops.

From the top of the massive spoil heap we watched as Emma walked up and down the grid she had surveyed in earlier that morning, with her well-practised and carefully measured tread. But it was impossible not to notice four areas of bright green grass which contrasted starkly with the darker shades of the sedge that covered the upper slopes of the hill. The only other area of grass was a strip that we knew from written accounts had formed on top of the track bed of the narrow-gauge tramway that was used to supply the camp and the works. This suggested that the grass was only growing on the better drained ground.

The tramway carried supplies of food, drink and coal to the camp and the steam-powered winches by each air shaft from the valley far below. These wagons were hauled up the steep slope by ropes which were probably attached to a steam winding engine at the top of the hill, close by Shaft 2. We also know from written accounts that this tramway was the scene of a tragic accident in September 1873 when the rope broke and a wagon, loaded with eleven passengers, began to run down the hill. The brakeman managed to hold it long enough for nine to escape, but two women failed to do so and were dashed to pieces at the bottom of the hill.

When Tony had finished his piece-to-camera, I walked over to the nearest patch of grass we had spotted from the top of the spoil heap, where I met a couple of the experts who had been brought in to advise us. Just by standing on it, it was immediately apparent that the grass was no more than a thin covering on top of a low mound of rubble; this in turn suggested to me that the stones were probably the collapsed gable end of a hut. Usually timber huts of this sort, at almost any time or place in Britain's history, had at least one end built from stone or brick, which was where the fireplace or hearth was positioned. The experts accepted that explanation, although we all agreed that we couldn't know for sure without excavation. At any rate it was something to go by, so I decided to place our first trench, which Phil Harding would excavate, directly over the most obvious heap of stones. It proved a happy choice.

We had just laid out the first trench and Phil and his team had begun to remove turf and topsoil by hand (the site was too inaccessible for mechanical diggers), when it began to rain. But this wasn't the thin, rather miserable rain we get on the eastern side of Britain. When the first drops hit my face, coming at me horizontally, I knew that we were in for a thorough soaking. I also knew that our time on site was already shorter than usual – thanks to the long journey at each end of the day – and that Phil's hut would take much careful excavation to reveal. So I avoided Phil's pessimistic gaze and headed off to the air shaft, where I planned to start two further trenches.

The first of the two new trenches revealed the position of the boiler house. This provided the steam for the beam engine which was used to hoist the rocks out of the air shaft and onto the wagons which then carried them along the top of the spoil heaps to the tipping area. We hoped that the second trench would find the massive foundations needed for the beam engine itself, but instead we came down on a less substantial wall which we soon realised had been built to enclose quite a sizeable pond or reservoir that provided water for both the boiler and probably the navvy camp, too. Then the rain really set in.

Towards the end of the first day I visited Phil's trench and was very surprised by what he'd found: there was no sign whatsoever of a gable-end wall and, instead of the single fireplace we had expected, Phil had revealed no fewer than two fireplaces. But these were not arranged next to each other, so they couldn't possibly have been built in a gable-end wall. That puzzled us and we were scratching our heads trying to work out what might have happened when Bill Bevan, one of the two experts I had met earlier in the day, suggested that the fireplaces had been positioned about a third of the way into the building. This arrangement allowed for a small and rather cosy two-roomed apartment for the hut supervisor and his wife, with a much larger space beyond. This larger room would also have been divided in two, with a smaller communal kitchen and a much larger dormitory, which would have held about twenty beds – sufficient for forty navvies working twelve-hour shifts, with two men to a bed (one sleeping while the other was working).

The heavy rain was actually quite helpful because it meant we had to face some of the problems that would have confronted the navvies as well. Water was pouring across Phil's trench and it was immediately apparent that no building could ever have been placed directly on that ground. They could only have been raised above it. This simple realisation threw entirely new light on the archaeological remains before us.

Bill Bevan's suggestion was based on some workmen's huts from the 1850s that he had excavated at a quarry site previously. These had been prefabricated units of a type that was then being exported from Britain to troops serving in the Crimean War (1853–6). I'm told that staff of the Midland Railway or its contractors had served in the Crimea and were aware that the accommodation huts were still in existence. The Midland was a notoriously thrifty company and they realised that these old sheds could provide a cheap solution to what was becoming a major accommodation problem in such a hostile environment.[25]

The prefab huts were built in much the same way as a modern garden shed, with separate wall and roof sections and a raised floor. In our case the floor and walls were raised on a continuous bank of stones mixed with cinders and a mass of fine coal fragments. At first we couldn't understand why the mix of cinders and coal extended beyond the stone bank, but as the rain continued to pour down Phil realised that it was superb stuff to walk on. It was hard; it did not stick to the soles of his boots and, more importantly, water drained straight through it – so it remained crisply dry. Obviously the navvies realised this, too, and they used it for all the paths around the camp. The spongy, reedy topsoil that lay on top of the paths was soggy and horrible, but as soon as we had removed it, the path below was as dry and firm as the navvies had left it in the 1870s.

By the start of the third and last day it was apparent that there had been four of these long navvy dormitory sheds, arranged in two parallel terraces close to the summit of Risehill, to one side of the tramway. The scale and the arrangement of the huts proved beyond doubt that they had been built by the contractors for their workforce and were a far cry from the sort of ramshackle accommodation that navvies would have built for themselves just thirty years earlier in the 1840s. Although not exactly well appointed by modern standards, these camps would have made life at least tolerable in these bleak and barren places during the winter.

We also knew from written accounts of later Victorian civil engineering work that the better built camps didn't just dig holes in the ground where convenient, but actually constructed communal toilet blocks. We found ours where we expected it, just downhill of the two terraces of huts – a short stumble away, after a long night on the ale on pay day. Again, it would seem that the wooden building was probably prefabricated, but the drain itself had been sunk into the ground and still contained 'cess', the contents of cesspits.

Now I've dug my fair share of cess over the years. I remember spending weeks in a complex of deep medieval pits in the Norfolk village of North Elmham, where the cess was a distinctive green colour – the result of biodeterioration over the intervening centuries. It did smell, but neither strongly nor of what one might expect. It felt more like we were digging our way through a vast and rather stiff Stilton cheese than anything else. But the stuff at Risehill was altogether different. Maybe it was its recent 'deposition', or maybe the high acidity of the surrounding soil and water had together conspired to keep it nice and fresh, but all I can say is that in terms of colour, consistency and, worst of all, smell, it was, as archaeologists like to put it, remarkably well preserved. Flippancy aside, sometimes the past can reach out and grab you most unexpectedly. The smell of that cess, although far from overpowering, did it for me. I was being filmed at the time, so I had to pretend that it was all horribly revolting; but in actual fact at that instant (and thinking about it on several occasions subsequently), I have to admit that I found the experience strangely moving. Nothing links one more closely or rapidly to people than smell – any smell.

Conditions in the camp provided by the railway contractor at Risehill were certainly harsh, if not actually squalid, but we know that there were many navvy camps along the upper reaches of the Settle–Carlisle Railway and sometimes these could be very grim places, especially those less formal camps where the huts were built by groups of navvies for themselves. Quite often these men would be working on more than one project, because the actual construction of the line was let to a number of main and sub-contractors.

Our excavation threw much light on unexpected aspects of the navvy life. Certainly conditions must have been unpleasant, especially during wet weather, but we do know that the men on top of Risehill were often skilled in various trades and this might suggest they were possibly a bit more mature and less prone to the excesses of drinking for which navvies were generally known. A picture of, if not gentility, then of something aspiring to it, is provided by the ash paths and the mass of glass and ceramic fragments, which one would normally expect to find in a middle-class suburb. There were relatively few beer or gin bottles or, indeed, glass or ceramic tankards. To my eye the finds did not resemble what one might expect to recover from, say, a hell-raising miners' camp in the Californian gold rush. They didn't resemble Calamity Gulch so much as suburban Clapham.

These results accord rather well with the picture of the navvies who worked in the Northern Pennines, as revealed by historians. Contrary to popular belief, most came from northern England, rather than Ireland, and most of their other workmates would have been from the Midlands or East Anglia. For too long the men who built the railways have been described as little more than drunken layabouts, but of course there was far more to them than this. Certainly they did let their hair down fairly often and in a spectacular fashion, as most people working in stressful conditions have to do, but they needed many skills other than just the ability to swing a pick. The railways worker also had a sense of his own worth which posterity has not always accorded him: 'Whatever abusive epithets his social superiors used, he called himself a "railway labourer" or "excavator" and almost never, at least not when a formal description was required, a "navvy".'[26]

So what lessons can we learn from the Settle–Carlisle Railway? From an historical perspective there can be no doubt that it was a grossly over-expensive project, both in human and financial terms, and it never repaid those huge costs. But as an archaeologist I am also interested in the local impact of the line.[27] Analysis of Census returns for parishes around the railway show that the line acted as a break on the economic decline of upland farms that followed the agricultural depression of the 1870s. More livestock, especially cattle, could be sent to markets by train. The same tendency can also be seen in the human population, which declined more slowly in those places within reach of a station. But as motor transport became more widely available (from about 1911), the beneficial effects of the railway begin slowly to decrease. Strangely, and bearing in mind that this particular line was never intended to serve local communities, its biggest impact was to be very much later when, thanks to local support, it managed to resist Dr Beeching's infamous cutbacks of the early 1960s. Again, in 1988, it was threatened with closure but an intense local campaign caused these plans to be dropped. Today it provides a major tourist resource in summer (complete with steam engines), while in wintertime it remains the sole reliable means of transport when the fells are thickly covered in snow.

And now for an unexpected footnote. If they are any good at their job, most archaeologists like to get away from their desks and out into the field. This applies as much to the writing of general books as to purely academic research. So, in April 2009, I made another visit to the area around Risehill where we had been digging the previous summer. It was a warm spring day and the first lambs were frolicking in the fields behind the station at Horton-in-Ribblesdale. A short distance up the line was the Ribblehead Viaduct and I was peering towards it, the way one does, when I noticed a slowly moving speck far away in the distance. I soon realised it was a train and instinctively stepped back from the platform's edge. Five minutes later it arrived, and didn't stop, being a long freight train hauled by a vast diesel locomotive.[28] Then another one went by in the other direction. This was not at all what I had expected. Of course, tourism is great and very important in its way, but it now appears that the much-loved tourist line is getting its hands dirty and returning to the real world. Nothing could have given me greater pleasure. I almost cheered when that second freight train rumbled its ponderous way through the little station.

No book about the archaeology of modern Britain could possibly ignore the motorways, whose construction involved the destruction of hundreds, probably thousands, of ancient sites of all periods. Sometimes, towards the latter part of the twentieth century, these were adequately excavated in a reasonably controlled fashion, but in the early days of their construction, especially in the 1960s and early 1970s, this rarely happened. Like many archaeologists at the time I objected vociferously to proposed road schemes all over the country, but now that most of the motorway network has been completed I find myself in the rather odd position of having to think about conserving these same roads that did so much harm to some of the monuments to our remote past.

The construction of Britain's motorways involved the discovery and excavation and destruction of thousands of hitherto unknown archaeological sites. And it wasn't just the roads; we must not forget that their construction also involved hundreds of thousands of tons of crushed stone, ballast and, of course, concrete. Wherever possible these materials were sourced locally, with the result that quarries and gravel pits expanded with unprecedented rapidity. I believe it is no exaggeration to say that the general threat posed by motorways was so severe that it provided the main incentive for the transformation of British archaeology in the 1980s. Faced by this new threat, archaeology grew from disconnected groups of amateurs to a properly structured profession.

With hindsight, one can realise that there was an 'upside' to what seemed at the time an orgy of wilful destruction. The new roads gave archaeologists a series of opportunities to examine in detail entire tracts of countryside, often in areas which were believed to be archaeologically sterile, such as the heavy clay lands of the English Midlands. And, of course, these places revealed a wealth of new material which had not been discovered hitherto, simply because these landscapes were believed to be empty. It was during the 1980s that we revealed the extraordinary extent and scale of Britain's surviving archaeological heritage. Rescue, one of the organisations set up by archaeologists to raise money and public awareness of the terrible destruction that was then taking place, estimated that on average there was a significant archaeological site in every square quarter-mile of Britain. To the best of my knowledge, that estimate still stands.

It has become very fashionable of late to complain about road-building and my immediate reaction is to say that the protesters have left it too late, because that particular horse has long since galloped over the horizon. Whether we like it or not, Britain has at last acquired a network of modern roads, albeit very much smaller than those of continental neighbours, such as Germany and France.[29] The construction of modern roads for motor traffic, let alone of motorways, did not begin in Britain until relatively late. Immediately after the war possibly the most travelled north–south route, the A1, or Great North Road, had no sections of dual carriageway, although a few, such as the Kingston Bypass, had been built in the 1930s. Construction of the new roads was not always straightforward. The first motorway, for example, the relatively short (8.26 miles, or 13.2 km) Preston Bypass, which is now part of the M6, was opened in December 1958, by no less a person than the Prime Minister, Harold Macmillan. Then, just forty-seven days after its official opening, it was closed for repairs to its asphalt surface, which was breaking up. This caused a huge political row, as the project had just cost the then huge sum of four million pounds.

The unfortunate Minister for Transport, Harold Watkinson, told the hordes of Opposition MPs baying for his blood in the House of Commons that these problems were due to bad weather: a hard frost followed by a sharp thaw. In fact, the archaeologist Dr John Prag of the Alderly Edge Landscape Project has recently suggested that the contractors used the wrong source of sand.[30] The sandhills they chose lay at the foot of Alderly Edge and were the waste product of copper mining dating to the 1860s. The extractive process in those days involved the removal of copper from sandstone by leaching in hydrochloric acid and even today these sands are so acidic that no vegetation will grow on them. Unfortunately a firm of contractors, whose management seemed to have little knowledge of industrial archaeology, then bought the land and used the sandhills to build not just the Preston Bypass, but the runway of Manchester airport as well – and very soon both required rapid repair.

Work on the first stretch of the M1 began the following year, 1959. The new roads were very successful, but soon began to develop new, unexpected problems as a result. One of the last of the major motorways, the M40, which offered a more westerly route to Birmingham from London, via Oxford, was opened in 1991, and was intended to relieve traffic pressure on the rather aged and over-travelled M1, which it may, or may not, have done. But it certainly added to the long queues on the M25. And here we come to an interesting dilemma.

Pressure of traffic on the M1 required it to be improved. New lanes were added and old bridges were sometimes demolished to make way for replacements. Some of the older structures were by now important in themselves and were worthy of protection. I think here of certain pillared bridges beneath that original length of the M1 begun back in 1959 (at Northampton, for example) which, although not to everyone's taste, do have a character all of their own and should not be demolished without careful thought.

I have said it before, and it bears repeating here, that archaeology can provide a fresh perspective on the present, because it is soundly rooted in the long-term processes of the past. For me the motorway system has many points in common with the railways of the mid-nineteenth century, which in turn have numerous similarities to the canals and waggonways of the eighteenth. In the 1840s there were numerous protesters when new railways were planned, and yet today most informed opinion would regard Dr Beeching's axing of so many of them in the 1960s as an ill-considered tragedy – a point that is proved by the now thriving Settle–Carlisle line. Surely there are lessons here for us today?

Although it will never be perfect, Britain now has a road system worthy of a modern commercial state. The next problem is already with us: the development of high-speed rail links. Then what about air travel, and links to regional airports? It goes on and on. That is why I passionately believe that the history of the development of Britain's rather chaotic transport infrastructure does have at least one important lesson to teach us.

We have seen how the canals and turnpikes developed piecemeal and how the rapid free-for-all growth of the railways produced anomalies like the Settle–Carlisle line. Then there was the short-sighted horror of Dr Beeching's 'rationalisation' in the 1960s. I know I am not alone in supposing that if we are to avoid some of the costly blunders of the past, it is surely time that a group of informed people (and not, please not, politicians) sat down and produced a well-thought-out and fully integrated transport policy. I cannot believe that such an undertaking is beyond the wit of man, because to judge by what they bequeathed us there seems to have been such a policy in Roman Britain. It is high time we created one for the twenty-first century.

CHAPTER FOUR

Rapid Expansion: The Growth of Towns and Cities

GOOD TRANSPORT LINKS between towns and cities only matter if the places in question are prospering. And if the story of Britain's towns and cities after 1550 is anything, it is a tale of growth, expansion and success. But this expansion was by no means uniform. Different towns prospered at different times and for entirely different reasons. Lately we have learned that there is no single, 'one-size-fits-all' explanation to account for these changes. Each place must be taken on its own merits and be assessed in its own contexts and circumstances.[1]

The study of urban archaeology in Britain has advanced at breathtaking pace in the last quarter of the twentieth century. One might suppose that the picture to emerge from this snowstorm of books, maps, papers, articles and internet files supports some of the theories about the origin and growth of towns that were fashionable in the three decades or so after the war. These ideas sought to systematise urban growth and development in a predictable manner. The mass of new urban research of the 1980s and 1990s took place during a period of unprecedented development, when developers were increasingly obliged to have their sites surveyed and excavated to a professional standard. But the results of all this new work simply failed to comply with theoretical predictions.

Rather like the planned villages of Scotland that we discussed briefly towards the end of Chapter 2, it would appear that towns and cities developed in a way that was unique to each individual case study. That is not to say, of course, that their developmental history could not be explained – in fact, far from it – but it could not readily be predicted using *a priori* models. Far from confirming what we believed we already understood, excavation was revealing things that were entirely new and unexpected. This disappointed a few people but delighted the majority – including those wet, tired and overworked excavators out there in some very deep, muddy and dangerous trenches in the heart of urban Britain.

Among other important things, urban archaeologists also rewrote the rules on health and safety: when I started digging in the 1970s I used to be 'banksman' (i.e. supervisor of a mechanical excavator) entirely on my own and wearing just a pair of trainers and cut-off jeans. These days I have to appear in safety boots, proper trousers, a high-visibility jacket and hard hat. There also has to be at least one other person on site in case I get whacked by the digger. And having witnessed one or two avoidable accidents over the years, I now take these things very seriously.

I ended *Britain in the Middle Ages** with the observation that at York and elsewhere it was almost impossible to pin down the end of the Middle Ages with any precision. One reason for this was that many later medieval houses and workshops continued in use well into the seventeenth century. Indeed, a few are still standing today. This is one of the factors to explain why urban archaeologists like to work on a fairly broad scale, because without some idea of a town's general development it can be very difficult indeed to explain what might have been happening at a specific time and place – especially given the fact that, due to the costs of such work, urban trenches can sometimes be very small indeed. In such cases context, in other words setting and situation, becomes all-important.

When I was writing *Britain in the Middle Ages* I found it relatively straightforward to draw general conclusions from finds and features discovered in individual excavations, and I'm thinking here of those remarkable revetments to the medieval London waterfront.[2] But when we get to post-medieval times this becomes increasingly difficult: every trench seems to be more than ever unique and increasingly site-specific. So although excavations have proliferated as the pre-financial crisis economy expanded, I have decided to concentrate on what I consider to be urban archaeology's greatest achievement: the development and creation of town plans, which illustrate in a very visual way

* Page 306.

how different places developed. In certain respects it could be argued that the town plans revealed by urban archaeology are trespassing on the territory of historical geographers, which may well be the case, not that it matters even slightly. Indeed, one of the best of the recent eight-volume landscape history of England was written by Brian Short, a leading professor of historical geography.[3] Very often it also becomes immediately apparent *why* those developments happened in the way they did, as the example from Sheffield will, I hope, soon make clear. So instead of excavations I will tend to focus on maps, plans and standing structures or fragments of architecture.

The principal exception to the 'no excavations' rule will be at Hungate, in York, where the great historic city which gave us those remarkable Viking houses at Coppergate is currently providing an intriguing glimpse into what one might term the prehistory of Victorian Britain. United by poverty, areas of the meanest houses such as these are sometimes referred to as slums. At the risk of sounding politically correct, I must register my dislike of this term, simply because it implies that the people who lived in slums ('slum dogs' in India) were somehow contemptible: slovenly and lacking in pride and self-respect. In reality they were poor, and nothing more.

It has also become something of a cliché to assume that all housing built for working-class people in the eighteenth and nineteenth centuries was inadequate. Inevitably, so the myth goes, it degenerated into slums. Laying aside the simple fact that people tend to try to improve their homes rather than destroy them, this view makes out that all working people were slobs. In reality, squalor only happened when people were forced to live in overcrowded conditions and where the drains, plus a reliable supply of clean water, were inadequate. Indeed, a recent archaeological survey of nineteenth-century workers' housing in east Lancashire has provided firm evidence that it was well designed, built and laid out. It does not conform to the widely accepted myth that such housing was always poor and the authors point out that, rather than urging the demolition of the many streets of terrace housing that still survive, politicians instead should be arguing for their preservation.[4] They are well built and could readily be converted to modern standards. More to the point, the arrangement of these houses suited the social life of the people who lived in them: close-knit communities were established and thrived. It seems that some of the current flatten-and-rebuild schemes, such as Pathfinder, have learned nothing from the mistakes of the post-war high-rise era. One is tempted to wonder why so many career politicians suffer from such historical amnesia. I suspect this failure of memory followed as a direct result of their move to the isolated world of the 'Westminster Village' where they quickly lost all contact with the lives of ordinary people.

Many town authorities have created computerised urban databases to provide context for their archaeological researches. These might sound rather tedious, and inevitably they tend to accumulate a certain amount of jargon and management-speak, but they are, nonetheless, fundamentally important – which is doubtless why they have been in development for the best part of forty years. Initially they were based around maps and card-index files, but these were soon replaced by various computerised and semi-computerised systems which were developed in leading historical cities, such as York, London and Norwich. Initially, too, the focus was on the Roman and medieval periods, but today the enormous speed and capacity of modern computers has meant that all periods are included, back, indeed, to the Palaeolithic (Old Stone Age) and forward to the present.

The compilers of the first urban databases realised that maps were of crucial importance and one of the earliest (1984) discoveries from such a map was the existence of Middle Saxon London (*Lundenwic*), which a distribution plan of pottery showed lay just outside the walled Roman city, in Covent Garden.[5] That research, by the much-missed Alan Vince, was an extraordinary breakthrough.[6]

Although urban databases developed through the pioneering efforts of individual archaeological teams, today they are coordinated at a national level, simply because it makes little sense if the various systems cannot communicate with each other in a comprehensible fashion. One result of this coordination is that some of the heterogeneity of Britain's urban histories is beginning to break down. Common themes are starting to emerge from the data and as these are identified they then, in turn, help to shape the direction of future research.

English Heritage began actively to support urban databases after their initial period of development, some eight years after Alan Vince's discovery of *Lundenwic*.[7] Much of this work has been based around a relatively new technique of analysis known as 'landscape characterisation'. Essentially, this approach is based on modern maps rather than a detailed knowledge of a particular area's historic and prehistoric past – and as such it has given many landscape historians serious misgivings. They see it as a somewhat facile, skin-deep approach that describes rather than explains. I'm not entirely happy about many aspects of it myself, but I have to admit that in general it does seem to work; I also think that something is a great deal better than nothing in a world where, without some form of containment or direction, development would soon obliterate some of the most interesting parts of Britain.

'Historic landscape characterisation', to give its full title, began in the mid-1990s at a time when I was quite active at English Heritage.[8] I must admit I was initially hostile to this new idea which had been developed by archaeologists in Cornwall, where it had then become an important tool for planners trying to curtail the rash of holiday-inspired developments that were then disfiguring large stretches of coastal landscapes. Despite my doubts, I soon realised that landscape characterisation was relatively quick and inexpensive to do and was certainly very much more cost-effective than an equivalent 'proper' historical survey. It could also be justified when confronting developers and their lawyers who could not argue with the evidence presented to them on detailed maps. It was a technique that was superbly equipped to deal with the intricacies of planning decisions, but as time passed archaeologists working within the planning world realised that its true potential lay in the creation of map-based plans for future development.

Today, of course, these plans for the future are based on a series of computer-generated map overlays, using GIS (geographic information systems) software. GIS allows archaeologists working in the various local authority planning departments to add and subtract sites, finds and monuments of various periods to a succession of maps. GIS and landscape characterisation began life as research tools of interest to planners. Now the situation has been reversed: they have become planning tools of interest to researchers. Had I, however, been able to foresee their future, I think I would have been surprised by the quality of the academic information they have yielded. But first some thoughts on the scale of the problem in England.

England is a highly urbanised country and the characterisation programme has to be sufficiently flexible to deal with the various types of towns, cities and the semi-urban, industrial and residential land-scapes surrounding them. So the full, all-singing and all-dancing urban databases are confined to the centres of just thirty-five major historic towns and cities. Next, more extensive (i.e. less detailed for so small an area) surveys of smaller towns are organised by individual counties. But today much of the landscape is in fact semi-urban and for these areas, for example Merseyside and the Black Country, a version of both urban and rural landscape characterisation has been developed. By 2006 some seven hundred towns and cities had been surveyed – around half the total number of towns in England.[9]

One important aspect of the more intensive surveys has been the fitting of digitally scanned ancient maps onto the modern Ordnance Survey system and, although the 'fit' is not always perfect, the appear-ance of an original map with finds from recent excavations superim-posed onto it in a series of overlays can be very striking when seen on screen (sadly less so on the page!). I was astonished when I saw Loggan's famous 1675 bird's-eye view of Oxford superimposed with considera-ble accuracy on a modern map of the city.[10]

One of the factors lying behind the early growth of industry in Britain was the development, in certain areas, of a dual economy. Most of these were pastoral areas without a particularly strong tradition of large estates and powerful landlords, so they generally tended to occur more to the west than the east. The area around Coalbrookdale (modern Telford) is a good case in point. Dual economies varied from place to place (in the Forest of Dean, for example, it was pastoralism and coal-mining), but the basic idea was that the family (often yeoman) farm kept livestock, but the wife (and children) supplemented this income by carrying out secondary processing of, say, wool – spinning it to form yarn, or fabric. Today we would see this as 'adding value'.

In the Sheffield area the dual economy provided full and part-time labour for a series of water-powered workshops (known as mills) along the various rivers that ran into the Don, from the west. Sheffield has long been famous for the cutlery and edge tools that were made in these small mills, the first of which were built in the fifteenth century, with many more in the sixteenth and seventeenth.[11] By the early 1600s

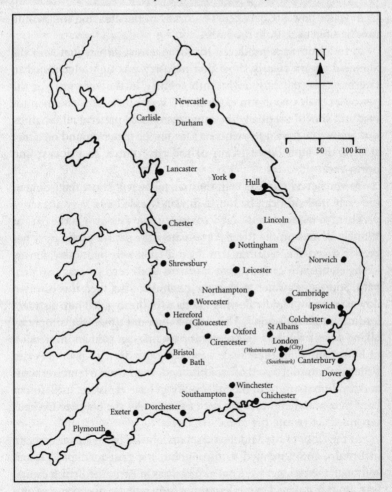

FIG 14 *A map showing the thirty-five major historic towns and cities of England. Each of these places maintains an up-to-date, computerised database of its finds, sites and monuments which are integrated within a series of period-based maps. London's historic core is divided into three: the City, Southwark and Westminster.*

the industry had become well established (the Company of Cutlers was formed there in 1624). The first rapid period of growth was from 1730 to 1790, but by the end of the century steam was beginning to take over from water power. Coal occurs naturally in the area and mills could now be sited back from the rivers.

A series of maps produced for the extensive urban survey of the Sheffield region clearly show that industry was tightly confined to riverbanks in the early eighteenth century, at the very start of the period of their maximum expansion.[12] Very much later, the map for 1950 still shows essentially the same river-based pattern, although by now industrial developers tended to favour the flatter ground on either side of the Don downstream of the city centre, to the east and north-east.

Anyone at all familiar with the area today will know that some of the early mill sites can be found in well-wooded and very attractive parkland to the west of the city centre. My own favourite is the park at Whitely Woods on the River Porter where the course of the river has been so diverted and dammed by the mills that were built there, mostly in the eighteenth century, that it is hard to discern its exact original path. Sometimes water follows the natural course, then it is diverted down a narrow, rapidly flowing tail race (or 'head goit') into a stream leading into a mill pond. This happens several times and simply by taking a stroll through this pleasant park one can gain an impression of how many mills there once were along the river. Today the Porter Valley is a tranquil haven for wildlife, and, apart from a few river walls and revetments, most of the mill buildings have vanished. I still find it hard to comprehend that the last of these mills, the Shepherd Wheel, remained active into the 1930s.

At the close of the Middle Ages, London was by far the largest city in Britain, and remained so throughout the post-medieval period. Although the changes were not as drastic as in Paris, the British capital was also transformed in modern times from a centre of commerce into the symbolic heart of a vast empire. The Great Fire of London in 1666 caused the City to be rebuilt in stone, with wider, grander streets which were laid out on the pre-fire plan. Personally, I have never regretted the decision of the city fathers not to sweep everything away, as Wren among others proposed. I like the jumble of thoroughfares, even if many of the post-war buildings along them can be less than distinguished. Like it or not, the place has character, which cannot always be said for the imposing and, to me at least, impersonal boulevards of

Paris. But before I start to receive threatening e-mails from every architectural historian in Europe, I will rapidly move on.

London is probably the most extensively excavated city in the world. It also boasts a series of splendid books covering everything from low life in the eighteenth century, to its many streams and rivers, most of which today flow in culverts below the surface.[13] So there is a vast amount of material to choose from. Of course the City, Westminster and Southwark, the three 'epicentres' of urban life around the lower reaches of the Thames, were always very important, but for my money the real archaeological gold lies further out, in what is usually referred to as Greater London, the area once governed by the late-lamented Greater London Council.[14] If anywhere can be explained by taking a broad-brush view, it has to be London.

By the eleventh century London was the richest and biggest city in Britain and the largest port in eastern England. In the Middle Ages, as now, much of the wealth was generated by the merchants and bankers of the City, but finance is only a means of facilitating, of scheduling production and supply. Sometimes financiers need to be reminded that you cannot eat or do anything useful with coins or paper money. They are merely symbolic expressions of wealth. As a consequence of this, outside the walls of the Roman City, London has always been a centre of production, marketing and exchange, first in Britain and then in Europe. From the period 1500–1800, London, along with Venice and Amsterdam, had established the regular long-distance trade links to justify a claim to be a world city; and by 1750 it had overtaken Paris to become Europe's largest conurbation.[15] By the nineteenth century its power was without rival or parallel anywhere on earth. We must leave posterity to judge whether that was a good thing for London, or indeed for Britain. But in history, where such things are rare, it was a fact.

The great effect of London on its hinterland and further afield was a direct result of the need to sustain a growing population.[16] In the mid-sixteenth century London was home to about 120,000 people; by 1700 there were half a million and by the first Census of 1801, nearly a million (959,000). This phenomenal growth represents an eightfold increase since the end of the Middle Ages. As London grew, so its influence on the rest of Britain became ever more disproportionate. In the century from 1650 to 1750 it has been estimated that no less than one adult Englishman in six had had direct experience of London life. During that period feeding the capital city largely determined the shape of the agricultural economies of Kent and East Anglia and the need to heat its houses caused London to double the output of Tyneside; without a railway or canal system, coasters plying ports along the east coast provided the most efficient means of moving such huge quantities of coal.

I mentioned that the rebuilding of the City after the Great Fire of 1666 essentially followed the original, medieval street plan, but I omitted to say that, although the Great Fire destroyed more than 13,000 houses, just over half had been rebuilt by 1673. This was deliberately done to reduce the gross overcrowding that had been such a feature of the City in late medieval times. It was effective, too, for although the City lost none of its financial clout, the number of permanent residents there fell sharply: by 1690 10,000 people had left and the population dropped to just 190,000. The important point to note is that by the late seventeenth century the City accounted for just a quarter of the capital's overall population. This represents a major change in the economic and geographical structure of the growing conurbation. By the early eighteenth century many trades and crafts had left the City and moved to areas further away, in some cases, such as the leather-working area of Southwark, to places where that craft had been plied since at least the Middle Ages.[17] The process of curing leather involves the copious use of stale urine which stinks to high heaven, so that industry had always been located across the river from the City. That may be one reason, but the leather-workers also enjoyed lower taxes and fewer restrictions south of the river. As we will see shortly there were also other, thespian, inducements that might have tempted people to live there.

Although the division of London into East and West Ends was already evident in the sixteenth century, it became more formalised after the Great Fire: the area in and around Westminster was the political and cultural centre; the City and along Fleet Street to the west provided commercial, legal and financial services; and industry, shipping services, docks and warehouses grew up along the north shores of the river, to the east. That, at least, was the general plan. During the eighteenth century the gentry and aristocracy added new estates in the

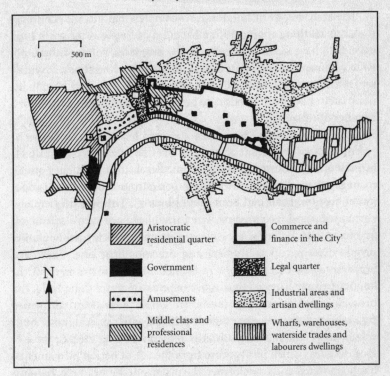

FIG 15   *A map showing how space within London was organised around 1750, largely based on a three-year detailed twenty-four-map survey by John Rocque (completed in 1749). By the mid-eighteenth century the growing conurbation north of the Thames was clearly divided into an essentially residential and political West End, a financial City and a maritime and industrial East End. South of the river Southwark was also prospering as a maritime and trading area, with leather-working (which became established here in the Middle Ages) still important.*

West End, such as those on land belonging to the Dukes of Bedford. These included what is possibly London's greatest contribution to urban architecture, the square, the first of which (St James's Square) was built in 1668. Squares continued to be built throughout the eighteenth century and as late as the 1880s; but by this time the builders had moved away from the West End to places like Chelsea, which had been outlying villages just fifty years earlier.

The archaeology of London is so complex that I cannot continue to sketch anything approaching a balanced overview in the space I still have. So I have decided to select a few examples, some of them not widely known, that illustrate aspects of life, at various times, in widely separated parts of the city. I'll start with something that has been in the news lately, but which I believe to be of more lasting importance for a number of reasons.

London was where Shakespeare earned his living and where he played such an important part in the creation of modern English. He himself is still something of an enigma but his extraordinary genius manages to inspire generation upon generation. Normally speaking, I'm not very enthusiastic about re-creations of anything extinct, except perhaps musical instruments. I'm particularly unenthusiastic about attempts at so-called historical re-enactment, which usually involve people dressing up as soldiers and precious little else. There are, however, a few exceptions. A re-created musical instrument in the hands of an experienced musician can be a wonderful thing and it can provide insights into the way music would have been performed centuries ago. Anyone even slightly familiar with classical music must acknowledge that the move towards authenticity over the past three or four decades (which partly arose from the use of period instruments) has invigorated and transformed the playing of, for example, Baroque pieces by masters such as Handel.

But until very recently nobody knew what it would have been like to have performed in, or witnessed, a Shakespearian play in an Elizabethan-style theatre. And there is only one contemporary illustration – and that by a Dutch visitor to London called Dewitt – of a London theatre (the Swan), drawn around 1596.[18] That sketch aside, we must rely for our reconstructions on contemporary bird's-eye views by artists like Wenceslaus Holler who drew the Globe in 1647, shortly before all London theatres were shut on Cromwell's orders. Theatre, it seems to me, is as much about space, acoustics, audience reaction and atmosphere as it is about stagecraft, declamation and theatricality. This doubtless explains the huge popularity of the faithfully reconstructed new Globe Theatre, on its original site in Southwark. Like countless others who have been there, I can vouch that it was a most evocative and moving experience.

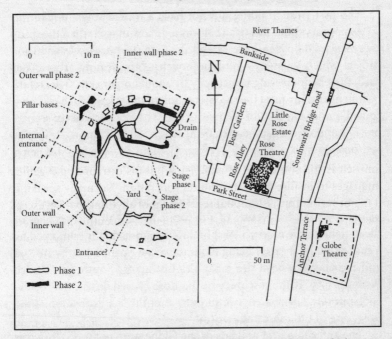

FIG 16   *A plan of the archaeological evidence for the Rose theatre, which was built in two phases. The inner and outer polygonal walls of the original building that supported the gallery are clear. The second-phase enlargement to the north made the theatre more oval than round and allowed the later stage to protrude further into the yard, where most of the audience would have stood.*

Given the paucity of original illustration, archaeology provides the best means of shedding fresh light on London's early theatres. It's a quest, moreover, which is still producing surprises. The original burst of activity was in 1988–9 when the Department of Greater London Archaeology discovered what are still the best-preserved footings of an Elizabethan theatre, the Rose, just west of Southwark Bridge Road, some eighty-five metres south of the Thames.[19] As the archaeologists predicted, these footings were polygonal, rather than circular, because the original builders had to work with straight lengths of timber. But what made the excavation so exciting was the revelation that the building had been extensively modified following its original construction in 1587.

The first Rose building did not have a roofed stage, unlike the contemporary Swan theatre. That was to follow in 1592 when the theatre's owner, Philip Henslowe, extended it to the north. This was a major project which involved rebuilding much of the seating around the yard, thereby increasing its capacity by about 20 per cent. This refurbishment also involved the reconstruction of the stage, which was now roofed, rather like that of the new Globe. The Rose was never seen as one of London's larger theatres, being described by Thomas Dekker in the prologue to a play he premiered there in 1599 as 'this smal Circumference'. Best estimates suggest that audiences there were probably in the order of two thousand.

The fact that the Rose was modified just five years after its opening paints a remarkable picture of a dynamic time, with many echoes of theatreland in the modern West End. This impression is reinforced by a succession of theatres being built: the Swan opened nearby in 1596 and the Globe, whose site today lies just across Southwark Bridge Road, in 1599. If the discovery of the Rose caused a fuss, that of the Globe in July 1989, barely two months after the last excavation at the Rose, caused little short of a storm.

The archaeological remains of the Globe were not as extensive as those of the Rose, but the theatre itself was larger and among the most successful of its time. The site revealed fascinating details, such as the discovery of a layer of hazelnut shells that were used as flooring between the two walls that supported the gallery. The Globe, too, was built in two distinct phases, the first of which was erected by a carpenter called Peter Streete, using timbers dismantled from a theatre north of the river, in Shoreditch. That theatre had been built by the well-known Burbage family around 1576. The original Globe theatre actually burnt down during the first performance of one of Shakespeare's later plays, Henry VIII, on 29 June 1613. Special effects can often cause problems and in this instance the fire was caused by sparks from a discharging cannon. Consistent with the energy of the time, the theatre was promptly rebuilt and reopened in 1614, although Shakespeare (who died in April 1616) was to produce no further plays there. The rebuilt Globe was demolished on Cromwell's orders in 1644.

The three principal theatres of the Shakespearian age were spaced out along Park Street (then known as Maid Lane), just back from the

Southwark river frontage with the Globe and Rose at one end and the Swan, to the west, at the other. These theatres were deliberately positioned outside the City of London to take advantage of Southwark's lower tax duties and generally less restrictive attitude. The Globe, of course, was where Shakespeare's company, the King's Men, produced some of his greatest masterpieces, but some of his earlier work (such as *Romeo and Juliet*) is known to have been produced at a theatre north of the river, in Shoreditch. This theatre, known simply as 'the Theatre', was the one that provided the timbers used in the construction of the first Globe.

The story behind the discovery of the Theatre is most intriguing.[20] In 1917 an antiquary named W. W. Braines was working through a succession of old maps and he came to the conclusion that the original site of the theatre was indeed in Shoreditch, west of the High Street and halfway along New Inn Broadway. Ironically, this is the site offered to the modern Tower Theatre Company by the landowner, a theatre enthusiast, for a nominal sum, for their new home. An archaeological assessment of the site in 2008 by a team from the Museum of London revealed the remains of a polygonal brick wall and part of the footings for the base of a pier or column. The bricks were undoubtedly of the right period, but the wall had partly been robbed out by people salvaging the bricks for use in other buildings. It would be hard to be certain that these rather slight traces were indeed part of a lost Tudor theatre, but the curve of the polygon (if indeed that's what it is) was of the right size. But the evidence that convinces me beyond much doubt had actually been revealed much earlier, in 1999, when a geophysical survey carried out ahead of a different potential development produced signals (known as anomalies) for a buried curved wall some four metres (twelve feet) inside, and concentric with, the footings found in 2008. The traces produced by the geophysics have to be the inner wall of the theatre, whose original diameter was some eighty-two feet – a size entirely typical of Elizabethan playhouses.

The burst of creative energy of the late sixteenth and early seventeenth centuries has been mirrored to some small extent by the spate of archaeological discoveries made during the credit-fuelled development boom of the later twentieth and early twenty-first centuries. In my blacker moments I used to fear that we were about to witness a modern equivalent of Oliver Cromwell's orders to destroy the Globe, such was the pace of development – but more recently there has been a slowing down, brought about by the economic decline. Sadly this has led to much archaeological unemployment, but things couldn't have continued as they were. Viewed realistically, it must signal a return to sanity. Anyhow, seen in the long term, London's story is one of almost incessant development, and sometimes the changes could be profound, even altering the height and shape of the ground beneath one's feet.

Like many other visitors to the capital, I sometimes like to take a stroll along the Victoria Embankment where the Thames is never far away and where the ground surface is sufficiently undulating to give an impression of what this part of the lower Thames Valley might have appeared hundreds of years ago, before houses covered everything. As one wanders along the footpath through the Embankment Gardens, one comes to the memorial to that great and largely unsung engineer Sir Joseph Bazalgette, who built London its system of sewers in the 1860s, following several waves of cholera and typhoid.

One of Bazalgette's huge brick-arched drains, the Northern Low Level Sewer, ran along the north shore of the river. Once built, it was buried and properly consolidated and named the Victoria Embankment. It gained London many acres of new land from the river and left the earlier river gates quite literally high and dry. The best-known of the river gates is Traitors' Gate, leading into the Tower of London. It was built on the orders of Edward I in the later 1270s, as a river entrance to St Thomas's Tower, which was then used as royal accommodation. By Tudor times the role of the Tower of London had changed from a royal stronghold to a prison for enemies of the Crown and the state. And it was then that the gate acquired its emotive name.

River gates further upstream were civil structures, designed to impress rather than terrify. These gates could be quite elaborate affairs, as they were often the main portals into smart residential developments from what was then the city's principal thoroughfare. So they needed to proclaim the importance of the individuals who built them.

A particularly fine example is the York Gate, which was built in 1626 by Nicholas Stone for George Villiers, the 1st Duke of Buckingham. Villiers was James I's favourite; never very popular, he was assassinated in 1628 after a series of unsuccessful European military campaigns for which he became the public scapegoat. But in 1624 he acquired the palatial York House from the Archbishop of York and York Gate was the imposing watergate he had built for the house, which was subsequently demolished in 1675 and a gridded network of streets laid out on its site. The principal of these, Buckingham Street, can be seen behind the gate. Then, in 1862, Bazalgette constructed the Victoria Embankment which left the erstwhile watergate stranded. Useless, it fell into disrepair and was eventually restored by London County Council in 1893.

In *The Making of the British Landscape* I came to the conclusion that although I didn't like bureaucrats very much, the main reason that rural landscapes survived the spread of town and suburbs in the twentieth century was because of the work of planners and the implementation of planning legislation. This process had its roots in the nineteenth century with the passing of the first of several Ancient Monuments Acts, which became law in October 1882. Since then the protection of ancient sites and buildings has been in the hands of officialdom, which has generally done the job quite well, if sometimes in a rather ponderous manner. But there is also another side to all this, with roots that are actually much older. I refer here to the unofficial, unpaid people who established the network of local history and archaeological societies that have stubbornly refused to die, despite ever-increasing competition from the internet – which the best of them have embraced, anyhow.

As a student I was taught that Britain's network of mostly county-based local societies which grew up in the nineteenth century was without rival in Europe, and I have found no reason to change my mind. They may not be 'official', but Heaven preserve anyone rash enough to cross swords with these deeply knowledgeable pillars of the local community. When it comes to their region they know every person and every place. What I also find remarkable when I talk to such groups is the fact that they can be extremely well informed about the bigger picture and make bold and imaginative use of the internet. I am glad to report that community archaeology is alive and proliferating throughout Britain.

One proof that community archaeology is thriving can be found in the 'Local' section of libraries and bookshops, which certainly include lightweight offerings on topics like *The Ghosts of South Borsetshire* and *Highwaymen Along the A123*, but their inspiration, if not their actual roots, can ultimately be traced back to the gentlemen's societies of the 1730s and 1740s, although, having said that, most county societies did not appear until the nineteenth century and only a few of these published regular journals before the 1850s.[21] Today the county societies retain their role, often as coordinators of numerous and sometimes shorter-lived local groups whose meetings take place in pubs, hotels, bookshops, church and village halls, not to mention a host of private houses. These groups are the backbone of local interest and they also serve an important social role, in drawing together a mix of different people with various backgrounds. Over the years I have been involved with several local groups whose members have come to the subject from backgrounds as diverse as the Church, farming, nursing, computer software, land working, garage mechanics and the building industry.

The diversity of people attending these groups is reflected in the approaches they take to the history of the area that unites them. Some are far happier working through historical documents in local government archives and in the records of family estates, or the longer established estate agents. Others like nothing better than to pore over old maps and then walk through the streets noting old buildings and surveying them. Increasingly people want more 'hands-on' involvement and organise excavations, many of which involve local children and young people. What makes these digs special for me is the fact that they are so well planned in advance. The people involved firmly believe they know what lies under the ground. Indeed, such digs sometimes leave no room for the unexpected, for the surprises that any experienced archaeologist knows will leap out of the ground and smack him across the nose. As I know both to my cost and pleasure, digs have a habit of making the most knowledgeable director look decidedly stupid.

Some local societies exist for a specific reason, such as the Shapwick project I discussed in Chapter 1, but the majority are quite content to take a broader view. Anything can be grist for their mill and it shows in the work they publish which can be, for me at least, fundamentally fascinating. Some years ago I spent a few days staying with a friend who lived in south-east London in a side street off Blackheath. We'd go for evening walks across the heath to pubs on the other side, and on one of these I noticed an extraordinarily elegant range of seven squarish houses, set in a gentle crescent and linked together by a classical colonnade. They looked out across the heath and I was immediately struck by their elegance. I must have been going home shortly afterwards because I never managed to discover any more about them, and didn't have the relevant volume of Pevsner's *Buildings of England* in my collection.

Twenty years passed and I had been approached by *Time Team* to be the archaeological director of a programme about the wartime archaeology of Shooters Hill, the highest ground on London's southeast approaches, for the series broadcast in 2008 (about which more in Chapter 8). Crew and contributors were put up in the Clarendon Hotel, an elegant Georgian building with commanding views across the heath. It was a fine evening and, as is my habit, I decided to reconnoitre the local pubs. The nearest one was already packed full of *Time Team* people who assured me warmly as I strolled by that the beer was first rate and that they were all thirsty. Fingering my slim wallet, I continued on my way. About fifty yards further on, the road began to swing away from the heath and a stand of tall trees appeared on my right. No sooner had I passed these, than the view opened up, the sun peeked out momentarily from behind a cloud and I could have sworn I heard the resonant chords of Beethoven's Pastoral Symphony mixed with thunder in the distance. Because there they were: those seven miraculous buildings, linked by what I now saw was a discontinuous colonnade.

Back at the hotel I mentioned the buildings to the manager who, it turned out, had an interest in local history. He pointed out a glass case in the foyer, which displayed books of local interest and a splendid historical map of the area, published by the hotel. From this I learned many things: that King Alfred the Great was the first Lord of the Manor of Lewisham, that both Elizabeth I's review of her troops and the ceremony marking the Restoration of Charles II took place on Blackheath; I further discovered that the Clarendon Hotel was built across the

Greenwich Meridian. All are facts which have enhanced my life, as such things can if you allow them to. Also in the case was a thick book by Neil Rhind, *Blackheath Village and Environs*, which is quite simply one of the best and most detailed accounts of local history I have ever read. Here, if anywhere, I would discover the story of those elegant buildings.

The story of The Paragon – and what an appropriate name that is – could be taken as a parable for those vast areas of post-medieval London beyond the immediate influence of the City and Westminster.[22] It seems another world, but it's also distinctively London – an enigma – which I think is why many people find the capital so appealing.

Today one can be walking on Blackheath and be dive-bombed by swallows, yet the South Circular Road is just a short distance to the south and in the not very far distance is the distinctive mass of the Canary Warf tower. So this would have been within comfortable riding distance of the City, if not on a daily basis, then for a few days at least. So when did Blackheath begin to feel the influence of its giant northern neighbour? At what point did it cease to be rural and become what it is today? Because much as I love The Paragon, those elegant houses are anything but rustic.

The small estate of 282 acres (114 hectares) on which The Paragon was later built is known as the Cator estate after a certain John Cator, who bought it at auction in August 1783 for the then knockdown price of £22,500. The estate then included a large mansion, known as Wricklemarsh, part of Blackheath village and a few houses on the edge of the heath. Wricklemarsh is mentioned in Domesday (1086) and although its medieval history is incomplete, parts of what was later to be the estate were owned by various country gentlemen.[23] Edward III and Richard II also possessed woodland there. The Crown owned hunting land all over England, so there is nothing very unusual in this, but in 1488 land was sold to Thomas Fetherston, 'a citizen and vintner of London', who doesn't exactly answer the description of an impoverished rural squire. But this is just a hint. Otherwise, records of the fifteenth and sixteenth centuries read like those of any other rural parish in southern England, with mention of leases, cattle droves and arable land. The landowners, too, if not local live in places like Reading.

The first indications of lasting change come in the mid-sixteenth century when separate parcels of land in Wricklemarsh begin to be owned by a single family and then by one man, Edward Blount (1559–1617), a lawyer in the Middle Temple. A wealthy, highly educated man, whose interest lay in London, was now the owner of a substantial manor house in what was essentially a rural estate, but still with many tenanted houses. This was the point when money earned in the City would be used to enhance the manor house, the estate and the reputation of the families that owned it. It was, however, a process that began gradually.

The next owner of Wricklemarsh, Colonel Thomas Blount (1605–78), was a colourful character and friend of the diarists John Evelyn and Samuel Pepys. During the Commonwealth he even spent time in prison for his religious views. He was a cultivated man – a member of the Royal Society – but was not closely involved with the City. In many respects he was typical of contemporary country landowners within reach of London: he had a wide circle of friends, but was not particularly concerned with the development of his estate. In fact, rather the contrary: his property accumulated mortgages and was eventually sold (in 1669) to a London merchant, John Morden, who needed somewhere safe to put his money.

Morden was very much a 'hands-on' City merchant, but he was also a generous man and established, in 1695, among other charities, Morden College, whose buildings can still be seen on the southern side of Blackheath. Future owners of Wricklemarsh, such as members of the Page family, were all closely involved with the City and the estate benefited greatly from their wealth. Improvements included the demolition of the old manor house and the erection of a vast stone-built mansion in 1724. So far the story is essentially one of wealth and patronage: royalty, for example, came to dine at the swanky new house more than once. But when did things really begin to change; when were others allowed to inhabit this highly desirable land? It's worth remembering here that during the latter part of the eighteenth century London's population was rising rapidly and these people needed somewhere to live.

The key change was the sale of the estate to John Cator in 1783 from its then owner, the wonderfully named dream reader of my books, a

Mr Page-Turner. The estate was now run by the man who would ulti-mately be responsible for the shape of modern Blackheath. While he was in charge, the vast Wricklemarsh House was demolished and the land made available for housing.

Cator was a timber merchant from Beckenham and, like many people associated with the building trade, he was also a developer. And like all successful men in that business he knew a great deal about marketing. It is immediately apparent from its elegant appearance that the fourteen houses (arranged in seven pairs) of The Paragon were aimed at 'the new upper middle classes, whose large families needed carriages, stables and servants' quarters'.[24] Cator leased the land on which they sit to Michael Searles, a practising architect, the son of a Greenwich surveyor and, like his father, also a property developer.

By the time Searles came to Blackheath he had designed a number of successful upmarket houses, including another Paragon in the New Kent Road. What I find so fascinating about this tale of lease and devel-opment is how modern it seems. First, Cator looks around for a part-ner with a good track record and they both put together a well-thought-out and carefully marketed plan. They knew it was a speculative and risky project and, indeed, it nearly did fall flat. But it didn't. The first of the seven double houses had been built by 1796 and the last by 1807. These were the honeypots to attract the influential people to the development. A short time later Cator and a series of other partners would provide not quite so lavish accommodation for the less well heeled, but still firmly middle-class people who also wanted to move out of inner London. So they succeeded and Blackheath has remained one of London's most attractive residential areas. A glance at the large cars along The Paragon crescent shows that after over two centuries their owners are as upmarket as ever.

In the early 1970s urban archaeologists across Britain began to wake up to the threat of massive redevelopment. In England the response was essentially piecemeal although there was a degree of coordination within individual towns and cities; this ultimately gave rise to the computerised urban databases that are now such an essential compo-nent of a planning office in any historic town or city.[25] In Scotland the approach was altogether more concerted.[26] The Scottish Burgh Survey came into existence in 1976 and has been an outstanding success. Historic burghs are surveyed in sufficient detail to recognise surviving areas of importance and places where ancient deposits are likely to survive below the ground. The results of the survey are published promptly and these volumes, many of them produced by Historic Scotland, provide the 'bible' that local planners and developers must refer to. These reports are also written with the public in mind and have played an important part in raising local awareness of Scotland's urban legacy.

Towns south of the border developed earlier than in Scotland, where the first to emerge were places like Dunbar, which were sited on an already existing settlement; in other instances, as we'll see in a moment at North Queensferry, they were placed on well-established routes or at places where ferries crossed major rivers or lakes. The Scottish Burgh Survey confirmed that many historic burghs were founded during the reign of King David I (1124–53), who granted the right to hold markets as part of the new burgh status. The formation of burghs then continued through the Middle Ages and into post-medieval times. Indeed, urban growth was an important feature of Scotland's era of industrial expansion.

The bald statistics are informative: 482 Scottish burghs were in existence prior to 1846 of which a minimum of 145 are medieval; these include 81 burghs granted by royalty.[27] Although the towns' origins lie in the Middle Ages the majority of early buildings in Scotland's historic burghs are firmly post-medieval (usually seventeenth century and later). This reflects the fact that most domestic and many public buildings erected in the Middle Ages were built of less durable materials, such as wood and plaster. So although they no longer stand, their foundations still survive below the ground.

The gardens of Scotland are among the finest anywhere and Maisie and I like to visit them whenever we can get away from the farm, but before we set out I fill a box in the boot with various regional guides for the trip. A couple of years ago we had been driving quite hard and for rather too long, to beat the Edinburgh afternoon rush-hour, and decided to pull off the A90 as soon as we'd crossed the Firth of Forth. While Maisie poured much-needed black coffee from the flask, I thumbed through the box and there came across the Scottish Burgh

Survey volume on North Queensferry, which a large road sign directly ahead informed us we were about to enter.[28] It proved an excellent diversion.

The name Queensferry is traditionally believed to have been derived from Queen Margaret, wife of King Malcolm Canmore (1058–93), who granted free passage across the Forth for pilgrims travelling to St Andrews. Today North Queensferry will be familiar to road and rail travellers as the northern landfall of the two great bridges that carry the railway (1890) and the road (1964) north from Edinburgh into the historic Pictish Kingdom of Fife and thence to the Highlands.

Travellers in the Middle Ages felt the need for religious protection which was provided by the chapel of St James (their patron saint), granted by Robert I to Dunfermline Abbey in 1320–22. This religious community ran the ferry and gave support to travellers throughout the Middle Ages. Early in the post-medieval period the wooden houses in the town were burnt by the English on Christmas night 1547, as part of Henry VIII's notorious 'rough wooing'. The chapel of St James was probably damaged in this attack, too. A century later, in 1651, North Queensferry was inspected by King Charles II, anxious to prevent Cromwell's troops moving north of the Forth from Linlithgow where they were then based. Subsequently Cromwell saw to it that the town was sacked and the chapel reduced to a ruin.

In the eighteenth century fishing continued to be important, but other local industries emerged: two quarries and a chemical works, producing magnesia (an important heat-resisting material), a blacksmith's works, brickworks and possibly also a saltworks. Despite these new industries the population of the village remained small, with just 312 inhabitants in 1793. The coming of the turnpikes in the 1770s meant that roads into North Queensferry and the ferry service itself had to be improved, as hitherto crossings had sometimes been irregular and were often bedevilled by unconstrained and illegal competition. John Rennie made proposals to improve the ferry pier and facilities around it, which were put into effect in 1809, by the new Forth Ferry Trustee Company; further improvements were made in 1828 by Thomas Telford. In 1821 the first steam ferry was introduced and seven years later the ferry was capable of moving up to a thousand head of cattle a day; the larger vessel also allowed carriages and wagons to be shipped across the Forth. In the early nineteenth century fifty post horses were stabled in the village. Most of the historic buildings in the town date to this period and to the mid- and later nineteenth century, when the town and its innkeepers enjoyed considerable prosperity.

The two events that transformed the town happened in the second half of the nineteenth century. First, in 1867, the North British Railway Company opened a railway line from North Queensferry, northwards. Then, in 1890, the magnificent Forth Railway Bridge was opened after eight years under construction and at a cost of £3.4 million. Although the new bridge took many through passengers away from the town, the ferry service remained the only route across the Firth of Forth for cars, lorries and pedestrians until the opening of the Forth Road Bridge (a suspension bridge which cost £19.5 million) in 1964, whereupon the ferry service closed.

As a child, Maisie used to cross to North Queensferry every year in the 1950s when her family headed towards Lossiemouth, on the River Spey, where her father had grown up and the family were still farmers. We chatted as we walked along the old main road towards the river and she described the hustle and bustle of the crossing, which must have been considerable as there were about 40,000 annual ferry crossings carrying some 1.25 million passengers, 600,000 cars and 200,000 vans and lorries.

We slowed down as we approached the water's edge, the point where the ferries used to leave, and I began to be aware of a strange feeling of being inhabited – taken over – by the past. It has happened to me on a few occasions. It's quite unpredictable. But I find I have to be surrounded by the physical remains of the past for it to happen. As, for example, quite recently when I filmed at dawn within the stones at Stonehenge; when I scrambled in the dark into the Bronze Age copper mine at Great Orme; on a visit to Ely Cathedral; and when I was lying down excavating a trampled sandy floor beneath Bronze Age posts at Flag Fen. But here at North Queensferry the feeling was completely unexpected and very strong. I suppose it emanated in some way from the massive railway bridge which completely dominates the Forth, but also from the unpretentious eighteenth- and nineteenth-century houses of the little town itself and the remarkable miniature light-house that still survives from the Rennie improvements. The lesson I took home from my visit to North Queensferry is that the past does not have to be ancient to be special.

The story of Britain's urban expansion during the industrial era of the late eighteenth and nineteenth centuries was essentially one of free-for-all privately funded expansion where developers bought fields and then covered them with houses. The great landscape historian W. G. Hoskins was one of the first people to appreciate that, if one looked at nineteenth-century town maps, one could quite clearly distinguish the shape of the pre-existing medieval fields that had been bought piecemeal, usually one by one and then built upon.[29] Sometimes enlightened employers realised that it was in their own interests to keep their workforce in better conditions and built so-called 'model villages', at places like Bournville and Saltaire.[30] I'll discuss one of the most remarkable of these, New Lanark, in the next chapter. In many respects these were one-offs, built by remarkably enlightened philanthropists for a very specific industry.

More often than not, employers who provided housing for their workforce did so for entirely practical reasons: in many instances they needed their labour to be close by the workplace, both because they were required at all hours of the day and also because the provision of transport from any distance would have been expensive. The principal, rapidly expanding industry of the mid-nineteenth century was the railway and each company was keen to promote its own 'image', or brand, in a way that we would take for granted today. The colour of the Midland Railway, for example, was maroon and its buildings echoed the great St Pancras Hotel, being generally ornate and Gothic, as befits a structure of the 1870s. The Great Western's colour was green and its style more classical and Italianate, which doubtless reflects the earlier date of its construction.

The earliest railway stations, like the principal London termini north of the Thames (Paddington, Euston, St Pancras, King's Cross and Liverpool Street), were placed on the very edge of the then built-up areas. Here land was cheaper and housing for the workforce could be built for less. One of the finest examples of such housing to have survived is the settlement of New Swindon, built on two fields bought from a local brewer in 1841.[31] Before the railways came to Swindon in the 1840s, the town's population was 2,459. In the last decade of the twentieth century it was 170,000, making it by far the largest town in Wiltshire. Some of this population increase happened in the 1950s, when Swindon was declared a New Town to house London 'overspill' population, but the main growth was in the later nineteenth and earlier twentieth centuries during the expansion of the railways, when Swindon was home to the main locomotive works of the Great Western Railway (GWR). Although the railway buildings are well preserved and of importance in their own right, New Swindon has increasingly been recognised as a very fine and substantially intact example of a mid-nineteenth-century railway village, which is located in an area south-west of the station. New Swindon is particularly important because the documentary evidence for its origin and development is so good. The overall plan was the work of I. K. Brunel, the GWR chief, or Company Engineer, and there are strong reasons for supposing that the first block, or blocks, of workers' cottages (built in 1842) were designed by him personally. Thereafter one cannot be certain, but we do know that he checked and supervised the drawings that left his office, which was responsible for the designs of most of the buildings in the village. Brunel had it arranged around a doubled-up central High Street, off which ran three blocks of housing, to east and to west. The roads between the terraces were named after prominent stations along the main line. The GWR had become financially overstretched in the 1840s and much of the work had to be contracted out using rents as an inducement. This arrangement was not very satisfactory and housing within New Swindon rarely kept up with demand during the rapid expansion, or 'railway mania', of the 1840s.

Brunel wanted his village to look good from the nearby main line, from which it was separated by a strip of designed parkland. The elaborate exterior of cottages visible from passing trains contrasted with far plainer interiors. As time passed, the exteriors became generally less elaborate. This is particularly evident when one compares cottages of the western (built 1842–3) and eastern (1845–7) blocks. The Company also provided shops for tenant shopkeepers (1845–6). A church capable of seating eight hundred and a parsonage were built with funds raised by public subscription in 1845. The church design rather unusually h as a tower and steeple on its north, rather than west, side, where it cou d clearly be seen from passing trains. The church and the look of the houses it provided its workforce with were both important elements in the GWR 'brand'.

The early life of the village was fraught with problems, especially during the post-'railway mania' financial recession of 1847–9. Housing was overcrowded and sanitation rudimentary. Cooking was done over open fires until the introduction of ranges in the late nineteenth century. In the 1840s there were serious cases of smallpox and typhus and an outbreak of typhus in 1849, caused by blocked cesspools. Over time, however, matters improved. In 1844 the GWR bought land for a park just west of the village. The Mechanics Institute and covered market provided baths and libraries, among other benefits. This Institute was the principal social centre of the railway workers and was first accommodated within the works, but was later (1855) moved to a handsome new building at the centre of the village.

Although several streets were demolished after the war, much of New Swindon survives and the stock of housing was extensively refurbished in the 1970s. At its peak in the 1930s the railway yards and works stretched for a mile and a half (2.4 km) alongside the main, London–Bristol line and employed over 14,000 people. Today the picture is very different: Swindon is better known for its software engineers than its railway mechanics.

I discussed medieval York at some length in *Britain in the Middle Ages* and I would like briefly to take the story forward, before I close this chapter, with another York excavation which has thrown light on far more recent, although almost as squalid, inner-city housing. Two centuries of decline in the late Middle Ages drew to an end in 1539 when York became the seat of the government of northern England for the King, until 1641. This new body made the city a major secular and judicial centre; it also flourished as the northern headquarters of the Church of England. As an administrative capital York now attracted lawyers, clerks, church- and businessmen of all sorts; as a result its inns and hotels flourished. During the Civil War only the outer suburbs were damaged, despite the fact that Charles I had his capital there for six months, in 1642.

After the Civil War, York became a resort and social centre for the northern gentry, whose legacy is the many fine Georgian terrace houses that still line a number of the city's streets. These new stone- and brick-built houses transformed the Georgian city. Many are particularly fine, the work of the noted local architect John Carr. The City Corporation realised that visitors and others prepared to spend money needed pleasant surroundings in which to socialise and in 1732 laid out the New Walk, a fine promenade with a long avenue of trees along the north-east bank of the Ouse. Next, the Corporation enclosed the Pikeing Well, a medicinal spring, in another building by John Carr. Carr did a lot of work for the Corporation, including the improvement of the bridges and some street furniture. Much of York's elegance is due to him.

In the Victorian era the Castle Yard was developed into a judicial centre, with a Debtors' Prison, Assize Courts and Female Prison. The arrival of the East Coast Main Line in 1839 had a major effect on the city's prosperity, which was symbolised by the demolition of the old station and the opening of the magnificent new one, in 1877. The new prosperity saw the construction of two new bridges across the Ouse and the opening up of the ancient city centre, by the insertion of Parliament Street in 1833–6. It was also during Victorian times that the chocolate and sweet industry developed, which benefited from the city's excellent road and rail communications. This and other industries attracted a new largely immigrant workforce which moved into the city centre, where slums soon developed. The middle classes then removed themselves from parts of the central area around Bedern and Walmgate.

It's true to say that archaeologists can still be remarkably snobby about aspects of their subject, especially those that are less ancient. When, for example, we find ourselves in the nineteenth and twentieth centuries I've noticed that people are sometimes inclined to smile indulgently, or raise their eyebrows, as if to say: 'Really? And you call that *archaeology*?' But even in these very recent periods a few topics have retained a degree of academic respectability – especially anything to do with the military or heavy industry. But try persuading a group of professional archaeologists that it can be important to excavate the remains of recent working-class houses and you could cut the collective scepticism with a knife. That is precisely what Peter Connelly has been doing at his remarkable project in Hungate, a district alongside the River Foss, not far from the famous Coppergate Viking Dig of the 1970s.

I first visited Hungate in May 2008, during their second season of work, and there I learned that they have the site to themselves until November 2011, by which time the developers, who have generously funded the project, want to start building work. From a purely professional point of view this places huge pressures on Peter and his team. I know how hard it can be just to meet deadlines on a month-by-month basis, but to pilot such a large undertaking to a successful conclusion in five years must be horribly daunting. Still, he seems to thrive on it.

I've been given many tours of archaeological sites by all sorts of people. As a general rule I find that graduate students and those freshly out of university are the best because they are enthused by the underlying research, which gives everything they do meaning. As people spend more time in the profession some of this enthusiasm can dim, especially nowadays when contracting firms are busy trying to complete a variety of sites to tight schedules and ever-tighter budgets. As we walked around the site and Peter gave me the tour he must have delivered hundreds of times before, his excitement was undiminished. After a few minutes it had infected me, too. I knew in advance from my background reading that this was an unusual project, but I didn't realise until I stood on a cobbled late Victorian lane listening to Peter holding forth about Georgian slums that what motivated him was the archaeology of urban poverty. As he put it, at Hungate they were excavating the origins of the welfare state.

When we think of Victorian social reformers we inevitably turn to the works of people like Henry Mayhew, writing in the mid-nineteenth century, but it is less well known that a few decades later the movement he helped pioneer had become very much more sophisticated and the first social scientists were drawing up detailed maps showing the extent of inner-city deprivation, house by house, in the most extraordinary detail. In London the series of twelve maps by Charles Booth drawn up in 1898–9 classified householders into four groups, ranging from the lowest ('Vicious, semi-criminal') to the wealthy upper and upper middle classes.[32] In York a very similar study was carried out at the end of the nineteenth and start of the twentieth century by the Quaker reformer B. Seebohm Rowntree, whose book *Poverty: A Study of Town Life* showed that the houses along Hungate belonged to the poorest possible group. Just across Dundas Street, which had been built in earlier Victorian times by private developers, the houses were a step better, belonging to working-class families with assured incomes. This contrasts with Hungate where the levels of poverty were dire.[33]

So the upper levels at Hungate were the floors and lower walls of the impoverished houses of the nineteenth and earlier twentieth centuries. Before then the area had been given over to allotment-style gardens in the sixteenth to eighteenth centuries. These plots used a quantity of manure and they accumulated two deep layers of what the excavators refer to as horticultural soil. Below this were a series of large pits, hearth and semi-industrial ovens. The pits were dug to extract clay and some were also used as waterholes by the Guild of Cordwainers, whose medieval hall stood close by the site. Cordwainers were shoe-makers and the pits were a useful and ready source of water. Over time they became filled with rubbish.

The later houses were arranged around a cobbled Victorian street, Haver Lane, and a small side street off it, known as St John's Place. The first house to be excavated was number 7, Haver Lane and a now famous picture of the area, taken shortly before its demolition in the late 1930s, shows it to have been unoccupied. The construction of the houses was undoubtedly poor: the walls have footings of just two courses of brick and are painfully thin, so the interior would have been bitterly cold in winter. The rooms of the houses seemed tiny, and of course some, especially the one at the very front, were only used on special occasions, such as marriages and funerals. The sanitary arrange-ments were, at best, minimal. There were no permanent bathrooms and the various household members shared lavatories, which were of a type that has long since vanished, in which waste water from bath-tubs and sinks drained into a cistern which automatically tipped over, flushing the individual toilets, which were sited alongside it, clean. That was the theory. In practice, particularly in hot weather or when water was short, the reality was very different. In such times they rarely worked properly; so waste accumulated, festered and blocked the system and became a potent source of disease. Even at the time, tipping-cistern toilets were widely regarded by the authorities as a major health hazard.

While the houses were what one might expect of a very low-cost private development (it was begun in late Georgian times, around 1815), the roads themselves were of excellent quality, with fine, well-fitted cobbles, side gutters, kerbs and narrow pavements. St John's Place had been given a tarmac surface. The inhabitants of Haver Lane were moved out by York City Council in 1936 and were given disinfectant showers and had all their goods fumigated in case they brought some of the disease of the slums to their smart new homes. This disinfection process has to have been mostly, or even principally, symbolic, as there is no evidence that the people, or their belongings were ever found to be contaminated in any way. It would certainly have been very humiliating and the City Council also made the mistake, common at the time, of splitting up the ex-'slum' community, which led to considerable bitterness later.[34]

This example illustrates some of the problems that can be encountered when well-meaning authorities attempt to 'engineer' or 'manage' the future of urban communities, in what they perceive to be their best interests. The mistakes that were made at places like Hungate were promptly repeated after the war when people from 'slum' areas in large cities were removed to the bright and breezy New Towns that were built in the countryside around them. This time the people were spared the humiliation of physical disinfection but in most instances, especially at the beginning of the process, their existing social networks were largely ignored – again leading to problems, some of which are still with us.

I suppose the main lesson to emerge from this brief foray into urban archaeology is that appearances count for little. Certainly Hungate could be cold, wet and miserable, as could Viking *Jorvík* a few centuries earlier, but in both instances the unpleasant living conditions were actually of secondary importance to the communities living there. What mattered to them was what matters to all but the most ambitious of people: the love, wellbeing and proximity of friends and relations.

CHAPTER FIVE

Dynamic, but Diverse:
The Development of Industrial Britain

I WILL START with a question: why were early industrialists able to develop and expand in Britain, rather than elsewhere? One answer is that the regional cultures of Britain in the sixteenth to eighteenth centuries tended to discourage entrepreneurs and emerging industrialists rather less than was the case in other European countries, such as France, where society prior to the Revolution of 1789 was still remarkably rigid, if not actually feudal in places. Holland, of course, was an exception and ought to receive far more credit for providing Britain with many of the commercial institutions and agricultural commodities that would prove so important in the eighteenth century.

There was also a mood of tolerance and a degree of military fatigue after England's Civil War and the peaceful change towards constitutional monarchy that followed from the Glorious Revolution of 1688. For these, and many other reasons, Britain was the principal birthplace of the modern industrial world. Incidentally, like many others, I was taught at school that Britain's 'unique' geology in which coal and iron occurred together, was the major 'cause' of the Industrial Revolution. But that simply isn't true. Coal and iron ore are found near each other in many parts of the world. But even this social explanation is something of an over-simplification. Yes, important elements of the industrial process – especially new forms of motive power and farm and factory machinery – did indeed make their appearance in mid-eighteenth-century Britain, but that is not to say that the rest of the world was doing nothing; the proof of this is that within a few decades industrialisation had become a world-wide phenomenon.

In Britain it has also been suggested that hard work was seen as a positive virtue by many nonconformist denominations, such as the

Quakers. The theory goes that this represented the first flowering of the Protestant work ethic, whatever that might mean.[1] I have to admit that coming from a once-Quaker family myself, I instinctively sympathised with that view, until I looked around at my living and dead relatives who include, at best, a thin scattering of entrepreneurs, bankers and business people, but also ex-hippies, a parson or two, a prison governor, social workers, teachers, a midden of farmers and even a former editor of the *Daily Telegraph*. Today we're a large and diverse family, that includes Anglicans, nonconformists, Roman Catholics and atheists, but somehow I can't see us inspiring revolutions. So I was pleased to discover that recent excavations at Coalbrookdale, of all places, have shown that some of the very earliest steel-making forges in the world were actually built and operated by practising Roman Catholics.

So far in this book I have tried to steer clear of iconic sites, but not to mention Coalbrookdale, near Telford, in Shropshire would be like omitting Stonehenge from an account of British prehistory. So the latest work is most welcome and gives me a good excuse to discuss this extraordinary place. Today this small and attractive town on a gorge in the Severn Valley has become a symbol of the industrial era. The Coalbrookdale coalfield in Shropshire extends some eight miles north and two miles south of the Severn Gorge.[2] Coal mines in the area became prosperous in Tudor times and by the mid-seventeenth century were some of the most technologically advanced in Europe. Other industries, such as potteries (Coalport china), tar distilleries, lead smelters, saltworks, ironworks and brickworks were attracted to the area by the cheap and plentiful supplies of fuel. So it was a diverse industrial landscape; but here I want to concentrate on the early development of iron and steel production.

When we come to look closely at a regional industry, known to have had ancient roots, the era of rapid expansion often appears to happen in the later seventeenth or eighteenth centuries; but as if to prove the very concept of a rapid Industrial Revolution wrong, the expansion phase of the iron industry around Coalbrookdale can be shown to have been well under way in Tudor times. This has been conclusively demonstrated by excavations at two quite separate sites.[3]

The first location is at Wednesbury, just over eighteen miles (thirty kilometres) south-east of Coalbrookdale, but in the same geological

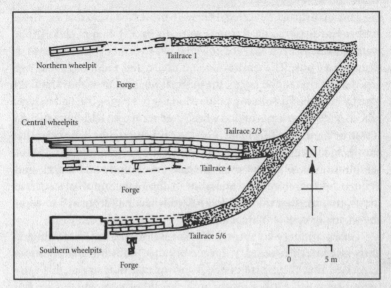

FIG 17 *Excavations at Wednesbury Forge, West Midlands, in 2006–7 revealed three tail races (two paired and one single) that powered five water wheels, whose deep pits survived, either complete or in part. Between the tail races were the buildings of iron forges whose hammers and furnace bellows were powered by the wheels. The forge was first built after the Dissolution of the Monasteries, in the second half of the sixteenth century, but was extensively reconstructed in the early seventeenth.*

landscape of coal, fireclay and ironstone – all essential ingredients for the operation of iron-working furnaces. We know from historical records that in 1585 William Comberford leased his forge to one William Whorwood, who proved an unsatisfactory tenant, so in 1606 he re-leased it to Walter Coleman of nearby Cannock Chase, but in a 'much decayed' state. Coleman was contracted to make the forge good and his structures survived below ground level, thanks to the rebuilding of the forge, in brick, in the later seventeenth century. The excavations carried out in 2006–7 showed the early seventeenth-century restoration essentially amounted to reconstruction, but in wood. The work was of a very high quality indeed and, thanks to the successful tree-ring dating of the oak wood, which probably came from the forest at Cannock Chase, can be firmly attributed to Coleman.

The excavators revealed the well-preserved remains of three timber-lined tail races fed from two pools by a system of sluices. The water carried in each tail race powered five overshot wheels housed in deep wheel pits. The central and southern tail races each had two wheels, but that to the north, the original one and probably first built shortly after the Dissolution of the Monasteries (1538–40), had a single wheel. A few fragments of one wheel were recovered and these suggest it was well and carefully made. During excavation it became clear that the wheel pits and tail races had all been stoutly engineered to resist the vibrations of a forge that used three or four powered hammers, plus bellows for the furnaces. The layout of the water supply system had been carefully planned, with the paired wheel pits staggered to allow the wheels to operate independently.

The excavators were surprised by the scale of the late sixteenth- and early seventeenth-century forge, because conventional wisdom suggested that the centre of the iron-working industry at this early period lay much further south, in the Weald of Kent and Sussex. But here were the remains of one of the largest ironworks in the country, whose origins almost certainly lay in the release of monastic capital, exploited by a new generation of independent entrepreneurs. A very similar situation can be documented, rather better in fact, at Coalbrookdale, where in the Middle Ages the Manor of Madeley belonged to the Cluniac monks of Much Wenlock Priory.

We know that a coal-mining licence was granted in the area as early as 1332 and that ironstone was mined here in the fifteenth century. Following the dissolution of Much Wenlock Priory in 1540, the lands and Manor of Madeley were bought from the Crown in 1544, by Sir Robert Brooke. Sir Robert was a remarkable man who rose from a yeoman background to become Speaker of the House of Commons. But he never lived in Madeley, whose industrial development was the responsibility of his son, John, and grandson, Basil, who proved to be an extraordinarily dynamic industrialist. Unlike the Darbys, who followed over a century later, these early ironmasters and their families were all devout Catholics.

When Sir John acquired the estate, with its two existing iron forges, he erected another, further upstream, later to be known as the Upper Forge. This was built at about the same time as William Comberford

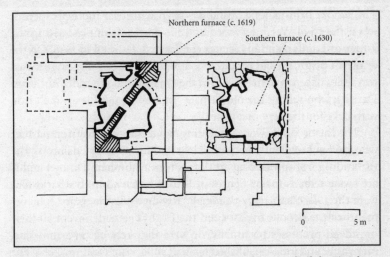

FIG 18 *The Upper Forge at Coalbrookdale, Shropshire, was built by Sir John Brooke who inherited the Madeley estate from his father in the 1550s. Sir John's son, Sir Basil, was a dynamic entrepreneur who in 1619 improved the Upper Forge by building the first English furnace to make steel from wrought-iron bars. This plan of recent excavations by the Ironbridge Gorge Museum shows the solid bases of the two round steel furnaces of 1619 and c. 1630.*

was constructing his forge at Wednesbury and it became the centre of the Brooke iron-making business. Sir Basil inherited Sir John's three forges in the 1590s and further enhanced what was now a substantial industrial empire that included coal-mining interests in Shropshire and further afield, in the Forest of Dean. He enlarged and embellished the manor at Madeley (his work still survives), but he is chiefly known for building the first cementation steel furnace at Upper Forge, in 1619. Cementation, incidentally, is the earliest process for bulk steel production and involves the heating of batches of wrought-iron bars. This was such a commercial success that a second furnace was constructed alongside the original, around 1630. Excavation undertaken by the Ironbridge Gorge Museum since 2001 has fully revealed the remains of Sir Basil's two original cementation furnaces.

Most of Sir Basil's iron and steel was used by the growing number of armament factories around Birmingham and the Black Country, but quantities were also exported abroad out of Bristol, via the Severn.

The Brooke iron-making business was growing ever more prosperous when the Civil War intervened and Sir Basil was imprisoned in the Tower of London and his estates confiscated. He died in 1646. On the return of peace, the old Brookes' Coalbrookdale ironworks were leased to a series of tenants that included the Quaker brass founder Abraham Darby I, who rebuilt the old furnace. In 1709 he used it to smelt iron with coke for the very first time.

The Darby family were pioneering eighteenth-century ironmasters, who have subsequently become celebrated for making Coalbrookdale the leading iron-producing area of its time.[4] Abraham Darby I and II are today seen as major figures in British history, but to what extent were their successes truly personal?[5] Laying aside the major achievements of the Brooke dynasty, did the Darbys actually invent all their improved processes personally, or were they relying on a first-rate, innovative and long-established team of supervisors and workers? The answer, of course, is the latter.[6] Abraham Darby I relied greatly on men like his apprentice John Thomas, from Wales, who was the first man to successfully sand-cast an iron pot. Abraham Darby III, who built the great iron bridge, learned his many skills while he was apprenticed to Richard Reynolds, who managed the Coalbrookdale ironworks between 1763 and 1768. Great ironmasters like the Darbys ought to be seen for what they were – captains of industry – and just like their modern equivalents their team, or teams, should also be given due credit.

One important aspect of the expansion of industry in the eighteenth century has been the way in which developments in one field gave rise to changes in another. We tend to think that in the eighteenth century the difficulties of travel meant that people and communities in places remote from London led rather insular lives. In fact, this was far from the case. Industrialists small and large kept in touch with each other and there was a great deal of cross-fertilisation between different industries. We must not forget that industrial expansion was as much about management and the organisation of the workforce as it was about technological improvement.

Abraham Darby I (1677–1717) was the first of the famous family of Coalbrookdale ironmasters to use coke in the process in which iron was smelted from iron ore. There were only four blast furnaces in the area when his son, Abraham Darby II (1711–63), blew his first one at Horsehay, just north of Coalbrookdale, in 1755. Under the supervision of Abraham Darby II, the team at Coalbrookdale refined and developed the techniques of using coke in a blast furnace. Initially water power was used but in 1743 steam was introduced. The earliest, Newcomen, steam engines were based on the atmospheric principle in which the weight of the atmosphere filled the vacuum left in the piston after a stroke, thereby returning it. But inevitably this was a slow process and these engines lacked the horsepower to drive heavy machines. So they tended to be used instead to pump and circulate water to drive water wheels. Iron cylinders for the first Newcomen engines were being cast at Coalbrookdale by the 1720s and by the 1730s iron wheels for the local wooden railways were being cast there; in the 1760s iron rails had been introduced.

Even by the later eighteenth century there had already been a long tradition of using iron in the area. Some local gravestones are made of iron, for example, as are mileposts along roads and lanes. Many eighteenth-century houses in the region have iron lintels, door and window frames. This is probably why so many important new applications of iron technology were made in Shropshire in the latter part of the century. Apart from bridges, these included iron-based boats, rails and the framework for multi-storey buildings, such as the mills of the growing textile industry.

Coalbrookdale foundries also produced the iron for Abraham Darby I's great iron bridge, which now gives its name to Ironbridge Gorge. For me this bridge is the most extraordinary and moving of all Britain's ancient monuments. I'd take it over Stonehenge any day. It's not just that it really was a very big 'first' – the first modern, large iron bridge in the world – but that it was also a major engineering feat in its own right. It's not generally known, for example, that preparation of its foundations took two years prior to its construction in 1779. It's certainly far better displayed than Stonehenge and one can walk across and beneath it unfettered by officialdom. One can also enjoy a meal or a drink in a pub overlooking it. Put another way, unlike Stonehenge, or indeed most churches and cathedrals, the iron bridge has not been removed from daily life. It's far from remote. It's still there in the heart of the community and doing what its builders wanted it to do, while looking stunningly beautiful even on those misty, rainy days that are such a feature of this part of Britain.

I suppose the most overquoted phrase associated with the idea of the Industrial Revolution has to be William Blake's 'dark Satanic mills'. Laying aside blight to the life of countless sallow-complexioned schoolboys named Mills, it successfully conjures up an image of Hellfire on earth. Certainly many mills (we would more simply refer to them as factories today) were indeed ghastly places in which to spend an entire lifetime, but as most of the early examples also depended on water to run them, their settings could sometimes be spectacular in the extreme.

I have always been a practical, hands-on archaeologist but I have to admit that although I have had an interest in industrial archaeology since my student days back in the 1960s, I nonetheless spent most of my professional life surveying and excavating various prehistoric sites. It wasn't until I became involved with Channel 4's *Time Team* that I was given the opportunity to direct a post-medieval dig. On *Time Team* one is surrounded by experts who gently dissuade one from making too many obvious mistakes, but I found that reassuring rather than a constraint. Certainly I have enjoyed the process and in a strange way I think my knowledge and experience of earlier archaeology has actually been beneficial. My first industrial site (in 2005) was a textile mill in what is now the heart of modern Manchester. The researchers at *Time Team* could not have chosen a better site. Shude Mill had originally been built by the great early industrialist Richard Arkwright (1732–92) and had subsequently been burnt down and then bombed during the Second World War. When we started our dig the site had been completely flattened and until our arrival had been used as a car park. Mercifully, it hadn't been covered in tarmac and just by walking across the compressed rubble one could clearly spot the cobbles and kerbstones of streets. In effect, we had been given a blank canvas with a few intriguing hints of what might lie beneath.

Whenever I take on a prehistoric site I always try to answer one central question: where did the people live? At the Shude Mill site the street (Angel Street) was still there, in use around the edge of the car park, and the demolished houses along it were on the land available to us. I won't discuss in any detail what we found at the mill site itself as there's a danger of getting bogged down in the intricacies of beam engine pits and water supplies. But the important point to note is that this mill was built by Arkwright at the very beginning of steam power, when people still didn't really understand it. I can remember that when the first microcomputers became available some time in the late 1970s we all imagined we would be able to catalogue every object we found, together with their contextual details, and, of course, all the information about layers, levels and so forth. But that proved impossible. The best we could manage was a few rather bare lists which we could then sort in a rather rudimentary fashion.

Something similar seems to have happened to poor Arkwright. As ever ahead of his time, he originally intended to run Shude Mill entirely by steam, but when it actually opened in 1781 the engines lacked the power to drive all the machinery; so he had them adapted to lift water from a nearby stream into a reservoir, where it was used to drive a conventional water wheel – which was able to cope. Arkwright had a reputation for providing his mill workers with good accommodation and when I turned the team's attention to the remains of the terrace houses that fronted Angel Street we discovered that he had provided each of the families that worked for him with three-storey houses.

The lowest floor was actually three-quarters underground. This cellar room was where the family ate, prepared food and washed. Above it were single ground- and first-floor rooms for sleeping. The cellar living room might sound bleak, and it certainly was when we excavated it in the rain, but with a fire in the grate, plaster on the walls and a meal on the table, I doubt if it would have seemed that bad to its occupants. Most importantly, with two other rooms upstairs, Arkwright's builders had given his workforce the space they needed. As I mentioned in the previous chapter, we must not be tempted into myth-making; much housing of the earlier industrial era was, by the standards of the day (and we must use no others), perfectly adequate. The problems, when they did occur, happened later. By the earlier part of the nineteenth century, when the mill had passed into different hands, each one of Arkwright's original single houses was being used to accommodate three families – one to a room. And by this time there could be no doubt: conditions must have been unspeakably squalid.

FIG 19 *Exterior view of a Manchester cellar house in Victorian times. Access to the cellar room at basement level was below the steps leading to the ground-floor room, from which internal stairs would lead to the first-floor room. This view is taken from* The Builder, *1862.*

This overcrowding simply reflected the downside of industrial success, followed by increasing competition which we can see in the population figures for Manchester which increased from 90,000 in 1801 to 400,000 just sixty years later.

With the possible exception of the great railway termini, the textile mills are the largest and most spectacular buildings of the industrial age. In part this reflects the sheer volume of the material that was

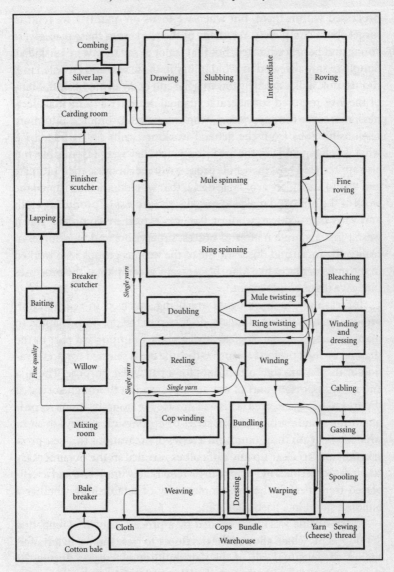

FIG 20 *A flow diagram illustrating the production of cotton textiles. The raw bales are delivered to the mill (lower left) and then pass through a number of different processes before they emerge as cotton cloth, yarn and sewing thread (lower right).*

processed within them, but when we focus on quantity we tend to forget about complexity. Yes, many of the workers in these places were young and poorly educated, but that is not to say they were unskilled. Simply to stay alive and to avoid injury in those vast and crowded mill rooms took skill, especially towards the end of an all-night shift. Many of the jobs required considerable manual dexterity and mental alertness; moreover the supervisors, who were often promoted into more responsible jobs from the general workforce, not only understood what was happening in the areas for which they were responsible, but also appreciated how the whole process worked, because their ultimate aim was to anticipate avoidable delays that would have interrupted the work of the mill. And make no mistake, the process of producing cloth and yarn from cotton, wool or flax was extremely complex.[7] But it wasn't just a simple matter of bosses, supervisors and workforce. In reality, the social and domestic life of the various groups who worked in the mills in places like Manchester were as complex as the processes that gave them employment.[8]

Increasingly, archaeologists are being involved in regeneration projects such as that at Hungate, discussed in the previous chapter. In many instances archaeological advice plays an important part in the shaping of such projects to ensure that the areas selected for preservation or display are the correct ones for a particular purpose. The first and most important part of any such project is a thorough survey of the area to be regenerated. This will involve the stone-by-stone recording of the standing buildings, a series of geophysical surveys to show what lies beneath the ground and a series of excavations to assess preservation and to clear up any difficulties revealed in the documentary research. Sometimes old maps can be remarkably imprecise and a well-placed trench might be the simplest way of establishing whether a building stood in a particular spot.

Much of this work was funded by a process known as 'enabling development', which allowed the developer to raise money in advance, against the eventual sale of the flats and houses created during the regeneration process.[9] Among other things this money would pay for any archaeological work, such as excavation or survey. It's an approach that makes plenty of sense, provided, of course, that the buildings in question are attractive to potential buyers and that the buyers themselves can get the necessary mortgages. Sadly, experience has shown that 'enabling development' could sometimes be more about development than enabling. And now, following the financial downturn, such projects are very much harder to find.

One of the most successful enabling developments, which involved the conversions of old textile mill buildings to accommodation, has recently taken place at an extraordinarily beautiful spot on the River Tay, about six miles north of Perth. Two of the Stanley Mills were converted to accommodation by the Prince of Wales's Phoenix Regeneration Trust and Historic Scotland and the money raised has gone into the restoration of the earliest mill, the provision of new displays and the conservation of surviving historic features, such as water-wheel pits and mill machinery. I found the displays imaginative and they successfully manage to convey an impression of the complexity of the various processes involved. The mills are best seen from the shores of the Tay immediately downstream, but I strongly advise against trying to walk out into the river on slippery rocks to get a good photograph. I got one, but nearly at the cost of my expensive camera and a good soaking.

The Stanley Mills had been positioned with considerable cunning by the then landowner Lord Nairne on the south, downstream, side of the Tay at a point where it passed through a long U-bend. Realising that there was a twenty-one-foot (seven-metre) fall on either side of the bend, in 1729 Nairne had a tunnel dug across the neck of the bend to take very fast-flowing water to a tail race, or lade, that ran his corn mills. More than half a century later, in 1785, the Duke of Atholl, plus a small group of developers that included the local MP George Dempster, approached Richard Arkwright to build and manage a new textile mill using the lade established in 1729. The mill in question was the Bell Mill, which was built between 1786 and 1787 and opened for business immediately. At least one other tunnel was dug to increase the flow of water to the new mill and the supply was so abundant that, unlike others which were converted to steam, those at Stanley continued to be powered by water, although in the late nineteenth century water wheels were replaced by more efficient turbines. However, despite the two natural advantages of a good water supply and a superb mill designer, the mills at Stanley never really thrived.

And this brings me back to one of the more abiding myths about the Industrial Revolution, which is traditionally seen as a time when innovation was followed by exploitation, further development and more progress – in a relentless process of industrial expansion. In reality the growth of British industry was a tale of fits and starts – of some successes but many failures, of which Stanley, I'm afraid, is one example. But it did get off to a good, confident beginning; next, in the 1790s, the Bell Mill was enhanced by an even larger mill, the East Mill. But other forces were also at work. The onset of the Napoleonic Wars in 1793 led to a recession in the textile trade and then, to make matters worse, the East Mill burnt down in 1799. As a consequence the whole enterprise went bust, and poor George Dempster MP lost the then equivalent of almost half a million pounds. Another attempt to run the mills at a profit was made in 1801, again with a good professional mill manager at its heart, but in 1813 this also failed.

Ten years later Stanley reopened and a new mill, the Mid Mill, was added and the burnt East Mill was replaced. Then, in 1848, fortune smiled with the arrival of the railway in the village of Stanley. This meant that raw cotton and finished goods could be sent to and from Glasgow in a few hours. The mills then stayed in business right through to the 1920s when they began a long period of decline, eventually closing for good in 1989.

As we have seen, some pioneering mill owners, such as Richard Arkwright, provided their workforce with good housing, although often it was allowed to degenerate into squalor in the nineteenth century. One of the most enlightened of the early industrialists was Robert Owen (1771–1858) who married the boss's daughter and in 1800 became a part-owner and manager of the New Lanark cotton mills in Lanarkshire.[10] The mill had been established in 1785 by a partnership between Richard Arkwright and David Dale and made use of the water power provided by the Falls of Clyde. Dale built three large mills, requiring about 1,500 workers, whom he then housed in long rows of handsome tenements.

Owen is widely regarded as the father of British socialism and had strong views on the importance of education and the influence of the environment in the creation of an individual's character. He put his beliefs into action when creating the new model community of New

Lanark, which featured a huge school and the wonderfully named Institute for the Formation of Character. Owen has undoubtedly been more politically and theoretically influential than David Dale, but we would be unwise to ignore the contribution made by his father-in-law. For example, three-quarters of the mills and most of the housing at New Lanark was built by Dale; he also established a school there, which in 1796 employed sixteen teachers for 507 pupils. The school was necessary for the simple reason that children also worked in the mills. Dale's housing was well laid out, spacious, and most of it survives to this day in the World Heritage Site.

Some accounts describe New Lanark in glowing, Utopian terms, but if there was such a thing I'm not convinced I would be happy even in this particular Paradise. Work in the mills, for example, was highly controlled and production revolved around Owen's own invention, his 'silent monitor', or 'telegraph', which was a colour-coded device controlled by supervisors which openly indicated to everyone the performance of individual workers ranging from black (bad) to indifferent (blue) to good (yellow) and excellent (white). The daily performance record was then taken from the 'telegraph' and entered into a register of individual performance.[11]

The system was not original and others, including enlightened educationalists, employed similar devices, but what made Owen's unique was the right he gave his workers to appeal directly to him if they considered their supervisor's assessment unfair. Owen's style of management was to be team leader, even if by our standards a paternalistic one, at a time when many industrialists were becoming increasingly autocratic. This style is reflected by the positioning of his own house in New Lanark, which is sited at the centre of the community, and, although detached, is by no means unusually large or extravagant. It embarrasses me to confess that when I first visited New Lanark I walked past it several times, before I read of its significance in the guidebook.[12] For what it is worth, his father-in-law's house next door is equally restrained and unpretentious.

Owen's great social experiment at New Lanark was a success and it provided an example to reforming politicians, industrialists and Utopian dreamers. Many of them, however, failed to appreciate that the New Lanark experiment only succeeded because the enterprise behind it was both efficiently run and financially viable. In the 1820s and 1830s other groups of people got together to form Owenite projects. Often these were less astutely organised, without a viable business at the centre. Doubtless there were many such projects that never got off the ground at all, but one did, and in the most unlikely of places – deep in peat Fens, near the village of Welney, on the borders of Cambridgeshire and Norfolk. If one walks across the site today it is still possible in a few places to discern the foundation of houses and streets and I have to admit I would dearly love to place a few well-chosen trenches in this remote corner of north Cambridgeshire.

The venture, which was set up in 1838, was known as the Mepal Colony and was backed by a local banker, one of whose daughters, Octavia Hill, was a socialist and co-founder of the National Trust. It was a noble experiment, based around the idea of self-sufficiency, with its own school buildings, windmill, central pavilion for meetings and a uniform; there were tokens for money and a motto, 'Each for All'. The colonists also produced their own newsletter, *The Working Bee*, which for a short time was read quite widely. The colony had the reputation for being the most radical of the Owenite communities but it was largely composed of people from towns who lacked rural experience. The land on which the colony sat was also prone to flooding so when Hill's bank withdrew its funds in 1841, to nobody's surprise the whole enterprise soon folded.[13]

The years of massive industrial expansion would have been impossible without a reliable supply of fuel and raw materials and, just as the industries in question started to expand from small beginnings, so the supplies they depended on had to keep pace, and change, when required to do so. Take fuel, for example: it is generally held that by the late sixteenth and early seventeenth centuries sources of timber had begun to run out and coal was adopted because it was a seemingly unlimited new source of energy. Recent research has, however, suggested that practices such as long-term coppicing, in which trees like ash and hornbeam were felled and their shoots left for a decade or more to provide long, straight logs for fuel, were well established at this time and could actually have provided much of the timber required by industry. So it now seems probable that coke was used for altogether different reasons that included, 'the inherent attractions of innovative coal-using processes'.[14]

Another major consumer of wood was the iron industry which used large quantities of charcoal to smelt iron ore. Whether or not timber supplies were actually becoming scarce, in 1715 the first Abraham Darby constructed his second blast furnace at Coalbrookdale. In this he was able to perfect a commercially reliable method whereby coke (in effect roasted coal) could be substituted in the process. Coke, incidentally, had first been made, not in Britain, but in China, probably in the thirteenth century.[15]

Mines and miners have always been an essential component of Britain's industrial past and they have always held a fascination for me, perhaps because, like many people who like the open air, I am also a little claustrophobic. So I find that going deep underground can be an unsettling, yet strangely exciting experience and I imagine that in the past many young miners felt much the same when they, too, ventured into a pit for their first time. For these and other reasons we tend to concentrate on the shafts and galleries of mines and pay less attention to what was happening on the surface around them. But in many cases this was where the raw products of the mines were converted into something suitable for transport. Coal is one of the few mined products that does not have to be sorted through on the surface, as the Duke of Bridgewater realised in the 1760s when he took his canal right up to the coalface of his Worsley mines. Most other materials need to be prepared if subsequent transport costs are to be kept to a minimum. This was particularly true in the years prior to the canals and railways; iron ore, for example, was usually calcined or burnt at the mine to remove impurities before it was crushed and taken away to be smelted.[16] But it was at lead mines where surface processing was so important and where the archaeological evidence, some of it now very fragile, still survives.

My introduction to the joys and miseries of the lead-mining life came in 1989 when I presented a children's television series for BBC1. Our twenty-five-minute programmes went out on those evenings when *Blue Peter* was not on air and for at least a couple of years afterwards I would find my hand being gripped in supermarket checkout queues by very small fingers accompanied by hugely smiling young faces. Ten years later I was in another supermarket when a very attractive young woman of about eighteen came up and greeted me like a long-lost friend. I have to admit that my composure slipped as she gave me a completely unexpected but wonderfully warm hug. Then we discovered that she only 'knew' me from that series, *Now Then*, all those years ago – and her confusion was immense, poor girl. From an entirely selfish point of view, I rather wish that sort of thing had happened more than just once.

In the late 1980s television digital graphics were just starting and many producers were keen to get their hands on the then state-of-the-art Paintbox software which *Now Then* used to conjure up long-dead children from history: a fixed camera, or locked-off shot of, say, a lake shimmered while a boy and girl wearing appropriate clothing of the time slowly mixed into vision. Today it sounds corny, but then, believe me, it was cutting-edge stuff. We filmed episodes at places as diverse as my own Bronze Age site at Flag Fen and a lead mine high in the Pennines at Killhope, Co. Durham.[17] The episode at Killhope was entitled 'Fourpence a Day', the rate of pay for children some 140 years ago.[18] And, despite being a children's programme, it made the serious point that youngsters were indeed exploited in Victorian Britain, and not just as chimney sweeps, but as an essential part of the ordinary workforce in mills and mines.

I hugely enjoy doing television and radio, but in common with most crew and production staff I don't like having to move on at the end. Normally, making a television programme can be quite a demanding process and one comes to rely very heavily on the creativity and patience of the people one is working with. Indeed, they can make or break a film. So it can be difficult to walk off the site with a cheery wave and cries of 'See you again', which one knows in one's heart aren't true. But, happily, there are exceptions, and as my experience at Killhope was to show, there are also surprises.

Maisie and I had been on one of our trips to northern England, which friends in those upland landscapes believe we take to prepare ourselves for what they imagine will be the flat greyness of a Fenland winter. In fact, we were simply on a short holiday after a hectic summer. We were driving through the Pennines, heading somewhere pleasant for lunch, when I spotted a sign for the Killhope Lead Mining Centre.

It had been raining all that day and showed no signs of clearing up. Neither of us fancied trudging around the Neolithic stone circle we had scheduled for the afternoon, so I pulled over, turned round and headed for Killhope, with Maisie looking at me rather strangely, as I hadn't bothered to consult her about the change of plan. Eventually, growing resentment from my travelling companion found its way past my memories of those happy days in 1989. An explanation was required so I explained why we had diverted. Maisie's immediate response was, as ever, practical: 'But do they do lunch?' 'Of course they do,' I replied breezily. In actual fact I had no idea, but prayed fervently that they did.

I needn't have worried, and after an excellent light lunch we were joined by the manager, Ian Forbes, who hadn't changed a bit in the intervening two decades. He said the same about me, which I knew wasn't true: he possessed the honeyed tongue of the North Pennines. We discussed old times and what had happened subsequently. It was apparent just by looking around that Ian had managed to build the enterprise into a substantial operation. But it wasn't overblown, nor was there so much as a hint of Disney. He ran the place for the County Council with a small and very friendly staff, but was still able to stay actively involved with industrial archaeology. As a result, Killhope has retained its authenticity.

We chatted over our coffee and Ian told us about various improvements to the place, and then quite suddenly he stopped. 'Do you know about our spar boxes?' he asked. Of course I didn't; in fact, I'd never heard of them. 'You're in for a surprise then', he said rather enigmatically and pointed out through the door to the mine shop where I could remember filming a scene in which I had to play a little jig on my 1870s concertina. Ian broke my reverie abruptly: 'We've converted the first floor. The stairs are at the back.' And with that he departed.

It was still raining, but Ian had just thrust a book into my hands and a glance at its cover more than whetted my appetite.[19] Rain or shine, I was going to see those spar boxes. And it was well worth the effort: the show was spectacular in the extreme. I simply had no idea that these things existed, but before I describe them I ought to say a word of justification for including them at all, because many people, I am sure, will not see them as belonging in the realms of archaeology, because they are neither broken nor bashed and never served a functional or utilitarian purpose. They are also very recent – most of them being made at the end of the nineteenth century – but by this point I do hope that particular argument can be seen as irrelevant. I regard spar boxes, which most would see as folk art, as an important part of the archaeology of the later industrial era because they are an expression of people's finer or even spiritual feelings. They demonstrate the need of ordinary working men to transcend the everyday world of toil down the mine; moreover, through the organisation of exhibitions and displays they also served an important social purpose. I cannot see why they should be considered less 'archaeological' than any other non-utilitarian aspect of the past, from Victorian clay tobacco pipes to Bronze Age goldwork.

Back in 1989 I spent the best part of a day filming underground in the Park Level Mine which provided most of the ore processed on the surface at Killhope. In those days the mine had not been made visitor-friendly, as it is today, and there was no lighting of any sort. I don't think I have ever experienced such utter, inky darkness before or since. You could almost feel it on the surface of your skin. We had powerful battery lights with us, but only used them sparingly, as their power soon gave out and they would shortly be required for filming anyway. As we walked along the tunnels we relied on the torches in our helmets and the expertise of the experienced Killhope guide. In the past all the miners had were candles which they would place in ledges close by their work. Today there are tens of thousands of little soot smudges left by those candles. Each smudge represented an event in somebody's working day – something I found then, and still find today, extraordinarily evocative.

Some of the scenes we filmed took longer than others and I remember the crew and the producer, David Collison, really struggling to get the lighting right for a particular shot. It didn't involve me and I found myself taking a short stroll back along the tunnel with a box containing the prop candles they eventually wanted to use in the film. Feeling bored, I lit one. And when I turned off the lamp in my helmet I immediately became aware of what seemed another dimension. The flickering flame revealed a hundred smaller flames reflected in the mineral crystals protruding from the tunnel roof and walls, which seemed to twinkle and shine with a light of their own. These crystals, mostly of the minerals fluorspar (hence spar) and barytes, occurred in many of the Weardale lead mines and they could not have been missed by the miners, some of whom would remove large or coloured ones and take them home, where a collection would slowly accumulate. Most people, myself included, are affected to a greater or lesser extent by the collection 'bug', and soon spar collectors formed groups where crystals were bought or exchanged. A next natural step was to make portable display cases in which the collections could be shown to advantage to other collectors. These boxes looked very good in their own right and soon took pride of place in the seldom entered front rooms of many miners' houses.

It wasn't long before these portable displays became objects in themselves and the crystals were an integral part that could not be removed. They were carefully lit using complex arrangements of mirrors. Many crystals were arranged to look like Aladdin's Caves; others formed large, sparkling pyramids; still others were built into strange twilight street scenes that somehow combined the menace of Jack the Ripper with showbiz glamour. Ian Forbes points out that the cave scenes follow in the general grotto tradition already established at landscape gardens such as Painshill, in Surrey, whereas the street scenes and house interiors owe more to the then current fashion for penny-in-the-slot peep shows. In common with most folk traditions, people drew on a large number of sources for their inspiration. Many of the later spar boxes were also fine examples of cabinetmaking, either purpose-built or converted from other pieces of furniture, and we also know the names of several spar box creators, among them William Ridley (1826–1910), of Allenheads.

Top-quality spar boxes featured in large public exhibitions in the 1880s and 1890s – the last one being in 1901. The shows were charitable, to raise money for the poor, and many were organised by the Wesleyan Methodists of St John's Chapel, Weardale. The Victorian spar box tradition seems to have fizzled out after that last exhibition of 1901, but, rather like the Settle–Carlisle Railway, it refused to die entirely and today artists from the area and further afield are creating traditional-looking spar boxes from minerals, but also more unusual creations using glass and other more contemporary materials. Much of the credit for the revival of interest in spar boxes must go to Ian Forbes and his upstairs museum at Killhope which has played a major part in preserving an important tradition. It's a good example of the way archaeology can rekindle local traditions and make them relevant to an increasingly homogeneous world.

I have already confessed that I will head rapidly in the opposite direction when I'm visiting a National Trust property and spot somebody dressed in antique costume, but I am not against re-creating structures from the past. We have seen that such re-creation has been outstandingly successful at the new Globe Theatre, and there are other fine examples, as we also saw earlier, like the more speculative gardens at Kenilworth Castle and the less adventurous restorations at Hampton Court and Kirby Hall.

Moving away from pleasure and leisure to the world of work, one of the best attempts at complete restoration is undoubtedly the North of England Lead Mining Museum at Killhope. What I like about this place is its absolute archaeological authenticity, being based on existing, surviving structures, combined with excavation carried out by leading industrial archaeologists such as David Cranstone.[20] It could be argued, of course, that reconstruction, if it has to involve excavation, is also destruction.

Strictly speaking that is certainly true, but I personally think it over-purist, if not over the top. If the reconstruction is sensitively done, I would maintain that its benefits, through education and information, far outweigh any harm done by limited excavation. Much more to the point, when they see sensitive re-creations a better informed public will come to care more about ancient sites and buildings and will then support their preservation, when and if they come under threat. That, surely, is the broader picture that the over-cautious 'purists' fail to see.

The extent of the surface workings at a lead mine has to be seen to be appreciated.[21] At Killhope the ore (galena, known in Weardale as 'bouse') was towed out of the Park Level Mine in single tubs by ponies. Immediately outside the mine was the washing rake where the bouse was tipped down into the Bousesteads and thence to the washing floor where various techniques were used to wash the galena-rich ore from the waste, which was then towed away to the dead heaps. Lead ore, like gold, is heavy and the washing process is similar to gold-panning, but on a vastly larger scale. The finest grains of galena were separated in

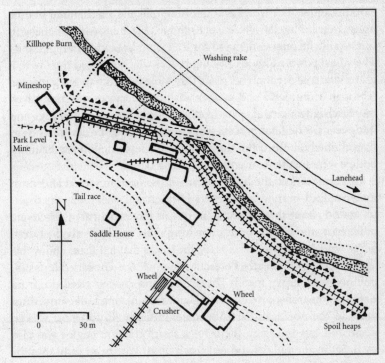

FIG 21 *A plan showing the organisation of the industrial landscape around the entrance to the Park Level Lead Mine at Killhope, Co. Durham.*

this way using mechanised paddles mounted in 'buddles'; from the mid-nineteenth century buddles were improved by the introduction of the Brunton buddle, which operated using a broad belt wound around two rollers. Most of this equipment was driven and operated by young boys (aged around ten and eleven) who worked the washing floors and wheeled heavy loaded barrows of rock and ore often in appalling wet and cold conditions (Killhope is 1,500 feet, or 460 metres, above sea level). From the washing floors the by now more refined, but still far from clean, ore was towed to the water-powered crushing mill.

The wheel for the Killhope mill was one of the few to have survived into modern times and although large, with a diameter of 10.26 metres (33 feet 8 inches), it was by no means the largest (the one at Nenthead nearby was 18 metres, or 60 feet). Today it has been restored to full working order. The wheel and crushing mill and mechanised buddle house were built relatively late in Killhope's life, in 1876–8, to cope with the steadily increasing demand for lead from later Victorian industry. The wheel powered huge crushing rollers which reduced the ore to a gravel-like consistency. This made it suitable for mechanised screening (through 'trommels') and further washing, processes which involved more rich language and terms like, 'jigs', 'jigger houses', 'middlings' and 'bingsteads'. The final process was known as 'dollying', in which very fine-grained ore from the slimes that were separated in the Brunton buddle were further concentrated using a 'dasher'.

Killhope sits in the heart of one of the best preserved and most intensive lead-mining landscapes in Britain and even today the country round about shows clear signs of this industrial past.[22] There are numerous worked-out mines, smelting mills and huge areas of dead heaps with distinctive flat tops for the tracks that fed them and where tip lines can still clearly be seen. Much of the countryside is still polluted with heavy metal. The dressed and concentrated ore from Killhope was transported to the Allenheads smelting mills some three miles to the north, in East Allendale. Initially, all transport was by horse and cart but from the 1870s a steam traction engine was also used. Sadly, the railway did not reach up to Wearhead until 1895, by which time lead-mining in the area had largely ceased.

One interesting link to the earliest days of the industrial era was the existence of a secondary economy in the area around Killhope. Many of the miners were also pastoral farmers who operated, with their families, smallholdings of sheep, pigs and the ponies used in the mines. These miner-farmers formed groups or partnerships to work the mines and prior to the 1680s it was traditional for certain families to remain loyal to the same partnership from one generation to another. In the Census of 1871 the population of upper Weardale was more than one thousand and about 85 per cent of the men and boys worked in the mines. When the mines closed, many families emigrated to America or Australia, or moved a shorter distance to the Durham coalfields. Today the population is around one hundred.

Inevitably the successful preservation and restoration of a mine like Killhope will have the effect of fossilising the perceptions of visitors, many of whom will leave with the impression that lead-mining in

Weardale was always like that. It doesn't matter that exhibits in displays stress change: the solid appearance of the machines, structures and buildings outside in the real Durham landscape convey a message of static permanence. This misapprehension is further reinforced by the prevalence of the Industrial Revolution concept, which suggests, by its very name, that there was just one episode of rapid change, culminating in places like Killhope. The reality is vastly more complex than that.

A recent study of lead-mining in Weardale has suggested that, far from a single phase of revolutionary change, there were no fewer than five in post-medieval times. The industry, however, is known to have roots in the Middle Ages, so the first recognisable phase of industrial-scale organisation was actually the second. This phase began at the close of the Middle Ages, in about 1566, with the appointment of the first so-called Moormaster of the Weardale mining field.[23] At this time the Bishop of Durham, who owned the land where the mines were sited, realised that the many small collectively operated mines on his estates needed to be controlled and coordinated by the new Moormaster. The Moormaster phase lasted from the 1560s to the 1680s and in theory, at least, the new coordination ought to have been beneficial. But in actual fact the tight system of control it brought to the industry tended to discourage both innovation and technological change. New inventions, for example in pumping and winding (i.e. winching), which had been made on the Continent, were not introduced to Weardale where the small mines struggled on, much as they had in the later Middle Ages.

However, big changes were introduced in 1688 when William Blackett founded the W. B. Lead Company, the company, incidentally, that operated the Park Level Mine at Killhope. William and two succeeding generations of William Blacketts had the vision and entrepreneurial flair to drive through change, which wasn't always in the miners' best personal interests. In effect, they ceased to be members of small collectives and became part of Blackett's Weardale workforce. The Blacketts were able to force the changes through because they had enlisted the financial muscle of outside backers in the then rapidly growing world of banking, stock trading and investment.

From the 1740s the entrepreneurial phase was followed by the industrial phase. By this time the industry in Weardale was sufficiently homogeneous to accept a number of major technological innovations, of which perhaps the most important was the introduction of blasting powder. By the 1750s it was in general use in all the mines. Shortly afterwards, in the 1760s, we see the introduction of wooden-rail horse waggonways. Taken together, these new techniques allowed mines and miners to exploit ever-deeper and richer sources of ore, which then had to be processed on the first purpose-built dressing and washing floors that also appeared at about this time. There were other important innovations, too: the first stone-built central building, or mine shop, was erected in 1766, and the first water wheel, around 1770.

Technology remained the driving force in the next, or mechanisation phase, which began in the 1810s and saw the introduction of more wheels and then of steam engines that drove a variety of washing and dressing machines, eventually culminating in fully mechanised dressing mills, which we saw were built at Killhope in the 1870s. This plant and equipment needed a good supply of water from reservoirs; it also required boiler houses and coal stores; other buildings included smithies, offices, stables, powder houses, workshops and weighbridges. All of these, together with the arrival of the railways in the mid-nineteenth century, had a major effect on the appearance of the North Pennine landscape.

The mechanisation phase went into a period of rapid decline in the later 1870s and 1880s when the introduction of cheaper lead from abroad undercut the British market. To make matters worse, the Ecclesiastical Commissioners, who still owned the land, decided to increase the cost of the mining lease. This caused the W. B. Lead Company to withdraw from mining in Weardale in 1883. They were replaced that year by a new firm, the Weardale Lead Company, which was supported by a number of backers, and the industry again began to prosper. As it prospered new techniques, such as the use of safer compressed-air equipment in the mines, were constantly being introduced. The final destructive phase began in the Great Depression of the 1930s and culminated in the closing of the last North Pennine lead mine in the late 1990s.

Lead-mining was not confined to the northern Pennines. It also occurred in the Yorkshire Dales[24] and one of the best preserved mining complexes is at Magpie Mine, on Sheldon Moor, in the Peak

District of Derbyshire.[25] This group of buildings was in some respects atypical, because many of the Derbyshire lead mines were very small in scale and have left little behind them, other than the ruins of stone 'coes', sheds where the miners kept their clothes and tools, and the openings of the mine shafts themselves, which still pockmark the landscape around Brassington, near Wirksworth.[26] Lead ore has to be broken up and crushed prior to smelting. This can be done using water power, as we saw at Killhope, but in Derbyshire most of the crushing was done in horse-powered mills where a horse walked a circle, pulling a long timber arm which turned the crushing mechanism at the centre.

Traces of the curved walls that enclosed these horse mills can still be seen in the landscape. In the Pennines some nineteenth-century smelting sites, such as that at Nenthead, had long flues which ran up the hillside leading to chimneys at the top. These served to remove the poisonous fumes from the smelting area, but this attempt at good health and safety practice was rather spoiled when children were sent up the flue to remove the metallic lead that had condensed along its walls. Their life expectancy must have been short.

The buildings of the Magpie Mine in Derbyshire belong to a number of different periods which reflect the long working life of the mine itself. The earliest records show that the mine was in operation by 1740, among several others in the area. Flooding was to prove a persistent problem, but this was dealt with by the installation of a Newcomen steam engine in the main shaft in 1824. This improved matters so much that in that year the mine produced 800 tons of lead, a British record that remained intact until 1871. The Magpie Mine closed in 1835 after a series of acrimonious disputes with other mines in the area and was reopened in 1839 by John Taylor, a famous mining engineer from Cornwall. He built a large engine house for a Cornish-style beam engine to pump out the mine. The engine worked successfully until the high price of coal in the 1870s caused it to be shut down. At this point the mine owners reverted to the traditional Derbyshire pattern of sough drainage in which a special deep tunnel, or sough, was dug to drain the water. At Killhope, incidentally, a similar gravity-based drainage system made use of the horizontal pony-sized tunnels that gave access into the mine. As soon as it had been successfully redrained, the Magpie Mine continued in use into the twentieth century. It closed for good in 1954, following the end of the Korean War which triggered the sharp fall in the price of imported lead.

I have tried to select case studies for this book that have left visible traces in the landscape, because, when all is said and done, archaeology is about tangible remains of things that can be measured, analysed or tripped over. So far in this chapter we've had quite a lot about the 'business end' of industry and how the workforce was housed, but not much on the effect of industrialisation on the surrounding landscape; nor, just as importantly, about the lessons this has to teach us about modern Britain. One of the things that has struck me very forcibly about historical archaeology is the way that it is almost self-consciously aware of its implications for the present and, indeed, the future. I find this a refreshing change from the ivory tower and rather arrogant study-it-for-academic-reasons-alone-and-to-hell-with-the-modern-world approach of many prehistorians, Romanists and medievalists.

While I was doing the preliminary research for this book I had to reject a number of possible case studies for various reasons, and, when I first glanced at it, I thought a recent collaborative research project into the impact of coal-mining on a South Yorkshire Coalfield town would probably be one of them.[27] However, I was about to turn elsewhere when my attention was caught by a series of maps that traced the growth of the small town of Wombwell since the late eighteenth century. There was nothing very remarkable about that, except for the fact that a medieval wood nearby had remained largely intact, when one would have expected it to have been obliterated. This intrigued me: why wasn't it destroyed, and what does this tell us about the impact of industrialisation on this small part of Yorkshire?

The town of Wombwell lies in gently undulating country that slopes eastwards onto the flood plain of the rivers Dove and Dearne, both tributaries of the Don. Today Wombwell lies on the fringe of Barnsley and as one drives through it the area seems unremarkable, consisting largely of post-Second World War urban and semi-urban sprawl, but there are areas of open country especially to the north-east, towards the two rivers, and on the higher ground to the west, around Wombwell Wood.

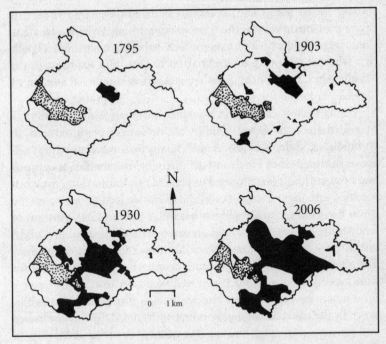

FIG 22   *A map showing the development of urban areas (black) and Wombwell Wood (stippled) in the town of Wombwell, South Yorkshire.*

In the Middle Ages this was an agricultural region, with three large Open Fields close by the then village of Wombwell and important 'ings', or seasonally flooded meadows, to the north-east in the flood plain. Wombwell Wood was one of those productive medieval woods that was never left alone for long. It was a common wood and provided the villagers with coppice products and grazing for livestock in its many clearings. In early post-medieval times things remained much as before, except that the wood was used to provide fuel for the charcoal-smelting iron industry.

By 1620 my old college, Trinity, Cambridge, acquired land in the area. This is interesting in its own right, as Trinity was one of the institutions that benefited greatly from the Dissolution of the Monasteries when its founder, Henry VIII, endowed it handsomely with former monastic land and money which was now free to circulate more widely through the economy. The last century of the Middle Ages and the first of the post-medieval was the time when, through royal involvement, Cambridge rapidly became a major force in both scholarship and politics; whereas following its foundation in 1209, and for most of the Middle Ages, it had been a rather lacklustre, provincial version of Oxford.*

Trinity College carried out a detailed survey of Wombwell in 1757, by which time the Open Fields were no longer being farmed 'in common', i.e. collaboratively. A later survey by the college in 1795 still shows the three Open Fields and the extent of Wombwell Wood, which had been enclosed (i.e. it ceased to be held in common) in 1764 when it passed into the possession of Thomas Turner, lord of the manor. So it was not until the mid-eighteenth century that medieval patterns of land tenure were replaced, after an extended and informal process of enclosure – and even then Trinity continued to receive tithes from Turner. By the end of the eighteenth century the charcoal market for iron-making collapsed and Wombwell Wood became a game reserve for a major new landowner. This assured its protection. Meanwhile, down by the rivers the annual flooding of the meadows was controlled and harnessed through the digging of new channels including, in Tudor times, the straight Bulling Dike, which still carries water to this day. This example shows that even at the close of the eighteenth century in regions that had for a long time been industrial, there were still significant areas of unenclosed fields, pastures and flood-plain meadow – all survivors from the Middle Ages.

The pattern of landownership inherited from earlier times was, to say the least, complex. At the point when the first collieries of the South Yorkshire Coalfield were opened in the mid-nineteenth century (two in 1855, one in 1856), they were served by a network of new railways and the population more than doubled between successive Censuses in 1851 (1,627) and 1861 (3,738).[28] At the same time, farmland shrunk by some 20 per cent. But even though the population of Wombwell had tripled (13,252) by the 1901 Census, and a new colliery had opened (in 1878), the area of farmed land in 1914 remained the same. This was because the increased population had been housed by infilling the many open

---

* King's College was founded by Henry VI in 1441 and Trinity in 1546.

spaces in existing urban areas. This process could not continue and by 1942 farmland had shrunk another 15 per cent, because of extensive house-building to the south-west.

This mini-blizzard of statistics has shown that even in the heart of the South Yorkshire Coalfield the rapid spread of something as 'dirty' (in terms of spoil heaps, dust and pollution) as the coal industry did not obliterate the rural landscape or economy. And we must recall that these were pre-planning days, when development was only constrained by market forces and existing patterns of land tenure. The coal mines had to contend with farming which has remained very important in the area until recently; as a consequence of this, landowners were not about to sell their productive holdings, unless the price was exceptionally good. But the pattern of farming never became fossilised. It remained competitive by serving the needs of the growing local urban population, by providing them with milk, and by adapting to changing global market forces. For example, the introduction of cheap imported Australasian lamb led to the collapse of the local sheep industry from some one thousand animals in 1866 to just two in 1914; the sheep were replaced by cattle which increased two and a half times between 1866 and 1942.

But now we come to the sad twist at the end of the tale – and remember we are now in the later twentieth century, when planners have acquired powers that even nineteenth-century colliery owners could never have dreamt of.[29] The collapse of the coal industry in the 1980s has led to the regeneration of the area and with it the destruction of the pit-head works, the removal of railways and the flattening of spoil heaps. Much agricultural land, by now in relative terms far less financially productive, has also been sold for retail parks, distribution depots, housing and light industry – again in the name of regeneration, the success of which can be seen in the last of the four period maps (Fig. 22). Of course, this process has created many new jobs, all of which are welcome, but at a very considerable cost to the area's ancient identity and distinctiveness.

While any visitor to the area would be able to spot Wombwell Wood, it would take a sharp-eyed landscape historian to realise that the grazing for the forty horses of the permanent travellers' site nearby is sited on the remains of the flood-plain 'ings', the remainder of which might soon form a regularly flooded wildlife and conservation area. These few features aside, Wombwell is now indistinguishable from hundreds of regeneration (I nearly said homogenising) projects elsewhere in Britain.

Earlier in this chapter I mentioned Coalbrookdale in the same sentence as Stonehenge, which, for a prehistorian, is high praise indeed and acknowledges the area's pivotal role in the development of the iron and steel industry. It has been described as 'the Most Extraordinary District in the World' and few industrial archaeologists would dispute this.[30] You invite problems when you exalt one particular site or area above all others. Take Stonehenge again: yes, it is indeed unique in having stones that are dressed square to fit around a huge circle and, yes, it sits within a rich landscape of other funerary and ceremonial sites, all of which surely proclaim its importance, too. On the other hand, there are hundreds of prehistoric sites of near-comparable importance in Britain and the general preoccupation with Stonehenge inevitably draws attention away from their diversity and sheer richness. What worries me in particular is that this 'Top Favourites' or 'Hit Parade' approach to the past does not reflect past perceptions. I very much doubt, for example, whether crowds attending the almost equally grand religious sites of Neolithic Orkney would even have been aware of Stonehenge's existence, although it is possible that the shamans who led the ceremonies might have been. The same could be said for Coalbrookdale and the iron and steel industry elsewhere in Britain, which is what I want, briefly, to examine next.

Ever since industrial archaeology came into existence in the 1960s, people have been concerned with working out, recognising and defining past industrial processes. This was usually done by first researching the documentary evidence, and then turning to excavation or survey to reveal precisely how the processes observed in the written sources were actually put into practice. The snag with this approach is that it is circular: so you look for evidence of something and, such is the way of the world, you usually find it. However, I think it would be much better if we could have the confidence to take excavation and field observations at their face value; otherwise, we will never be able to question what we believe the documentary sources are telling us. And this is precisely what has been happening in a recent study of a nine-teenth-century steam forge within the important iron and steel industry of Monklands, in central Scotland, which grew in size following the foundation of the Carron ironworks in the mid-eighteenth century. This was the first ironworks in Scotland to smelt iron using coke instead of charcoal.[31]

The Monklands were the most industrialised part of Scotland in the nineteenth and early twentieth centuries, when there were some seventy workshops and factories in the parishes of Old and New Monkland, Lanarkshire – midway between Glasgow and Edinburgh. The case study that interested me was the survey and excavation of a series of mid-nineteenth-century furnaces at the Moffat Upper Steam Forge, near Airdrie.[32] The excavators, however, had two big problems to contend with. First, most of the existing historical sources were principally concerned with the early (later eighteenth- and early nine-teenth-century) development of iron-making that followed the foundation of the Carron ironworks in 1759. But the Upper Steam Forge was considerably later (it was first known to be in production in 1845) and was a much smaller workshop than those normally discussed in mainstream historical literature. And if it was possible to make things worse, the site had been completely flattened.

Industrial expansion in the Monklands area began with the opening of the Monkland Canal in 1793. This brought down the price of coal, but the iron and steel industry did not begin its period of rapid expansion until the 1820s, followed swiftly by the construction of a series of new blast furnaces in the 1830s. By the mid-century there were some sixty blast furnaces around Coatbridge, the centre of the industry, and by 1845 Scotland was producing 25 per cent of the top-quality pig iron used in Britain. The so-called puddling furnaces of the Upper Steam Forge were used to convert pig iron into malleable or wrought iron, a process introduced to Monklands by English and Welsh workers in 1839. Soon the wrought-iron industry was thriving. Puddle furnaces are less expensive to build and many of the new works required far less capital to establish than smelting blast furnaces. As a consequence, many were set up by teams of iron-workers, with the help of backers.

Shortly after excavation began, it became apparent that Upper Steam Forge was neither a Carron nor a Coalbrookdale. For a start, it was only in use for a couple of decades and had wooden, not stone, walls and had never been the source of major technical innovations. Instead, it was a relatively humble workshop with a couple of furnaces and a single expensive tool, a three-ton Nasmyth mechanical hammer. But careful chemical and metallurgical analyses of the deposits on its floors revealed much new information about the day-to-day processes that took place there.

One might suppose that during an industrial revolution competition would be rife, and, rather like in the early days of micro-processors, all small companies would be eager to embrace the latest technology. That may indeed have been the case in some places, but the floor deposits at Upper Steam Forge showed that some of the processes used there were actually conservative, if not outdated. They indicated, for example, that the puddling furnaces were lined with gritty sand, a practice that was being generally abandoned in the mid-nineteenth century, because it led to loss of iron in the slag.

Much industrial archaeology is inevitably concerned with breakthroughs and 'firsts', but sometimes we can become too focused on these things, and to such an extent that we actually stop researching into the ordinary and the mundane, as if they didn't matter. That would be to deny one of the prime purposes of archaeology: the re-creation of daily life in the past. Over-concentration on innovation, for example, might draw our attention away from the organisation and practice of day-to-day production on the shop floor. We assume that most workshops operated in the same way, but the excavations at Upper Steam Forge suggest that in actual fact each workshop had its own, individual, even idiosyncratic, way of doing things, which was based on the practical experience of the men working there, many of whom would have come from different parts of the country.

I don't want to end with a damp squib, but I feel quite strongly that the story of Britain's industrial past has concentrated too much on the great innovations and breakthroughs. They are, after all, what gives the subject excitement, but they do not necessarily reflect what was actually happening out there in the real workplace. Sadly, life is not about innovation alone. As any innovator will tell you, the bright idea was just the start of the story and led to years and years of development, which often involved false turns and journeys up blind alleys. And while all this was going on within the laboratories and factories of the most innovative industrialists, the daily tasks of processing finished goods and raw materials had to continue, both there and elsewhere. That is why case studies that examine the archaeology of industrial *process*, rather than innovation, are so important because they seek to reveal the variety and complexity of what actually happened, rather than what *ought* to have taken place.

CHAPTER SIX

Capitalism Triumphant:
Markets, Trade and Consumers

So FAR WE HAVE concentrated on the actual remains of past industries – on mines, mills and machines – and we have also taken a very
quick look at housing. I cannot deny, either, that my approach has been
very conventional, often as much historical as archaeological, but I'm
also fully aware that the academic study of trade and industry has
moved on from such narratives. So I would like to open this chapter
on trade and commerce with a thought on how historical archaeology
itself is beginning to reflect aspects of its subject matter: the emergence
of a modern world where trade and communication are becoming
increasingly important.

Today archaeologists are as concerned with the products of the
mills and potteries as they are with the processes of their manufacture.
British ceramics, for instance, were exported widely across the globe
and they now provide an important dating tool for researchers working abroad.[1] Similarly, Britain imported goods, food and raw materials
(such as cotton) from overseas. Sometimes these patterns of trade
could be complex. In the eighteenth century, for example, vessels from
ports like Bristol and Liverpool took trinkets and other manufactured
goods to Africa in exchange for slaves, who were taken across the
Atlantic to plantations in the Caribbean and North America. The ships
then returned to Britain with cargoes of rum, sugar and cotton. This
pattern of trade has come to be known as the now infamous 'North
Atlantic triangle'.

Britain is an island and in archaeology there is a natural tension
between those who wish to examine connections with other countries
overseas and those who prefer to concentrate on what makes Britain
unique – on its own forms of distinctive insularity. This dichotomy

may be acceptable (just) for the periods prior to 1550, but it becomes unsustainable after that. As I mentioned much earlier, it would be impossible, for example, to attempt a study of the cotton industry of north-west England without also paying close regard to the changing political system in the southern United States. Similarly the archaeology of modern London has to take account of the fact that the capital had become a world city by the eighteenth century.

This chapter will be about trade, and overseas trade usually begins at home, where products are developed, manufacturing processes perfected and distribution networks established. Only then do the majority of manufacturers feel sufficiently confident to turn their attention abroad. And this brings me to one of Britain's oldest and most successfully traded items, pottery – or ceramics, the preferred archaeological term, which lumps together everything from coarse hand-made earthenwares to fine bone china. All ceramics are fashioned from clay, with or without the addition of other ingredients, and all are fired to such a degree that the clay's physical and chemical composition is altered irreversibly.[2] An air-dried or lightly fired pot will revert to clay if it gets wet, while a ceramic vessel will remain unaltered. It goes without saying that this chemical stability is the reason why pottery survives so well in the archaeological record and why it remains such a good indicator of past exchange and trading networks.[3]

When we think of the natural resources that brought Britain to commercial and industrial pre-eminence in the eighteenth and nineteenth centuries we tend to think first of coal, which became the universal fuel; then of iron, which became the raw material of change; and finally perhaps of wool, which provided much of the wealth that funded early post-medieval expansion, and without which later textile industries would never have started. I would add a fourth commodity to this list, namely clay. In Britain we take clay for granted. It seems to be everywhere and its main purpose on my farm is to form sticky and intractable mud in which wheels revolve to no purpose and a surface upon which water simply sits, stubbornly refusing to drain. Without clay, I sometimes think, my farming life would have been a lot simpler. But in actual fact clay can be very useful stuff, even on farms, where in the form of 'marl' it can be added to thin, chalky soils to make them more water-retentive and give them extra 'body', better able to retain fertilisers. Many chalk hills are capped with deposits of glacial boulder clay which often include deep marl pits dug in the post-medieval period.

The geology of Britain is extraordinarily varied, and there is a huge variety of clays and mudstones, all with their own distinctive properties, some of which can be unexpected. Take, for example, the Oxford Clay, which formed in Jurassic times about 160 million years ago. This sticky clay formed in a shallow, muddy sea and is still crammed with organic material.[4] Today it outcrops around Peterborough and in northern Bedfordshire, and when fired it gives off a raw, sulphurous smell that still reminds me of the years I spent excavating downwind of the London Brick Company's Whittlesey brick works. As a consequence of this, I've long been fascinated by bricks and was intrigued to discover that in the 1870s somebody realised that when heated to just 400°C, the carbon in the Oxford Clay starts to burn and takes over the process, roughly doubling the temperature (to 1050°C); in effect the bricks then self-fire, thereby saving the manufacturers fortunes by way of fuel costs.[5] This Fletton process (thus named after the Peterborough suburb where it was discovered) transformed the brick industry and led directly to the construction of hundreds of thousands of low-cost suburban London houses from the 1890s onwards.

The clay that occurs in Staffordshire is very different and far more variable in content and quality, but it does make good ceramics, as the local inhabitants discovered in the Middle Ages, when they used various local clays to fashion a number of distinctive styles of pottery. But in the post-medieval centuries this pottery industry had to change significantly if it wanted to thrive. From the eighteenth century, for example, the earthenwares that were mainly produced from the local clays began to fall from favour and the top end of the market began to demand pottery with a white body that resembled the fine china that was then being imported from the Far East in increasing quantities. So the Staffordshire potteries of the famous Six Towns* (reduced to five in the novels of Arnold Bennett) had to import new sources of raw material, first from Dorset and Devon, where so-called 'ball' clays produced a whiter body, and then from even further south-west,

* Stoke-on-Trent, Hanley, Burslem, Tunstall, Fenton and Longton.

around the St Austell area of Cornwall, where millennia of naturally decaying granite had given rise to true china clay, which, when other ingredients had been added (mostly flint and bone), produced a fully vitrified (glass-like) bone china.

The Cornish clay was taken to the Potteries by rail, ship and canal, while flint was removed from East Anglia by sea and canal and taken to specialised mills in Staffordshire where it was fired, or calcined, in purpose-built kilns and then crushed in water-powered roller mills. Animal bone was treated in a similar way in specialised mills, one of which still operates: the Etruscan bone mill (built 1857) on the Trent and Mersey Canal, near Stoke-on-Trent.[6]

The production of fully glazed and vitrified ceramics required very high temperatures. Prior to the later eighteenth century most pottery kilns were fired by wood, but, as supplies of this are believed to have become more scarce and as higher temperatures were required, it was replaced by coal.[7] This switch involved technical and mechanical changes to the kilns and their stoke holes. It was also difficult to find the right kind of coal, which was needed to produce both short and long flames. I was surprised to discover, for example, that the twentieth-century potteries of Limoges in France actually imported their long-flame coals from Abercarn, in Gwent. In the Staffordshire potteries Wedgwoods, for example, converted to coal between 1768 and 1806 and Mintons from 1796 to 1803.

I can well remember travelling through the Potteries in the 1950s and being amazed by the sight of so many distinctive bottle kilns, where the vast bulk of the pottery was fired. They occurred in clusters surrounded by other buildings, which I now realise were used to house coal, make and decorate the unfired pottery and then store the finished wares. These groups of buildings were known as 'potbanks' and they were very characteristic of the Six Towns. Today, a handful remain. There were four main types of bottle kiln which are generally distinguished by the way in which they draw in the air needed to produce the high temperatures (1300–1400°C) required by china and stonewares.[8] The 'classic' bottle kiln is the 'hovel' type, so-named from a bottle-shaped brick-built outer shell, or hovel, whose sole purpose was neither to fire pots nor to contain heat, but to induce a strong draught of air to feed the fires of the kiln that it completely enveloped.

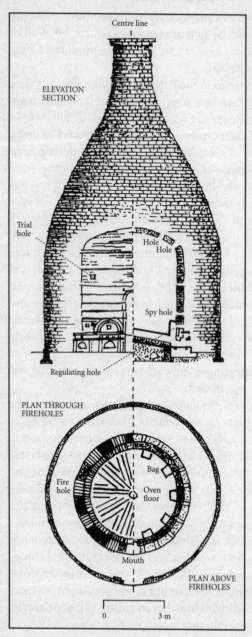

ELEVATION
SECTION

Centre line

Trial
hole

Hole Hole

Spy hole

Regulating hole

PLAN THROUGH
FIREHOLES

Fire
hole

Bag

Oven
floor

Mouth

PLAN ABOVE
FIREHOLES

0   3 m

FIG 23 *The firm Wengers Ltd of Etruria, Staffordshire, built many of the kilns used in the Potteries. This drawing, based on their catalogue of c. 1938, shows the constructional details of the traditional 'hovel' type of updraught bottle kiln. The kiln was fired through stoke holes below the ware chamber where the pots to be fired were stacked. Air from the outside was drawn down through the mouth of the bottle-shaped hovel and into the kiln through the holes beneath the oven floor. It was then heated in the fires, passing up through the stacked pottery and out through the holes in the kiln roof.*

Excavations have revealed the footings of hovel kilns at Hanley and at Topsham in Devon that can be dated to the 1690s, but the vast majority were built rather later, mostly in the mid-eighteenth century. Fine examples of hovel bottle kilns have been preserved at the Gladstone Pottery at Longton, Staffs. I have to say bottle kilns look lovely today – anything that is or was truly functional is endowed with a beauty born of purpose – and this is enhanced by their highly skilled, almost sinuous brickwork. But the fumes they omitted were once toxic and blacked out the sun, especially after the introduction of coal. And we should also recall the poor firemen who stoked the kiln, from a walkway within the hovel, in extremely hot and cramped conditions.

One feature of archaeology that has always fascinated me might be described as cultural conservatism. In theory, at least, accountants and engineers would have you believe that if entrepreneurs and industrialists were given absolute freedom to make decisions, they would always opt for the most efficient and lowest-cost option. But happily human beings – and here I include businessmen – aren't so predictable, and often they let other arguments affect their judgement. Moreover this is something that has been going on for years, because for some reason that only the Almighty in his infinite wisdom can comprehend, the British have always had a predilection for things that are round. So they invented circular henges and throughout prehistory they lived in roundhouses, while their neighbours across the Channel chose to dwell in more capacious, rectangular halls. Perhaps it was the same genetic or cultural predisposition that made the British develop bowler hats and circular, bottle-shaped kilns, while the rest of Europe, from Denmark to France, opted instead for homburgs and rectangular kilns fed by a cross-draught.[9]

The continental style of kiln may indeed be more efficient,[10] but the British bottle kiln was actually easier to load, and of course later, in the nineteenth century, there were abundant supplies of coal relatively close by, so efficiency *per se* was not necessarily the main criterion for making a decision. Having said that, the contrast between the sort of kilns used on either side of the Channel is very striking and does need to be explained.

There is now abundant evidence to suggest that the earliest bottle kilns were based on the shape of later medieval domed kilns, which were incapable of raising temperatures as high as the 1000°C required to fire the stonewares that become popular in early post-medieval times. So eighteenth-century potters opted for a new kiln design that nevertheless mirrored what had gone before, as this shape was familiar to the workforce and accommodated the working practices employed in their various yards and workshops. Pottery-making was essentially a conservative craft and it suited the potters to stick with something familiar which could be shown to work. There was simply no need for a radical departure from tradition. And besides, raising money to build these expensive kilns would also have been more straightforward if the financiers thought they were venturing their capital on a well-proven technology. Today it is easy to forget that traditional bankers have always avoided unnecessary risk.

I mentioned earlier that industrial archaeology has been mainly concerned with innovation and the development of production techniques. This might be all well and good in certain heavy industries where the requirements to produce more and better iron and steel at lower and lower cost were fairly straightforward. But when it comes to the production of smaller items that will only sell if the market demands them, then the market itself has a direct influence on the production process. So in practical terms it became simpler to treat producer and consumer as integral components of the same cycle of market, production and trade.

The idea that pottery could be traded and exchanged is nothing new and in Britain goes back to prehistoric times when high-quality ceramics were traded over hundreds of miles. After the departure of the Romans in the early fifth century, the trade resumed quite quickly and then gathered pace, so that during the Middle Saxon period (AD 650–850), certain distinctive types of pottery, such as Ipswich Ware, were traded not just across the whole of southern England, but also in bulk.[11] It would not be an exaggeration to describe the production of Ipswich Ware, for example, as semi-, or indeed fully, industrial. The trade in pottery increased throughout the Middle Ages, when we also see the widespread introduction of glazed vessels. Anyone who has taken part in an urban excavation of the later Middle Ages will be aware that by this time domestic pottery was being produced in vast quantities.

Then, in the sixteenth century, many new forms of pottery, of decoration and production, too, were introduced from the Continent.[12] The causes behind these quite sudden changes are most probably to do with the Renaissance which witnessed the widespread movement of artists, craftsmen and ideas between royal courts and the rise of a new prosperous middle class keen to emulate princely behaviour. The new vessels, technologies and the fresh market opportunities gave rise to a number of distinctive regional ceramic styles and traditions which emerged and flourished throughout the sixteenth and seventeenth centuries.

By now readers will be aware that I am not fond of 'revolutions', but the changes to the ceramic industry in the sixteenth century have indeed been described as a 'ceramic revolution'. Then another took place just two centuries later and certainly in this latter instance, if not the former, the term does indeed appear to be justified, because of its rapid and major effect on the industry (if not on society as a whole). Even though the new British bottle kilns resembled earlier models, that resemblance was actually superficial: what mattered was the controlled heat they generated and the sheer productivity of their output. Both of these were revolutionary, as indeed were the new styles and forms of the ceramics they produced. But none of these things would have been relevant if there had not been the international markets to sustain an industry, which was rapidly growing into something truly massive. There were other important regional ceramic traditions, for example, in Shropshire, London, Devon and Derbyshire, but here I want briefly to consider the Staffordshire Potteries where the changes of the eighteenth and nineteenth centuries amounted to nothing less than complete transformation.[13]

The pottery industry of the early eighteenth century was diverse, ranging from very small-scale, rural itinerant potters to educated capitalists such as John Dwight, who established his Fulham pottery in the later seventeenth century. People like Dwight operated sophisticated production units in urban situations and served very different niche markets, but the growth of this diverse industry was a reflection of its structure. Paul Courtney has described the situation at this time: 'The transport revolution of, first canals and, then, railways had yet to happen, but a growing population, rising standards of living and demand-led competition for markets, especially after 1650, was producing some of the conditions for a supply-led revolution – that is, led by technological and organizational innovation.'[14] In the Potteries of north Staffordshire this supply-led revolution was to continue and gather pace throughout the eighteenth and nineteenth centuries.

From the mid-seventeenth century (and as early as the 1610s, in Virginia) fine-quality earthenwares and salt-glazed stonewares were being exported from the Potteries to specific regional markets in North America and the Caribbean. From the late seventeenth century until about 1740 a large number of successive micro-technological and production improvements effectively transformed the north Staffordshire pottery industry. Twenty years earlier we see the first appearance of entrepreneurs from outside the pottery industry, whose finance and marketing skills helped to hasten the pace of change. At the same time there arose an informal network, or pool, of shared knowledge, which allowed the many workshops to serve the changing needs of niche markets both at home and abroad.

The first stage of the ceramic revolution, during which the main technological advances had been made, was completed by the 1740s. This triggered a second phase of even more rapid growth, which was characterised by a large number of minor developments that added further variety to the texture and appearance of the increasingly large range of ceramics being manufactured at any one time. Perhaps the culminating development was the introduction of transfer printing in the 1780s, and with it the first truly modern-looking domestic pottery. It was a simple technique that could be done in-house. Designs were printed onto tissue paper which was dampened and then very carefully wrapped around the unfired, unglazed cup, teapot or whatever. It was then fired and in the process the design was transferred to the clay.

This was the era when creamware was to replace Chinese porcelain on the dinner tables of the British upper classes of the 1760s and 1770s, largely thanks to Josiah Wedgwood's inspired top-down marketing to influential households. But the success of creamware, which was produced from ball clays, was relatively short-lived, being replaced around 1800 by bone china, which, although not technically a true porcelain,* was translucent, evenly textured, very attractive and relatively cheap to produce. It was to be the dominant British porcelain style throughout the nineteenth century.

The scale of the eighteenth-century ceramic revolution in north Staffordshire was astonishing. Josiah Wedgwood himself estimated that in 1710–15 there were some fifty potteries employing about five hundred people. In 1762 local manufacturers claimed there were 150 potteries with some seven thousand workers; by the end of the century the number of potteries had probably doubled again, and the staff employed risen to around 15,000.[15]

The men behind the more successful potteries realised that marketing and distribution were all-important, and the brothers John and Thomas of the leading ceramic dynasty in the area, the Wedgwoods, invested heavily in local turnpike roads. They followed this by helping to fund the Trent and Mersey Canal, which gave far better access to the port of Liverpool and was to be of benefit to the Potteries for many years to come. The Wedgwood brothers have been described as 'pottery capitalists' because they dealt widely in land, buildings and factories, had interests in coal mines and were the biggest moneylenders in Burslem, where they built the largest house (the Big House) in 1751. In the later eighteenth century, Wedgwoods had several dealers in various towns and cities, including in London (37), Bristol (22), Newcastle upon Tyne (8), Sunderland (8), Manchester (6), Liverpool (4) and Gloucester (4). Even by modern standards this was an extraordinarily well-organised marketing network.[16]

If the British market was well organised, the export trade was certainly not ignored either. In 1785 the Staffordshire potters' Committee of Commerce reported that five-sixths of the area's earthenware production was exported. In the late eighteenth century Europe was the main market and between 1760 and 1780 Josiah Wedgwood was selling to Russia, Spain, Portugal, the Netherlands, France, Italy, Germany, Sweden and Turkey. At the same time, and into the nineteenth century, markets in Africa, Asia and the West Indies were also developing, but David Barker of the Potteries Museum at

---

* True porcelain is a mixture of china clay and chinastone fired to c. 1200–1350°C and was first produced in quantity in Europe at Meissen in the early eighteenth century.

Stoke-on-Trent believes that the United States was the key market, where exports of 1.2 million pieces in 1770 increased to almost fourteen million in 1830 (albeit with minor hiccups during the War of Independence and the War of 1812). The American market continued to grow and by 1835 had overtaken Europe as the main consumer of British ceramics, by an extraordinary 17.5 to 10.8 million pieces.[17]

I was going to say that these figures came as a great surprise, but to be honest they didn't, because I can well recall back in the 1970s, when I was an assistant curator in the Royal Ontario Museum, Toronto, I worked as a volunteer on an excavation of a nineteenth-century native American settlement site. In my naïve fashion I applied to go on the dig expecting to find quantities of unglazed, hand-made, Iroquois-style pottery, but no. Instead, my meticulous trowel revealed numerous sherds of white and blue willow pattern plate – all the way from Stoke-on-Trent. If I'm honest, I must admit it was slightly disappointing.

During the nineteenth century both the British and worldwide markets for the products of the Potteries grew, but price competition also increased and the smaller workshops began to be replaced by pottery factories. Indeed, much of the growth in the industry during the nineteenth century was achieved by employing more and more people in ever-larger factories, rather than through automation or mechanisation. The power for many potters' wheels, for example, was provided by women and children. This, of course, was because labour was plentiful and cheap.

Inevitably, the history of the Potteries tends to revolve around the great innovative producers, such as Wedgwoods, whose history has become well known. So rather than concentrating on the great and the good, I thought I would take a closer look at a smaller manufacturer whose potbank and works have been preserved as the Gladstone Pottery Museum in Uttoxeter Road, Longton, now a part of the south-eastern approaches to Stoke-on-Trent.[18] But here we encounter a phenomenon we have met before, at places like the picturesque Stanley Mills on that bend in the River Tay. The general history of an industry is not necessarily mirrored on the ground, in individual case studies.

The Gladstone Pottery began life in the 1780s, at the time when the ceramics industry in north Staffordshire was going through a period of rapid expansion. Burslem, just north of Longton, was the largest pottery town, but much of the land available for development there had been taken up. Then in the 1780s the Longton Manor estate was sold off and many skilled and experienced potters from Burslem bought land there. Among them were the Shelleys who already ran a local firm. By 1787 they had built a thriving pottery at the south end of Lane End, close by the newly opened Uttoxeter turnpike. Everything seemed fine: the new potbank made the Shelleys' own earthenware and to diversify the business they also decorated plates and dishes made by Josiah Wedgwood at Etruria. The firm, under the two Shelley brothers, Thomas and Michael, established a good local reputation, yet in 1789 they went bust and were forced to sell up.

William Ward, a potter, bought the works for £900 and promptly sold half of it off – something that today would be frowned upon as 'asset stripping'. Undeterred, he then divided the land that he had retained into smaller potbanks, keeping one for himself, which he worked, and eventually sold, in 1818, to John Hendley Sheridan, for £1,222 – quite a tidy profit. Sheridan, a developer and prominent civic official in Stoke, let the potbank out to tenants whom he seems to have selected with some care, supplying them with houses, workshops and new kilns. This development, which was arranged around a courtyard, in a pattern that was becoming typical of smaller works in the area, had been completed by 1840.

The most successful of Sheridan's tenants was Thomas Cooper whose enterprise thrived during the 1850s when he employed forty-one adults and twenty-six children. During that period he bought himself a comfortable house adjoining the potbank and expanded the enterprise into neighbouring properties which he demolished and rebuilt, in conjunction with Sheridan. As we saw in Chapter 1, many Victorian enterprises, both urban and rural, were the successful result of partnerships between tenants and landlords – and this was no exception. Most of the buildings now visible were built by Cooper in the 1850s.

Sadly, the phase of expansion didn't last long and in 1876 the works were sold to a local company, Hobson and Co. The pottery probably acquired the name Gladstone after a visit by the Prime Minister in 1863, when he laid the foundation stone of the Wedgwood Memorial Institute. Thereafter the Gladstone Pottery had a complex history, but it never seems to have thrived in quite the same way as it did under

Cooper, and it even closed for a time during the Second World War. The kilns were last fired in March 1960, and in the early 1970s the site was scheduled to be demolished for development. At this point a successful and far-sighted local tile manufacturer, Derek Johnson, stepped in, promptly bought the site with its buildings and made them over to the Staffordshire Pottery Industry Preservation Trust, which opened them as a museum in 1974. It had been a close-run thing.

I want now to move on from bricks and mortar to something very much more abstract and philosophical. I'm talking here about nothing less than the nature of things – of objects and possessions – and of our relationships with them. Like most people who earn their living by excavating artefacts, or by picking them up off field surfaces, I sometimes pause to wonder how people would have thought about them in the past. I remember when the thought first struck me. It was the summer of 1971 and I had been excavating the contents of a small Neolithic pit on the outskirts of Peterborough, which revealed a finely made, leaf-shaped flint arrowhead. When I held it up to the sun, it was translucent and the even ripples of the flakes that had been so skilfully removed from both surfaces deflected the light in an almost magical way, subtly changing colour from deep rich browns to ochres and creamy yellows. As I stared at it I wondered whether the man who had made it some five thousand years ago thought it as beautiful as I did. The more I looked, the more convinced I became that this was more than a mere utilitarian object. It had been fashioned with love and must have been intended to be beautiful.

This then sent my thoughts in other directions: what were Neolithic ideas of beauty and were they all necessarily, like those expressed in this arrowhead, similar to our own? Was the arrowhead fashioned with such care to reflect well on its maker, or its user, assuming, of course, that they were different people? Conversely, could it have been made so well as a mark of respect for its eventual prey – be it human or animal? But the question that intrigued me most was this: was the care taken to make such an ordinary object as an arrowhead something that arose through habit (in other words that was the way arrowheads had always been made), or was it part of a living tradition in which some arrowheads were made well and others not so well? I find the 'living tradition' idea fascinating because it suggests that people had active relationships with objects whereby some were regarded as special and others taken for granted.

As I write I cannot help thinking about my mobile phone, which I lost three days ago and only noticed that it was missing this morning. It almost certainly fell out of my pocket when I was turning the hay with my aged tractor. Doubtless it is now sliced up and bound into a bale, to annoy me no longer with its irritating metallic ring, which I never managed to change. That's another way of saying that my relationship with it wasn't exactly active, unlike some students I know, who would be less likely to lose their phones than amputate a limb. On the face of it, of course, one could simply write off the need of the current younger generation to possess the most up-to-date phone as a fad, a fashion or, at best, as technological one-upmanship. But in fact there is far more to it than that; because it's all about the relationship of people to things and of things to people. As Marx observed, it's a dialectical, or two-way, process. Things affect us as much as we affect them. This observation leads me to question a widely held assumption about eighteenth-century attitudes towards objects. Were they mere things, that could sometimes symbolise rank and status – to be possessed and discarded – or was there more to them than that?

It would probably be no exaggeration to say that there was an explosion of pottery production in the eighteenth century but this time the explosion was more like a firework: yes, there was a quantitative and qualitative 'bang' made possible by new production techniques but these improvements were accompanied by a shower of bright lights, different colours and sparkly new styles. There were similar developments, too, in the world of textiles where the great mills were now producing a wealth of new fabrics in a huge range of materials and an endless variety of colours, textures and finishes. From at least the sixteenth and seventeenth centuries, workshops sited in the larger towns and cities were able to produce the leather straps and laces, the metal buckles, glass beads, rings, loops and other accessories needed to complete the perfect garment.[19] This was the period when the concept of fashion in the rapidly emerging 'polite society' became important, not just for women, but for men, too. This was also the period that saw the emergence of the first modern novels and as a student I can well remember reading Tobias Smollett's *Humphry Clinker* and Henry Fielding's *Tom Jones* and thinking that these people were almost exactly like us. I think I might be forgiven this, as young Tom's lusty pursuit of various young women was precisely what I was then attempting to achieve for myself, but with notably less success.

When we read books of the period or visit the country houses of such members of the 'polite society', it is very easy to assume that they were, indeed, exactly like many of us today: 'dedicated followers of fashion'. The idea that the eighteenth century witnessed the rise of the first consumer society gained respectable support in 1982 with the publication, by three highly distinguished historians, of *The Birth of a Consumer Society*.[20] The book appeared in print at a time when Mrs Thatcher's government had launched the Falklands campaign and her government's free-market, consumer-led reforms were starting to produce the dividends and bonuses that would prove so popular for the next quarter of a century. Given these historical contexts it is hardly surprising that the book was received enthusiastically by both general and academic readers.

Although the basic economic thinking behind *The Birth of a Consumer Society* may be valid in general terms, it has more recently been criticised for making the less justifiable assumption that eighteenth-century 'consumers' were just like their modern equivalents.[21] This view is based on the idea that people's relationships with objects were the same in the eighteenth century as they are today. In actual fact such relationships are, and always have been, complex, as I hope my flint arrowhead example illustrated. Archaeology surely teaches us that even today very few people see themselves as mindless followers of fashion, bent on finding the latest thing, only to discard something perfectly usable, as the clichéd concept of the throwaway society would have us believe.

Like many others in my profession, my first degree is in Archaeology and Anthropology; and from the very outset I was taught that one must try to avoid judging other communities and cultures by the standards of twentieth- or twenty-first-century Western morality.[22] Archaeologists believe that this must also apply to past communities, too, whether they be foreigners or British, Bronze Age or Georgian. Having written those pious words, I also freely acknowledge that such intentions are impossible to achieve, but I suppose they do give us something to aim for. And that brings me back to the idea of the eighteenth-century 'consumer society', which I am now quite convinced is a later twentieth-century concept that has been misapplied to an earlier period.

We certainly know that production of luxury ceramics, textiles and other goods increased by leaps and bounds during the eighteenth century. We also know that many of the objects bought by the aspiring middle class echoed the tastes of the Court and of the aristocracy. As time passed, many of these objects, once thought of as high-status, were bought by a more diverse selection of society. In crude terms, upmarket objects, such as ceramic vessels, moved downmarket when they became more plentiful and cheaper to produce, as one would expect in an industry led by the supply side. But that is not to say that all of these purchasers were aping higher echelons of society.

People also bought things for other reasons: maybe they just liked them or found them useful; maybe, too, they made them feel comfortable; we mustn't leap to the conclusion that every member of polite society was solely concerned with appearing 'upwardly mobile'. Today many objects are seen by economists and marketing gurus as possessing a social dimension. Seen in this way, relatively ordinary objects can be given added status: works of art by fashionable artists, flashy cars and four-wheel-drives, designer handbags etc, etc. The cost reflects the status, ranging from a Damien Hirst pickled pig at the top, to a personalised number plate at the bottom. But Heaven alone knows how future archaeologists will be able to decide which was considered the more valuable. This was not necessarily the case three centuries ago. This is because eighteenth-century England had its fair share of unpleasant people; it was not populated with City yuppies, nor was it modelled on New Labour Islington; and there is no evidence that everyone was desperate to claw their way to the top of the social ladder, regardless.

One danger of interpreting a society nearly three hundred years old in the light of such a period-specific modern attitude is that it obliterates the subtlety of what actually might have happened in the past. If that is so, then what is it that some archaeologists believe motivated people in the eighteenth century to buy the bright new pots and textiles, if they were not driven by the aspirations that took such a firm hold in the final decades of the twentieth century? To answer that question we must head in an entirely new direction.

I want now to change both gear and scale, away from the worlds of macro-economics and the transformation of society to something altogether more intimate. I mentioned earlier how I had speculated about that flint arrowhead and how its role might have been understood way back in the Neolithic. Such thoughts would have been anathema to many archaeologists just forty years ago. In those days it was believed that we could never progress beyond mere objects and the immediate circumstances in which they were found. So if my flint arrowhead had been found in a grave, I could speculate about the status of its owner, but I could not then consider the state or structure of the society in which he lived. All of that intellectual stuffiness (at the time it was regarded as necessary rigour) has since changed and today almost anything goes; new ideas are encouraged and are then judged on their merits.

One result of this intellectual freedom has been to liberate archaeologists to study the role of objects within a particular society, but using sources of information that until quite recently would not have been seen as strictly archaeological, no matter what light they threw on a particular problem. Happily, these rigid attitudes are fast disappearing and, just as with ideas, almost anything goes when it comes to the discovery of new sources of information. These days, the learned journal *Post-Medieval Archaeology* is as likely to contain articles about the role of stars in promoting relations between native Americans and colonists in seventeenth-century Chesapeake, as more conventional excavation reports.[23] And although a few Oxbridge dons might splutter into their glasses of port, such papers do indeed enrich life for the rest of us.

If we are to understand how objects were regarded in eighteenth-century society we must look for contemporary sources that show what people were actually thinking.[24] These sources include the so-called Courtesy Books which were intended for men and women who wanted to be members of polite society. These inexpensive books were readily available, but it would be a mistake to assume that they were only guidebooks for the aspiring social climber. Because, as I have repeatedly noted, we cannot assume that everyone was seeking social advancement. Indeed, the Courtesy Books themselves suggest that most people simply wanted to feel at ease in what was becoming an increasingly important part of society. I cannot think of a modern equivalent for them other than, perhaps, the magazine sections of Sunday newspapers with their weekly columns on shopping, food, wine and fashion – and, of course, social cartoonists such as Posy Simmonds.

The first Courtesy Books were published early in the eighteenth century and remained popular, reprinting regularly, for the next hundred or so years. From these books and from other sources it becomes clear that in Georgian England objects were used both to maintain social values and to manipulate the way individuals chose to be perceived. This is far more subtle than the simple, catch-all notion of a consumer society. The Courtesy Books make it clear that a member of polite society was someone 'who knows how to act with the objects that surround them. To demonstrate ineptitude with objects was to signal rusticity and ignorance …'[25]

Another equally unknown source of information about people's attitudes to objects in the eighteenth century is the so-called 'it-narratives'. These popular works of fiction took objects, rather than people, as their principal characters and 'described their lives, their owners and the circumstances they found themselves in as they circulated through society'.[26] A few titles give a flavour of the genre: *The Adventures of a Pin* (1790), *The Adventures of a Black Coat* (1760) and *The Secret History of an Old Shoe* (1734). Novels, too, can be used, especially (as one might expect) those of Jane Austen, even though they were written somewhat later: *Mansfield Park*, *Emma* and *Persuasion* demonstrate in the author's own words the 'remarkable closeness' between objects and people.

There is a wealth of material in these sources to show that objects signified their owners' role and status within society. They were not seen as a means of moving up through it; on the contrary, in fact, they suggested instead stability and permanence. If you moved above or below your given station in life you then became uncomfortable with the objects around you – and with which you had to relate. The latter was important because it was widely held that objects somehow possessed character and could influence people.

The 'Sensibility of Things', for example, was important to C. Gildon, the author of the it-narrative *The Golden Spy* (1709), which was about a gold coin with 'Observation, Memory and Reflection'.[27] One could also argue that the very existence of it-narratives in the first place implies that ordinary items of daily life could be seen to possess volition, personality or identity. Objects were especially thought to be endowed with character and judgement when it came to assessing the suitability of a new owner. Interestingly, however, money seems rarely to have changed hands when the heroes of the it-narratives were transferred between owners; this, again, is not what one might have expected in a consumer society based on monetary value alone. It also argues strongly against the idea that in Georgian times objects were seen as mere commodities, to be used only for the acquisition of greater influence and social status.

The idea of a consumer society began to gather credibility in the twentieth century, but even then the demand was led by the supply side. Just like the ceramic industry in the eighteenth century, it was the makers of plastic consumer goods and domestic appliances who had to create the need and market for their products in the mid-twentieth century.[28]

If the mills, mines and factories of Georgian Britain were to continue to expand it would prove necessary to export their products abroad in ever-increasing quantities. And, of course, by Victorian times a growing workforce, demanding (just as today) cheap food, would need to import grain and other commodities from overseas. Even fertilisers such as seabird dropping guano were imported in huge quantities, this time from the Peruvian coast in the nineteenth century. I shall briefly discuss port development shortly, but first I would like to draw attention to an aspect of industrialisation linked to trade that has been almost wholly neglected. I suspect this was because it did not involve Big Names: neither great entrepreneurs nor high-profile industrialists. Yet heroes there were, aplenty. I refer to the rapid expansion of the British Royal Dockyards which began in the late fifteenth century under Henry VII and continued for the next four and a half centuries, although here I will mainly be concerned with the eighteenth.[29] There have been many naval histories, but only recently has our attention been drawn to the shore installations that serviced the rapidly expanding fleet, without which, of course, Britain would soon have failed as a globally trading nation.[30]

I was in two minds whether to discuss the supply and maintenance of the Royal Navy in Chapter 8, which is all about defence and fortifications, but in the end I decided against it, in part because I am convinced that the main reason why this unique and extraordinary aspect of Britain's industrial past has not received the popular attention it deserves is precisely because it has been relegated to the realm of 'big boys' toys'. It's an arcane world of guns, cannons and fortifications, where men knowingly discuss the merits of various weapons nobody in their right mind has ever heard of, as if they had personally been under attack from them. I sometimes think of these people as 'special interest groupies', but their knowledge can be exhaustive. The main problem with such attention to detail is that larger truths often fail to emerge into the full light of day unless a rather special person can create the interest.

Jonathan Coad has done more than anyone else to demonstrate that the archaeology of naval dockyards is a microcosm of early industrial Britain.[31] He has also shown that it is extremely early and highly important. To give just one example, a good case can be made that some of the specialist facilities required by the ships of the rapidly expanding navy, such as rope works and sail lofts, were among the earliest true factories in the world. The complex blocks used in the block and tackle of the rope rigging of Georgian warships were made in the Portsmouth Block Mills, which can claim to be the world's first instance of mass production using machine tools.[32] But before we take a closer look at Chatham, the best preserved of the eighteenth-century dockyards, we need a few key historical markers.

In the Middle Ages the Crown resurrected the navy, as and when political events dictated. Sometimes it could be quite large, as during the reign of Henry V (1413–22). Incidentally, I was the archaeological director of shore operations when *Time Team* investigated Henry's flagship the *Grace Dieu* which lay in the mud of the River Hamble, just upstream of the Solent. Until I took part in that dig I simply had no idea that medieval warships could be so vast: it has been estimated, for example, that her mainmast was some 200 feet high and measured a massive 7 feet in diameter at the base.[33] But although the ships themselves could be impressive, there was no administrative mechanism in the medieval Court to ensure that the navy was maintained and serviced by shore facilities in times of peace. Consequently, it usually wasn't.

In 1485 all that was to change when Henry VII ordered the construction of a dry dock at Portsmouth. Dry docks, which could be drained to allow ships' hulls to be worked on in the dry, were the most expensive items of capital equipment needed by the navy.[34] The yards that surrounded them, where ropes, sails and other equipment were stored and repaired, were the servicing facilities of the dry docks – hence dockyards. In the sixteenth century other Tudor monarchs established dockyards at Deptford, Woolwich, Chatham and later at Sheerness and Harwich. Plymouth Dock (from 1823 known as Devonport) was built in the 1690s beside a naturally sheltered harbour, but in a largely rural area of south Devon, and a New Town had to be built to accommodate the many people who worked there. Although it only became fully operational by 1700, the placing of a major new naval shore base so far to the south-west was tacit recognition that Britain's sphere of naval interest no longer lay in the Channel and North Sea alone, but had extended significantly towards, and into, the Mediterranean. By 1711 some 6,500 people were directly employed by the Royal Dockyards, but this figure would be greatly increased if one included outside subcontractors and suppliers. In effect, even by this early date servicing the navy had become a major industry.

The industry then grew relentlessly. In the 1760s there were some 430 warships serviced 'by what by then could reasonably claim to be the greatest and most complex industrial organisation in the western world. By 1814 the number of warships had risen to over 900, supported by shore establishments employing nearly 17,500 people.'[35] By the early nineteenth century there were ten additional naval bases overseas, extending from Jamaica to Madras, and employing some two thousand people.

During the seventeenth century its location in the south-east, with ready access to the North Sea and Channel, meant that Chatham was the principal naval dockyard, but in the following century the shift in emphasis towards the south-west saw the rise of Plymouth and Portsmouth relative to Chatham, which continued, however, to be one

ABOVE: The potbank at the Gladstone Pottery's Roslyn Works, Longton, Staffordshire.

BELOW: A view across the Albert Dock, Liverpool, designed by Jesse Hartley, the city's dock engineer from 1824 to 1860. The Albert Dock opened in 1846 and featured a series of uniform warehouses at the water's edge. Goods were offloaded from ships and taken into the warehouses through the three large openings in each block. In the background can be seen the two pinnacles of the Royal Liver Building (1908–10) and the dome of Mersey Docks and Harbour Company Offices (1907).

ABOVE: The recently restored Swiss Bridge in Birkenhead Park, Merseyside. Birkenhead Park was the first municipal public park in Britain and was laid out to designs by Joseph Paxton, from 1843. This park was an integral part of William Laird's New Town of Birkenhead, which was centred around Hamilton Square, to the east. After 1850 there was a rapid increase in the number of new urban parks in Britain and elsewhere, many of which, including Central Park in New York, were much influenced by Paxton's Birkenhead.

BELOW: Hamilton Square, Birkenhead, Merseyside. This large and very grand rectangular square was built between 1825 and 1844 to the designs of James Gillespie Graham, who had previously worked on the later stages of James Craig's New Town, in Edinburgh. No two sides of Hamilton Square are identical and the east side includes the fine, if slightly later (1883–7), Town Hall. The west range (seen here from the south) was built between 1839 and 1844.

ABOVE: A view of the 768th (2006) annual Corby Glen Sheep Fair, in the southern Lincolnshire Wolds, near Bourne. This is the oldest continuously held sheep fair in Britain. The charter was granted by Henry III to the son of a local landowner, Hamon Pecche, and his heirs 'of a weekly market on Thursday at his Manor of Coreby and of a yearly fair there on the Vigil, the Feast, and the Morrow of the Feast of the Assumption. Given by the King's hand, 26 February 1238.'

BELOW: The chancel of St Mary's Church, Bottesford, Leicestershire. This fine, mostly late medieval (Perpendicular) space is uniquely cluttered with the tombs of eight successive post-medieval Earls of Rutland, plus their wives. This view is looking towards the north wall and the tombs (l.–r.) of the 8th Earl (d. 1679, by Grinling Gibbons) and 5th Earl (d. 1612) with 1st Earl (d. 1543) in the foreground; this is one of two at the centre of the aisle leading up to the altar.

ABOVE: The church of St John the Evangelist at Little Gidding, near Peterborough. This small church has a nave and chancel and was entirely rebuilt by Nicholas Ferrar when he and his family established a religious community here in 1626. He is buried beneath the table-top tomb on the path leading to the main west door. The main seventeenth-century church is brick-built but the idiosyncratic stone west front was added in 1714. The wood-panelled interior is remarkably complete (*photograph: Maisie Taylor*).

LEFT: The gravestone of Elizabeth Cuthbert (d. 1685) in the south nave aisle of St Magnus Cathedral, Kirkwall, Orkney. The cathedral boasts an exceptionally fine collection of post-medieval carved tombstones, many of which were originally positioned on the floor of the nave, but were later moved to the aisles for their protection. Elizabeth Cuthbert's husband, James Wallace, was Minister of the Cathedral.

RIGHT: The Sight of Eternal Life Church, Shrubland Road, Hackney, east London. This is a fine example of a so-called 'Tin Tabernacle' church. These buildings were erected from pre-fabricated kits in the mid-nineteenth century. This example dates from 1858.

BELOW: The Union Workhouse, Gressenhall, near East Dereham, Norfolk. This building was erected in 1776–7 as a House of Industry, following the purchase of a small farm in 1776. It was substantially modified in 1835–6 to include requirements of the 'new' Poor Law Act of 1834, which stipulated that men and women, including married couples, should be housed in their own wings, entered through the two widely separated doors, visible here. The chapel (with the bellcote), on the extreme left, was erected by private subscription in 1868.

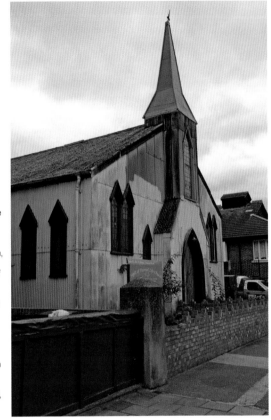

ABOVE: Many of the bridges for military roads built in the Scottish Highlands in the eighteenth century were severely functional. The principal exception is this magnificent bridge, built by General George Wade in 1733 across the upper reaches of the Tay, at Aberfeldy (Perth and Kinross), which was designed by Robert Adam.

BELOW: The Second World War defensive landscape of the southern Wash at Lawyers' Creek, near Holbeach St Matthew, Lincolnshire. These defences were usually placed on the inland side of flood banks. The example shown here is of a Lincolnshire-type three-bay infantry pillbox, entered from the rear, with two covered sections and an open central area to allow anti-aircraft fire.

ABOVE: This example of the very rare Ruck machine-gun post in the defensive landscape at Lawyer's Creek has three embrasures for guns and is mounted high on a sea bank to cover a sharp bend.

BELOW: The Carmarthen stop line was laid out in 1940 and 1941 as part of measures to protect the port of Milford Haven. It ran from Pembury, overlooking Carmarthen Bay and the Bristol Channel in the south, to Cardigan, in the north. This view shows the last defences at the northern end, a line of anti-tank cubes ending at a pillbox in remote countryside at Blaen-nant-gwyn, near Cardigan. Beyond the pillbox to the sea in the distance, the fissured landscape of steep-sided valleys was not considered passable by armoured vehicles. Note the original earth coverings of the cubes and pillbox.

ABOVE: This view of the Carmarthen stop line is from a gun emplacement overlooking the mouth of the River Tywi at St Ishmael, near Kidwelly, close to the southern end of the line. There is a wartime painting of a cigar-smoking Mickey Mouse giving potential attackers a V- sign and a defiant British Bulldog showing them his raised tail (inset).

BELOW: Excavation of a series of Second World War defensive works at Shooters Hill, south-east London, revealed the complexity of planned urban defences. The work began in July 1940, shortly after the retreat from Dunkirk, and was completed in 1942 when the threat was perceived to have diminished significantly. This view shows the excavation of a spigot mortar, an anti-tank weapon, which would have been mounted on the stainless-steel pin, or pintle. The weapon was fired by soldiers of the Home Guard who were protected by a shallow trench, seen here lined with corrugated iron. Ammunition and supplies would have been kept in lockers within the trench.

of the three principal naval bases, until its closure in 1984. In 1761 the Navy Board ordered the wholesale modernisation and enlargement of Plymouth and Portsmouth and this was followed by a more piecemeal programme of improvements to Chatham. The result was that when Britain entered the wars with Revolutionary and Napoleonic France in the 1790s the Royal Navy was supported and equipped by the most modern dockyards in Europe.

Unlike the other naval dockyards, those at Chatham, Plymouth and Portsmouth were homes of the fleet; they possessed large natural harbours where ships could either be laid up or moored, ready for immediate use if required. They were also ordnance and victualling yards and by the end of the eighteenth century all three had naval hospitals; rather surprisingly, they only acquired barracks towards the end of the nineteenth century.

Chatham is important because it escaped both the serious wartime bomb damage of Devonport and the post-war naval development of both Devonport and Portsmouth. Its Georgian naval buildings are particularly fine. They include large timber-framed workshops and mast houses, which were started in 1753, but before their completion were modified (in 1755) to form an immense (119 x 55 feet, or 36.2 x 16.7 metres), roofed, open space where a master shipwright and his assistants could draw out a complete and detailed cross section of a warship. This was where the lines of HMS *Victory* were first drawn out while her masts and spars were made in the workshop below. Other fine buildings at Chatham include the only known purpose-built sail loft to have survived in a Royal Dockyard. But the Navy Board were careful with their money and the wooden pillars that still support the ground floor are from a seventeenth-century warship, which we must presume was being taken apart at the time. The building was completed in the mid-1720s. Other important facilities included the ropery, where rope and cordage continue to be made and maintained, using the original Georgian and Victorian machinery. In its heyday it was capable of producing rope in vast quantities from hemp stored in purpose-built warehouses. Although less celebrated, we ought perhaps to treat Chatham Dockyard with all the care, love and respect we accord to royal palaces and cathedrals. It is every bit as remarkable.

* * *

Trade, like the industrialisation that accompanied it, happened in different ways in various places, and not necessarily all at the same time. Most of the research has been at sites where early industry is well attested, such as Coalbrookdale, or around major towns and cities where modern development has provided the resources for large excavations; this probably explains why more outlying parts of Britain appear not to have played such a major role. However, a recent survey of the Whitehaven coast of Cumbria by David Cranstone and Simon Roper has shown that the roots of industry there lay firmly in the Middle Ages and that the process of rapid entrepreneurial expansion – a revolution if ever there was one – happened rapidly, but in the earlier seventeenth century.[36]

The Whitehaven survey was commissioned by the National Trust who needed a management plan for a three-kilometre length of shoreline, a full kilometre wide. The obvious signs on the surface were of modern coal-mining but on closer investigation the specially commissioned survey was able to demonstrate that coal was being mined and salt extracted as early as the thirteenth century. This medieval industry was organised by the St Bees and Wetheral priories, and seems to have involved the very early use of coal to boil water – a technique that was not widely adopted elsewhere for some two centuries. However, the process of industrialisation along the Cumbrian coast seems to have changed gear sharply in 1630 when Sir Christopher Lowther took over the existing coal mines and saltworks and transformed the industry, building new units and exporting coal to Ireland. The Lowther estate enterprises prospered and eventually, at the turn of the seventeenth and eighteenth centuries, led to the building of a new harbour and planned residential town at Whitehaven. By 1690 this new town rivalled Liverpool to the south, with a population of some two thousand, and for a while in the mid-eighteenth century was Britain's sixth largest port.[37]

In recent years historical archaeology has become better informed about places like the Whitehaven coast, Coalbrookdale or, indeed, the early textile industry around Manchester and it could be objected that such studies show an unhealthy interest in too much detail. That is until one reads them. Only then does it become clear that these regional projects are actually concerned with the inter-relationships of the various interests involved in the development of entire landscapes, including landholdings, fields, settlement patterns, housing, workshops, mines, factories and infrastructure.[38] This broadening of scope at the regional level has given rise to a number of general questions which require a wider overview if they, too, are to be answered satisfactorily. This is undoubtedly one of the principal reasons why historical archaeology has turned its attention to countries outside Britain. It also helps to explain why associated topics, such as naval protection and processes of trade, are coming under closer scrutiny.

Today large ports like Europort at Rotterdam are scenes of vast bridge cranes, stacks of containers, trucks, railways and precious little else. The scale is such that humans appear to be ants. But it was very different in the quite recent past and I can still vaguely recall a visit I made with my father to the London Docks in the 1950s, when the family firm had invested money in a shipload of sugar from Peru. I remember standing on the deck and looking down into the darkness of the great hold where four stevedores were shovelling raw sugar into large tubs that the cranes then winched out. The conditions the men were working in were quite appalling: hot, airless and with an overpowering sticky-sweet smell. But the scale was undoubtedly human and not too dissimilar from what I might have seen there two hundred years earlier, where men would also have been working with their hands and minds (having done my fair share, I detest the idea that manual labour requires no brains).

In the later twentieth century ports and their dockside facilities have come under close archaeological scrutiny as part of the process of regeneration of many of Britain's redundant docklands. In most instances the original docks that were built close to city centres have closed in favour of new container facilities in deeper waters further out, where larger ships can be dealt with more cost effectively. So the old London Docks have closed and the ships now berth at Tilbury, in Essex, and in Liverpool the new container port is well to the north of the old docks which have been redeveloped as offices and leisure facilities. I freely confess that my immediate reaction on hearing that this was to happen was one of gloom, but over the years I have made a series of visits to Liverpool and I have to say the authorities there have done the conversion very well indeed. Although one could never hope to recapture the hustle, bustle and smells of the original docks, the buildings have been superbly restored and, of course, there is the sea – or, rather, the Mersey estuary. Seagulls and salt breezes do their bit to restore some of the lost atmosphere of the time when Liverpool was one of the premier ports of the British Empire.

We tend to think of Liverpool as a relatively recent phenomenon, mostly of the eighteenth and nineteenth centuries, and as such it has become identified with the trading side of the Industrial Revolution. But as with the revolution, Liverpool had been active and under way as a trading centre long before 1750, even laying aside the opening of the first dock in the early eighteenth century, which I'll come to shortly. The town had already ceased to be a fishing village in the later Middle Ages and now earned its income from regular trade with Ireland and Scotland. In the sixteenth century regular contacts were established with the Atlantic ports of France, Spain and Portugal and with North America by the mid-seventeenth.

At this point I should acknowledge that, together with Bristol, Hull and London, the merchants and shipowners of Liverpool earned much of their wealth through the despicable slave trade. Nothing can ever undo that. It was a part of the so-called 'North Atlantic triangle', which I mentioned earlier in this chapter. But so far as I know, although they were treated as commodities, slaves were never accommodated in the warehouses that still grace the old dock area. Of course, we have lost quite a few of these large industrial buildings, but enough survive to provide a remarkably vivid picture of dockside life in the eighteenth and nineteenth centuries.[39]

Had I been offered the entire coastline of Britain to build a port, I doubt whether I would ever have selected Merseyside, where the tidal range is huge and the river's flow both fast and treacherous. But there were other more important factors in Liverpool's favour. Communications with major production centres inland were good and became even better during the eighteenth and nineteenth centuries with the arrival of canals and railways. Most importantly, it faced west – towards the Atlantic, the Americas, Africa and thence to the Far East.

The huge tidal range and other problems caused by the silting up and movement of natural and artificial channels led the port authorities to opt for enclosed docks which vessels entered at high tide. The huge dock gates were shut before the tide began to ebb, and the ships within the dock could then be loaded or unloaded safely. It was an expensive system to build, but it worked efficiently with warehouses close to the water's edge where goods could be stored directly off the vessels. We are fortunate to have an accurate illustration of the first Liverpool dock, which opened in 1715. It shows the dock crowded with vessels.[40] Apart from expense, the main problem with the system was its lack of flexibility, which meant that it was difficult to modify or expand a dock. As a result, it was found to be simpler and more cost effective to start again and build afresh. This process of constant renewal, as a series of larger docks was constructed to accommodate the growing size of vessels, has left Liverpool and archaeology the finest set of historic dockyards anywhere.

I mentioned earlier that historical archaeology makes use of any source of information that can be found to throw light on daily life in the past. These resources include a wealth of topographical prints and paintings, mostly housed in the reserve collections of the museums, galleries and archives of Britain.[41] Just as we might take a photograph of where we live, people in the past also wanted to record their surroundings. Sometimes they had the talent to do this themselves and there must be tens of thousands of watercolour paintings of nineteenth-century Britain, mostly done by the women of middle-class Victorian households, sometimes under the supervision of a visiting professional artist. Until recently, people have taken such things for granted, but increasingly we realise their value as historical documents and, indeed, as artworks.

In addition to informal topographical paintings and drawings, a number of artists and printmakers realised that there was a market for their work in the various towns and cities of Britain, whose populations were becoming increasingly prosperous. These people were educated and were prepared to buy views of their towns provided, of course, that they were detailed, were preferably annotated and reasonably accurate; otherwise they would have made their owners look ridiculous. These views became known as 'prospects' and their greatest exponents were the Buck brothers, Samuel and Nathaniel, who together perfected the art of the topographical print.[42] Their output was prodigious and the accuracy and quality of their illustrations was generally first-rate. The timing of their work was unintentionally superb, as it provides the single best historical record of England and Wales immediately before the impact of the Industrial Revolution. The Bucks are best known for their Principal Series of (eighty-three) Town Prospects, which appeared between 1728 and 1753. The prints of this series are panoramic and highly detailed; some, such as the series of five showing London from Westminster to the City, join together to form a hugely long composite view. The Principal Series was preceded by the First Series of (ten) Town Prospects, drawn by Samuel alone; these were published between 1721 and 1725.

I mentioned that the Buck brothers were not the only publishers of topographical prints, but they were the best and among the most profitable. The production of a prospect was a commercial operation that depended for its success on finding a list of subscribers prepared to pay a good price for the finished work. It required very careful marketing before it had actually been produced, although preliminary sketches would have been done and the actual point from where the prospect would be drawn would be known, and often advertised. Pricing was crucially important and it helped if the list of subscribers could include some big names, which were often then emblazoned across the print as dedicatees. The Prospect of Wakefield, for example, is conspicuously dedicated to Lord Carmarthen; that of York to Thomas Earl of Stafford.[43] The Principal Series was marketed very much better than the First Series, of mainly northern town views, and the list of subscribers for the five London prospects of the Principal Series numbered some 1,350 people, including a generous sprinkling of bishops and bankers. Some would have been surprised when they received their sets of London prints to find that they had also paid for a view of Portsmouth – 'as advertised' (but in much smaller print).

But to return to Liverpool and its docks and warehouses, one of the most important to have survived, largely intact, is the Albert Dock, which opened in 1846. Its designer, Jesse Hartley, was appointed engineer to the Port Authority in 1824 and the Albert Dock was the culmination of a distinguished career. Like the very first dock at Liverpool, his consisted of a square basin enclosed but now surrounded by uniform warehouses and other buildings.[44] By the time Hartley had completed his Albert Dock, Liverpool had become the dominant exporting port in Britain, with no less than 45 per cent of the total trade, when measured by value. And this despite the abolition of the slave trade in 1807. By this time, too, Britain's export market was starting to extend beyond the North Atlantic, to India, China and South America. The figures give some idea of the scale of Liverpool's growth during the nineteenth century: in 1800 some 4,000 vessels arrived in the port; by 1871 that figure had risen to over 19,000.[45]

The archaeological evidence for the prosperity brought to ports by merchants, shipowners, shipbuilders and ship repairers was not confined to the waterfront. In fact, its lasting legacy was to the townscape not just of Liverpool, but of Birkenhead, on the other side of the Mersey. In recent years Birkenhead has undergone something of a revival, with the general recognition that its park, which was designed by Sir Joseph Paxton and opened in 1847, was the most successful of the early urban parks, and its influence was to be widespread both in Britain and abroad, for example, in Central Park in New York.[46]

The increasing prosperity of the rising middle class led to the construction of a number of classically-inspired developments in Britain's towns and cities. The schemes themselves were generally excellent, but as they often relied on the fickle property market for their full realisation, what we see today is not always true to the purity of the original inspiration. Of course, there are exceptions: Bath is a fine example of later eighteenth-century town planning.[47] But one of the best, if perhaps less known, of these early grand designs is that by James Craig of Edinburgh's New Town (1767), which, although very fine indeed, is by no means what its designer had originally intended. By contrast, most of the West End of London's planned developments of the later eighteenth and early nineteenth centuries, for example in Belgravia and the Duke of Bedford estates in Bloomsbury, were better capitalised and were able to draw on a larger and more prosperous property market; as a consequence their realisation has generally been more complete. The Lowthers' plan for their Cumbrian New Town at Whitehaven was another well-managed success.

Other planned urban developments in the industrial north-west, however, encountered problems at this time, including William Laird's scheme for Birkenhead. But these were unexpected problems, born of success and expansion. Laird was a hugely successful shipyard owner and in 1825 commissioned an architect, who had earlier been a part of the Edinburgh New Town project, to lay out Hamilton Square. This was to be the focus of his new town. Sadly, further progress towards the completion of Laird's plans fell victim to the town's rapid development and was swamped by unplanned commercial growth. A similar fate awaited other orderly developments in the north-west, at Ashton-under-Lyne (1780s and 1820s) and Barrow-in-Furness (1856), where the smoke and grime of industry confined middle-class house-buyers to the burgeoning suburbs.[48]

Any discussion of trade in post-medieval Britain must inevitably concentrate on the urban changes brought about during the early industrial era. So I want to redress the balance and close this chapter with some thoughts on trade in rural Britain at this time. We saw in the first chapter that the world of agriculture had gone through some major changes which resulted in the growth of the new farming areas. These regions only worked because they could sell their products, first by way of markets situated around the region's periphery and latterly through others sited close to roads and railways. Often the roots of these markets were very ancient indeed.

Fairs and markets have been an essential feature of British rural life since the Neolithic period. Fairs are usually annual and last anything from three days to six weeks. Markets are generally weekly and last for a day. Both are important socially, especially in those areas where the rural population is widely dispersed. They are required not just to trade surplus goods, but for livestock farmers to acquire new blood lines. Even today the oldest of the livestock fairs, the Corby Glen Sheep Fair, in south Lincolnshire, which was granted a charter by Henry III in 1238, specialises in the sale of breeding ewes and rams. It is still held close to the Feast of the Assumption in late August or early September, in time for farmers to acquire rams for the new season. Lambs conceived in October would be born twenty-one weeks later, in March, to coincide with the first flush of new spring grass. In lowland counties, such as Lincolnshire, this would also fit in with the arable cycle, but in upland areas the tradition was to lamb later, usually in April, when weather conditions had changed for the better. Today, as in the nine-teenth and twentieth centuries, the Corby Glen Sheep Fair is accompanied by a three-day fun fair – a remnant of the lively social side of most farmers' fairs.

The fair used to be held in the village but has recently moved to a field just outside, where the photograph shown in the plates section was taken. We bought a couple of fine Lleyn rams there in 2006, after an excellent day out in the Wolds. Then the 2007 fair was cancelled because of disease scares and, as a consequence, those of 2008 and 2009 were called off at short notice. In an early draft of this manuscript I wrote: 'It's a sad reflection of our times that the future of this most ancient country festival is now in serious doubt.' I can now report that the 2010 fair took place, as usual in early September. Hooray!

The 2006 Corby Glen fair was a very large gathering and I well remember walking across the field trying to spot anything that might give future archaeologists a clue that so many people and livestock had ever come together in that particular field. Apart from a few crisp packets that might have accumulated in a field dyke, and some possible soil phosphate enhancement caused by sheep droppings, there was nothing that would have betrayed its location to posterity. It can be salutary to remind archaeologists that documents can sometimes record quite major events for which there is virtually no 'real' evidence in the ground.

Before the Norman Conquest fairs were held by common agreement, but after 1066 these customary markets became regulated, usually by the granting of royal charters, which were keenly sought by medieval landowners because of the taxes they could collect if the market was held on their land. Nearly three thousand markets were authorised in England during the thirteenth century, but numbers fell in the next century, following the economic decline and the Black Death of 1348–9. Sometimes the larger annual fairs would be held outside towns and villages, but weekly markets and smaller fairs took place in formal marketplaces or on village greens where the fair was marked by a market cross. Public markets, where a variety of goods, including groceries, were sold by merchants and stallholders began to be housed within buildings from the seventeenth century onwards, although a few medieval examples (such as Leadenhall Market, London, established in 1493) are known.[49] Livestock markets were generally held in the open air until the later nineteenth and early twentieth centuries when open-sided roofed structures were often erected close by railway sidings. Today most livestock markets are held under cover.

We know from anthropology that trade is not just about exchanging goods and services for money at a profit. It is also about social relations with people, some of whom may not be particularly friendly. So the rules of engagement must be stated clearly in advance of any meeting, and the place where the transaction takes place must be seen as neutral. For these and other reasons, trade can be seen as a means of maintaining peace, even if sometimes it may be to one party's consistent advantage, as the history of the British Empire indeed makes so clear. Although some may regret that Britain no longer dominates world trade, it seems to me that at long last we are seeing the repayment of some very long delayed imperial debts. If the past is anything to go by, it will be a process that will last for centuries rather than decades.

CHAPTER SEVEN

The Big Society: Faith, Justice and Charity

HUMAN SOCIETIES are greater than the sum of their parts. But if it is to survive and prosper, every social group, be it village, town, city or nation, requires somewhere for those parts, the people, to meet. Of course these places don't have to be roofed, and most weren't in earlier prehistoric times, but as communities became bigger and meetings were needed in winter, large communal buildings became necessary. The 'excuses' or reasons for convening the meetings could vary from one culture to another. Religion played an important part, but so too (as we have just seen) did markets, the administration of justice, local and wider government and, of course, pleasure in the form of feasts and parties. But it would be a mistake to assume that any one of these gatherings was convened for a single purpose, despite what the organisers themselves often believed.

Take the case of religion. It was possible, indeed probable, that other business would be transacted outside the church or temple before or after the ceremony. That is why even today members of congregations often foregather in the churchyard, ostensibly to have a few words of farewell or greeting with the vicar or minister, but actually to talk among themselves. These informal sub-meetings are essential because they oil the wheels of society. It is in small gatherings of this sort that the preliminary moves that will ultimately lead to new marriages, business partnerships and property deals are made; and it would be a huge mistake to think for a moment that churches, to name just one public building, were erected to the glory of God and for the conduct of services alone. There was far more to them than that.

Although it could be argued that the Middle Ages bequeathed Britain the richest possible architectural legacy, it must also be admitted that there is also a certain uniformity to it. Put at its simplest, you don't get pointy arches in Norman architecture, or wide windows in Early English. In part this can be attributed to the development of stone masons' technique, but I also believe it mirrors a society that accepted a single version of Christianity and a style of feudalism that, if not wholly uniform, was at least structured in ways that would have been recognisable to people travelling across the country. So although one can indeed discern differences in, say, the monastic architecture of the Benedictines from that of the Cistercians or the Cluniacs, I would hesitate to do so myself and would need to be accompanied and encouraged by a specialised architectural historian, were I to attempt it.

In the post-medieval period this architectural uniformity begins to break down and we also see churches that had been built in the Middle Ages being used rather differently. Both, however, reflect broader changes that were happening within society, which is why I wanted to emphasise that churches were places where other, non-religious communications and transactions also took place. So I will begin this chapter with two examples of churches that are personal favourites. The first example shows how medieval buildings were adapted to play new roles, the second how a new building was created for a specific purpose that, at first glance, might seem medieval but was actually rather more personal and modern.

I must confess that I adore church architecture and never miss an opportunity to pop into one of Britain's 14,000 or so medieval churches, provided, that is, the doors aren't locked, as is too often the case nowadays. I usually have a copy of Simon Jenkins' *England's Thousand Best Churches** or one of the Nikolaus Pevsner county guides with me to help unravel the architectural history. Pevsner, who was something of a purist when it comes to ecclesiastical architecture, will often bemoan the fact that later tombs and monuments have 'spoilt' a fine old medieval church. But have they?

Surely even the original master masons never intended their buildings to be architectural museums. Certainly they built them for primarily religious reasons, but they were also men of the world and

* Penguin Books, 2000.

they must have known that they would be used for all sorts of different purposes, including the expression of personal loss and the promotion of family prestige, through the erection of grand tombs. Now I concede that Westminster Abbey is so stuffed full of monuments that it can sometimes be hard to appreciate the great building in which they sit, but one glance up and into the window tracery and vaulting of the roof will transcend the clutter at ground level. Up there is where the builders still express the purity of their original intentions. Down at ground level the place is merely human, but on a very grand scale.

A friend of mine once described the monuments in a church we were visiting as 'the detritus of history'. I know what he meant, but as an archaeologist who spends his time dealing with the detritus of prehistory I had little sympathy with this view. Far from being rubbish, I find that church memorials can reach out across the centuries and touch me personally in a way that a well-executed pilaster or balustrade never can.[1] Besides, memorials can tell some fascinating human stories about individuals, and, perhaps just as important, about the standing and status of local families.

After the Dissolution of the Monasteries, the early post-medieval period witnessed the rise of individual wealth and influence. It was then that many aristocratic families felt able, or obliged, to express their new-found prosperity in the form of fine church memorials. I cannot think of a better illustration of the changes that happened during this fascinating time than the interior of the parish church of St Mary the Virgin, Bottesford, in Leicestershire.[2] Within a century or so, the post-medieval tombs are all about people, rather than the Almighty alone. Sure, there may be a rather perfunctory 'To the Glory of God', but they then go on to list details of the men and women buried beneath; very often too, their wives, husbands and children (who are frequently represented by charming, idealised miniature statutes) and the principal achievements of their lives.

Bottesford lies just 3½ miles (6 kilometres) to the south of Belvoir (pronounced Beevor) Castle, the ancestral seat of the Earls of Rutland. St Mary's is the church where the tombs and memorials of no fewer than eight successive Earls, together with their wives and children, can be found. The monuments line not just the walls of the chancel, but the central aisle as well! Reading between the lines, this crowd of monuments obviously rather annoyed Nikolaus Pevsner, but I have to say I find them a joy: a series of superb celebrations of Tudor, Jacobean and early Georgian magnificence, blissfully insensitive to their surroundings, and only competing with each other in splendour.[3]

There are earlier aristocratic tombs and monuments at Bottesford, but the principal sequence starts with Thomas Manners, the 1st Earl (d. 1545), and ends with John, the 8th Earl (d. 1679). Their artistic and architectural confidence speaks volumes about the social changes that had begun and then gathered pace during and after the English Renaissance.[4] Incidentally, the family later became even grander, as Dukes of Rutland and Marquises of Granby, and it was 'the Great Marquis' (1721–70), who was an MP at twenty-one and a brilliant leader of cavalry during the Seven Years War, but is chiefly known for the many Marquis of Granby pubs which were named in his honour and still survive.

I said I would start this chapter with two examples of churches for which I have a soft spot and the second is possibly my favourite, not so much for its architecture, or even its setting, but for something intangible that I can only describe rather feebly as 'atmosphere'. I have admitted before now that I'm not a believer in God or religion, but I found the tiny church at Little Gidding, in Huntingdonshire, quite haunting the first time I visited it. In many ways it recalled that day ten years ago when I walked out across the wind-swept sands of the foreshore at Holme-next-the-Sea, in Norfolk, to view the gnarled roots of the four-thousand-year-old, upside-down oak tree at the centre of the site now known as Seahenge.[5] Both the church and the timber circle were small, even tiny, by the standards of others we know, but both too told remarkably vivid human stories. At Little Gidding we have records of the Ferrar community who rebuilt an earlier church there, and at Seahenge we have the extraordinarily detailed evidence of tree rings and axe marks to help us re-create those few weeks in the late spring or early summer of 2049 BC, when maybe two hundred people convened behind the coastal dunes to create a monument to their ancestors.

Although the church of St John the Evangelist at Little Gidding is located just three miles west of the A1(M), some eight miles south of Peterborough, it still manages somehow to be remarkably peaceful.[6] One might suppose that such a location would bring the noise and constant movement of modern British life uncomfortably close, but in fact the surrounding landscape, which conceals the tiny church and its hamlet, still manages to be remote and rural. I was delighted to see fresh dollops of mud on the road and the two offending tractors had to pull over to let me past as we drove down the narrow lane to the church, on a freezing cold afternoon early in January. Both drivers gave cheery waves as if they had known us from childhood. When we arrived I was also delighted to see the car park empty and we sat there for a few moments with the windows wound down, collecting our thoughts. There wasn't a breath of wind and the only sound was the calling of rooks high in the trees of the thick wood behind the church. I remember thinking that the sounds could have been nature's call to prayer, but the unseen birds were probably just thinking about their new season's nests, much as they would have done at this time and place back in the 1630s.

'Little Gidding' is, of course, the title of the last of T. S. Eliot's *Four Quartets*, which is probably why the name will be familiar to most people. Eliot visited the church in May 1936 and signed his name in the visitors' book. Another poet, Stephen Spender, described 'Little Gidding' as the furthest point in Eliot's spiritual exploration, so he was clearly deeply moved by his short stay, just as we were. Later Eliot was to play an important role in saving Little Gidding church from decay and neglect. Apart from Eliot, distinguished visitors included King Charles I who came no fewer than three times, in the 1630s, in 1642 and on 2 May 1646, when he sought refuge from Parliamentary troops, who were both numerous and popular in the area, Oliver Cromwell having been born and brought up at nearby Huntingdon. Other well-known names at Little Gidding included the poets George Herbert and Richard Crashaw, both of whom were personal friends of Nicholas Ferrar, the remarkable man who founded the religious community there, around 1625.

Artefacts can tell us about people but rarely about individuals, and when they do we almost never know their names. As a prehistorian I have found one-to-one links with the past have been very rare indeed, and I have already written about my first such experience when I came across the fingerprints of somebody from the Bronze Age on a clay loom weight.[7] My second encounter had nothing whatsoever to do with my professional life and purists might say that it wasn't even archaeological, although a most remarkable artefact was at the centre of it all. Ten years ago, along with hundreds of others, I went to Buckingham Palace to receive an MBE, not for archaeology but for 'services to tourism'. Such occasions are all about standing around and getting into line and I remember thinking as I looked in a mirror at all the other black-and-white tail-coated figures that we looked like so many Holstein cows waiting to be admitted to the royal milking parlour. Anyhow, I had the extraordinary good fortune to spend half an hour standing directly alongside that remarkable triple portrait of King Charles I, by Sir Anthony van Dyck. The picture shows his face from the left, the right and the front. I couldn't take my eyes off it. Yes, it did prove the cliché correct: like everyone, his left and right sides were different, but all three views, especially the main one, showed a kind, intelligent but, sadly, a very weak man, too. The slightly watery eyes did it for me: they screamed, or rather, whimpered, weakness. And I felt so sorry for him.

Ferrar had always been a man of a contemplative frame of mind, but he also lived in the real world and in 1622 took over as Deputy Treasurer of the Virginia Company from his elder brother, John, who admired him greatly and wrote his biography. Unfortunately for Nicholas, however, the Company was disbanded in 1624 on the orders of the King and Parliament, as part of a policy aimed at appeasing Spain. Bruised by this, he decided to withdraw what family money he could salvage from the Company and retire to the countryside and live a life of prayer.

In the seventeenth and eighteenth centuries many people living in and around the Fens suffered from malaria (the disease was endemic there), and Nicholas Ferrar was no exception. When he retired to his new home at Little Gidding in 1626 he was already much weakened by the sickness, which was to kill him eventually, in December 1637. But during the intervening years he and his close family established the small religious community based around Thomas Cranmer's English Prayer Book (1549). This featured hourly gatherings in the house and the small church that Ferrar rebuilt entirely, on the site of a slightly larger medieval precursor which was much decayed and had been used as a barn.

The main work of the community was the production of illustrated 'Concordances' or 'Gospel Harmonies' which were versions of the Bible that had been edited, essentially with scissors and paste so that the various well-known stories were mounted alongside each other, allowing ready comparisons to be made. King Charles I was much impressed by the quality of the work and Ferrar give him a special royal Concordance.

Ferrar had a formidable family. His mother was very religiously inclined and liked to listen to long sermons. In fact, I suspect she would have driven me to violence, because no sooner had the family moved to Little Gidding than she urged that the church be rebuilt, despite the dilapidated state of the house. A few weeks before his death, Nicholas passed the running of the community to his nephew John, who died early, in 1640. Soon the small community was falsely condemned as popish and was ransacked by Puritans in 1646. It came to an end in the 1650s, but Ferrar's original vision continues to inspire and the community has been revived at least twice subsequently; there is still a religious presence at Ferrar House, albeit more loosely structured than in the seventeenth century.

On the face of it, then, the Little Gidding community might be seen as essentially medieval; after all, it did share the form and structure of many monastic services, which had been used by Cranmer as the basis for his English Prayer Book. But there the similarity ended. Ferrar's community was essentially idiosyncratic and could never have happened in the Middle Ages when few men – not even royalty – considered themselves more powerful than the Church. Ferrar was the son of a prosperous Tudor merchant, so he didn't even have the authority of an established aristocrat, yet he and a few like-minded individuals established a religious community that was admired by some of the greatest minds of the time, including a rather sad and lonely King. Although structured in an altogether different fashion and with disciplines that are unheard of today, in many respects Ferrar's community had more in common with some of the 'alternative' experimental communities of our own time than with the rigidly structured, even corporate, monastic traditions of the Middle Ages.

Churches were the principal public buildings in Britain throughout the Middle Ages, but all of that was to change in post-medieval times with the increasing importance of secular interests. So I want to conclude this brief discussion of the ecclesiastical world with two case studies: first, of graveyards and gravestones, and then of a Nonconformist chapel.

The study of graveyards illustrates some of the problems that still confront post-medieval archaeologists. I suppose, like the world of industrial archaeology we discussed in Chapter 5, this study reflects the transition from a series of hobbyists' pastimes towards a discipline that is attempting to provide explanations of general relevance. Although thousands of graveyards have been plotted and planned, there has still been no attempt to draw all the information together to tell a coherent story. One reason for this is that most graveyards are of primary interest to local people, local historians and those who chase after genealogies – an increasingly popular pursuit. But at last graveyards are now being recognised as uniquely important resources not just of local stories, but of past attitudes to life and death.[8] The development of graveyards, and the position of the gravestones within them, can reveal a great deal about the changing social structure of a town or village, which is why it is absolutely essential that they should remain in place and never be moved to the cemetery's edges, even if it does make for easier maintenance. Personally I detest neatly mown graveyards and would much prefer to see long grass, butterflies and wild flowers surrounding the graves. Even in death, it would seem, we must bow to the modern obsession with neatness.

I have already discussed how successive waves of plague, and a general decline in the population from the mid-fourteenth century onwards, changed the labour market profoundly and led to the gradual decline of feudalism. This process was to gather pace rapidly in early post-medieval times and we see increasing importance being attached to individuals. Whereas medieval tombs might sometimes commemorate a knight and his lady, those of post-medieval times routinely portray successive wives and children who are often shown kneeling piously around the outside of the tomb. Ladies frequently become the object of memorials in their own right in the sixteenth and seventeenth centuries, as can be seen in the particularly fine collection of seventeenth- and eighteenth-century tombstones preserved in St Magnus Cathedral, Kirkwall, Orkney. These vividly carved and stylised tombstones made an instant impression on me when I first visited that fine cathedral some ten years ago. They really are extraordinarily direct and striking.

One of the finest is the gravestone of Elizabeth Cuthbert, who died in 1685. Although the wife of a then famous man (he was Minister of the Cathedral), her tombstone remains hers alone and it is rich in the symbolism of the time. As Sarah Tarlow puts it, the carving has a 'strong upward dynamic'.[9] It is arranged in three zones. At ground level a skull and crossbones symbolises mortality and an hourglass the brevity of earthly life. Above her head she is being offered the crown of eternal life and overhead is the arch of Heaven (complete with a crescent moon and stars), and above that two winged angels. So, although the gravestone is devoted to an individual, the message it conveys is essentially a general one: the inevitability of death and the hope of a life everlasting. Skulls, cadavers, hourglasses and snuffed-out candles are so common on tombstones and memorials of the seventeenth and earlier eighteenth century that they must have seemed almost clichéd to mourners at the time.

By the nineteenth century we see the widespread introduction of mass-produced gravestones. These almost never include skulls and other reminders of death. Instead, the emphasis has moved on to the individual making the (assumed) journey to the afterlife. The journey is taken as read and now the text of the tombstone provides details of the individual's life and relationships: 'Beloved wife of John Smith and mother of Elizabeth etc, etc'. Often the inscriptions reflect the rather sentimental language that was fashionable, stressing in fulsome terms how good the person was and how much they are missed by their survivors. In Victorian times the departed soul's journey is not seen as a passage to the next world so much as a sea voyage, where the survivors are left standing at the water's edge, alone but soon to be reunited: 'not lost but gone before'.

The single most important development in post-medieval church architecture must surely be the building of many thousands of Nonconformist chapels and meeting houses. These have recently been the subject of four major surveys by the Royal Commission on the Historical Monuments of England.[10] Like their other projects, these are superb reports. The buildings themselves were often deliberately designed to avoid a feeling of 'churchiness', which was too close to the Anglican Church that these people were escaping from. Some of the very best (one of my personal favourites is the Wesleyan chapel at Little Walsingham, Norfolk) recall contemporary domestic architecture but add an air of dignity or reserved transcendence which I find quite captivating. We tend to forget that many of the smaller chapels – and I think here of the numerous Primitive Methodist chapels that can still be found across Fenland – were erected by public subscription, often in the teeth of fierce opposition from the established Church and the local gentry. Given such fraught origins, it is hardly surprising that sometimes these splinter groups had to adopt gradual measures to get established at all. And this brings me to my final religious case study.

The 'Tin Tabernacle' in Havelock Street, Desborough, Northamptonshire, was built in the late nineteenth century as a temporary chapel, roofed and clad with corrugated iron. More importantly, it has recently been the subject of a careful excavation.[11] Sadly, however, the Desborough building is rather incomplete, so to give an impression of what these structures might have looked like in their prime I have illustrated the best preserved example in Britain, in Hackney, east London, which I am glad to report has been Listed at Grade II.

Today the Desborough church is used as a garage, having endured a period as a small fire station, a process which involved the insertion of barn-like double doors into its west wall. This wall forms the approach to the building which was made even less auspicious when the fire brigade tacked square-section modern wall sheets onto the earlier galvanised corrugated iron. But go round the back and the building's true origins become apparent.

I've come across corrugated iron on more than one occasion when excavating on modern sites, but until I read the report on the Tin Tabernacle I had no idea it was so old. The earliest corrugated-iron sheeting was being mass-produced in Britain in the 1830s, but it was not until the invention of galvanising (which involves the addition of a thin coating of zinc to prevent rusting) in France (1837) that it took off as a cheap and popular building material. I suspect it will be with us for some time to come, because, unlike plastics, it doesn't go brittle after exposure to sunlight. I have long been an admirer of sheds, many of which are made from old doors and corrugated iron.[12] These, surely, are the new and genuinely vernacular architecture and I wonder how long it will be before the authorities in their wisdom decide to Schedule an entire allotment garden, plus its sheds? But I digress.

The Tin Tabernacle is located near Station Road in Desborough and it seems reasonable to suppose that the materials for its building were transported there by rail. In the late nineteenth and early twentieth centuries buildings like these were important because, being very cheap to buy and build (they cost around £100 at the time – the equivalent of about £8,000 today), they allowed small projects to get started. The Desborough building is based around a timber frame and is lined on the interior with thin tongue-and-groove pine panelling. Most probably it was bought in kit form from a number of companies that are known to have supplied such buildings. The actual foundations were minimal – usually a dump of brick rubble – and the sites were often small, having been donated by local landowners and developers. Once a sizeable congregation had been established, it might then become feasible either to move to somewhere better, or else demolish the temporary building and erect another in its place.

I began this chapter with the thought that ancient and modern societies have only held together if the people comprising them are able to assemble. Traditionally, such gatherings have been based around religion which has provided the necessary social adhesive. In more recent times, as British society has become increasingly diverse we have seen the rise of many Nonconformist Christian sects and the appearance of entirely new, non-Christian faiths. We tend to think of the latter as essentially a modern phenomenon, but in actual fact Jews formed a significant sector of British urban society through most of the Middle Ages. Several synagogues have exceptional architectural merit and have been Listed. Arguably the finest, and oldest, is the Bevis Marks Synagogue of 1699–1701, on the edge of the City of London, which was founded following the Jewish resettlement of 1656, during the Commonwealth, and has been in continuous use since its completion.[13]

Mosques are now adding a welcome splash of exotic colour to many urban Victorian streets, but one of the earliest, and finest, may still be seen in the centre of, not Bradford or Burnley, but that epitome of middle-class respectability, Woking, in Surrey. Here the Shah Jehan

Mosque, which is northern Europe's oldest surviving mosque, was built by a most remarkable man, Dr Gottlieb Leitner, the son of Jewish converts to Protestantism, who founded his Oriental Institute there in the early 1890s.[14] Leitner died in 1899, ten years after the completion of the Shah Jehan Mosque. Sadly, his plans to pair the mosque with a Hindu temple fell through after his death, but the planned church of St Paul's was finished and can still be seen in Oriental Road. I need hardly add that there are lessons here for us today.

Religion and justice have always been different sides of the same coin. Today that link is still remembered when witnesses in court take their oath on the Bible. In the Middle Ages the Law and the Church were closely united, but after the Reformation those links became less direct, and had more to do with maintenance and enforcement of morals and morality than with the actual administration of justice. Certainly as late as the nineteenth century vicars or priests played significant roles at executions, in prison life and, indeed, in the dispensation of Poor Law relief, but as time passed the links between a single official religion and the judicial authorities grew weaker.

It would be a mistake, however, to see the administration of justice as a simple process in which the powers that be sought to maintain absolute standards of morality. Even in modern theocracies, as we are currently witnessing in places like Iran and Saudi Arabia, both power politics and popular pressure for reform can add many levels of complexity to an ostensibly simple picture of good versus evil. This is particularly true in periods of major social upheaval or change, such as the enclosure movement of the late eighteenth and early nineteenth centuries.

We saw in Chapter 1 that the widespread reorganisation of much of Midland and eastern England marked the birth of what was to become a new kind of rural Britain. These new landscapes were controlled by farmers and landowners and as part of the process most of the once communal moors and commons were in effect privatised. So far I have viewed these transformations as essentially an economic process that brought wealth to an increasingly large middle class of yeoman farmers, the more successful of whom were now the owners of small and medium-sized estates. But I want now to turn my attention to the impact of enclosure on non-landowning folk in rural communities who now found themselves faced by an altogether different world, in which they didn't even have access to common land and were now forced to play a marginal or at best minor role, usually as labourers. I intend to investigate their lives through their attitudes towards death.

The remote rural gibbet, with or without a dangling corpse, has become an essential background feature of any eighteenth-century costume drama, and gibbets have become a symbol of the harsh justice of the time. Two hundred years later they can still send a chill through the bones, even if they are known to be relatively recent replacements, like that at Caxton, which is visible on photographs taken in 1900. Like many others it's located at a crossroads, in this instance of the world's first turnpike and the Cambridge–Bedford road.[15]

When I was a boy, we used to drive past the Caxton gibbet on our way to Cambridge from our home in north Hertfordshire, and I can remember returning home and lying awake, haunted by thoughts of the poor unfortunate, slowly writhing away the final minutes of his life, watched by a small crowd of people by the roadside. In my nightmares I was next in line for the noose, but mercifully I'd awake before that dreadful moment came. Of course, I didn't know it then, but gibbets were not the same as gallows, where criminals were executed. Gibbets were where their bodies were exposed to the elements, to rot and decay (a process often slowed down by the application of coats of tar), without the benefit of burial in hallowed ground. Even in post-medieval times it was still widely believed that it was possible to make the criminal suffer further beyond, or rather outside, the grave. Suicides, too, were seen as having offended God and man, which is why their bodies were buried outside churchyards, at parish boundaries or beneath roads, where their ghosts would be confined, unable to haunt the living.

A recent study of gibbets and the 'deviant dead' in Norfolk has revealed a more complex story than the usual 'and let that be a warning to you all' explanation we were taught at school.[16] For a start, the act of hanging the dead body from a gibbet, whether chained or unchained, was often accompanied, not by cowering dread, but by celebration and drunken revelry, especially if the victim was known to have been guilty of a serious crime or crimes. Very often gibbets were positioned on open moor or common land and were removed when these were enclosed in the later eighteenth and nineteenth centuries. This positioning on unenclosed common land was certainly about visibility and display, but it also provides us with some important clues about people's attitudes to their surroundings in the later eighteenth century.

The location of most eighteenth-century Norfolk gibbets on common land and along parish boundaries provides us with a fascinating insight into contemporary attitudes to the land in a time of rapid landscape change. The origins of these practices lie in the Middle Ages, and even earlier, in Saxon times, when gallows and executions often took place at boundaries. Somewhat later in the Middle Ages the Crown took control of local justice from the major landowners and gallows were often positioned in empty spaces, atop mounds or sometimes on prehistoric barrows where they could be seen as symbols of royal authority, visible across large distances, especially from roads and settlements.[17] Of course, perceptions will change through time and we must not simply assume that Saxon and medieval beliefs continued unaltered into the eighteenth century, but it would nonetheless be fair to say that certain core values remained substantially the same.

The church and the parish were seen as a key element in the personal geography of most people, just as today we would see ourselves as being English, Welsh, Scottish or, indeed, British. Prior to enclosure the manor and the parish were the units around which people arranged the day-to-day management of the Open Fields. In later medieval and early modern times the system changed somewhat, but labourers, smallholders and small yeoman farmers still worked together as part of an agricultural community. The ties of community were further reinforced by annual ceremonies where parish boundaries and the edges of common land would be perambulated, and the principal points – which often had names that recalled death or burial, such as 'Piggs Grave', 'Mark's Grave' or 'Gallowshill Lane' – were rehearsed and remembered by all members of the community, but especially by the young.[18] Common land and the boundaries of the parish had become, in effect, symbols of the identity, strength and cohesion of the community itself. They provided far more than the mere 'sense of place' of modern times.

It has long been known that the actual process of enclosure often involved the destruction of ruins or prehistoric monuments that stood in the way of efficient arable farming, but less attention has been paid to the destruction of gibbets which had come to play an important part in most people's sense of local identity. That identity was, of course, being fundamentally damaged by the process of enclosure which is probably why the destruction of gibbets caused such public anger, at the time – but was soon forgotten. In her study of Norfolk gibbets, Nicola Whyte notes that the crowds 'that assembled to observe the removal of the gibbets probably constituted some of the final displays of communal sentiment before the commons were enclosed'.[19] Maybe that is why seemingly miraculous events were noted at these rather grim occasions: a starling's nest, complete with its young, had to be removed from the body of the criminal Stephen Watson in 1801. Echoing this, a few years later, the skull hanging from Bennington's gibbet revealed a blue tit and her family of nine or ten.[20] It's ironic, but once loathed criminals had acquired a new life within, rather than on the fringes of, the societies they had once preyed upon.

These grisly monuments were so potent because they were erected during the lifetimes of the people who had then to witness their destruction; but they had also come to symbolise the cohesion of the entire community which most people – rightly, as it happens – believed was being undermined by the increasing power not just of the existing gentry, but of a new rural middle class. It was a time of great change and we should not forget that to most ordinary country people much of it would have been very painful.

I shall finish this chapter with some thoughts on two topics which illustrate very different aspects of collective life in rural and urban Britain in the eighteenth and nineteenth centuries. The first has to do with buildings, the second with landscapes.

Most people are probably unaware that the large and sometimes rather stark but elegant, often Georgian-style (but usually early Victorian) buildings on the outskirts of many towns and large villages in England were, in fact, workhouses. These were built, in theory at least, for the relief of the poor. Very often today they have been converted into flats or retirement homes, but at least one, in Southwell,

Nottinghamshire, has been preserved as a museum by the National Trust. The former House of Labour and Union Workhouse at Gressenhall, Norfolk, also retains many original features, although its larger rooms have been converted into offices and an excellent Museum of Norfolk Rural Life.[21]

Many workhouses were converted to old people's homes and geriatric wards when the nineteenth-century Poor Laws were eventually replaced by the National Assistance Act of 1948. Money was short in post-war Britain, but the continued use of these institutions that had been so feared and dreaded by generations of working-class people caused huge upset. I shall never forget visiting an elderly lady when I was a young child in the early 1950s and being startled when she burst into tears, tightened her grip on my mother's hand and pleaded with her not to let 'them' put her in the workhouse, which had, in theory at least, been closed down some five years earlier. Looking back on this sad incident many years later, I began to realise that it was the moment when the distant past suddenly became real, a part of my own life, and not something remote, to be studied in a library or probed in an excavation.

But why was that elderly lady so terrified? In the Middle Ages the relief of poverty was paid for by the tithes returned to the parish church. In the early modern period the Poor Laws of 1536 and 1601 allowed begging to continue and made the relief of poverty the responsibility of the parish, much as it had been before.[22] It was by no means a perfect system, but it seems to have worked reasonably well. Unfortunates who had fallen on hard times were looked after by those who would have known them and who would have understood the reasons why they had come to such a sorry state. It was, however, a fairly makeshift system which began to creak when both rural and urban poverty increased during the eighteenth century, largely as a result of people leaving their parishes of birth to find paid work elsewhere. This was the period when the first workhouses began to appear and with them we also see initial indications that poverty was something to be despised. The term 'pauper' began to be used, and some workhouses insisted that their occupants wear a distinctive uniform (rather like the equally unenlightened current proposals for those on Community Service orders). By this time, too, many of the people in the workhouses would have been from outside the parish.

The Poor Law Amendment Act of 1834 rationalised the system, but in the process did much to humiliate and dehumanise the 'paupers' in its care. Central funds were administered by a commission which organised parishes into groups, or unions, who provided large union workhouses, such as that at Gressenhall in Norfolk, which combined the parishes of Mitford and Launditch. These union workhouses were run by boards of governors which included Church of England ministers, local magistrates and members elected by ratepayers (i.e. payers of local taxes). The regime within these workhouses was harsh, ostensibly to deter the lazy from 'sponging', but also because politicians hoped it would keep potential voters happy. So food was extremely plain, deliberately intended to be inferior to that which even the poorest working person could afford. But perhaps the nastiest requirement of all was the enforced separation of couples, with men and women housed in separate wings, which were entered through different doors. In pre-pension times the circumstances of many elderly couples without families to support them were such that they were forced to retire to the workhouse. In hindsight, the inhumanity seems tinged with vindictiveness: unmarried mothers, for example, had to wear distinctive clothing and were denied the only decent meal of the year, Christmas dinner. Many of the people sitting on governing boards disliked the new system and in some union workhouses older couples were allowed to live together; at Gressenhall that welcome reform occurred in 1853.

Some workhouses were successfully managed and, although conditions remained harsh throughout the nineteenth and into the twentieth century, this was also a reflection both of the original 'new' Poor Law Act and of the finance available at any one time. It could be said that governing boards made the best of a bad job. To return briefly to Gressenhall (which most would agree was generally well run), despite improvements in the second half of the nineteenth century, particularly to the nutrition and education of children, poor people in west Norfolk still regarded the place with horror.* As late as 1897 the local

---

* By no means everyone administering the new system approved of it. The notable Fenland magistrate and farmer, John Peck of Parson Drove (Cambridgeshire), thought the separation of men and women inhumane and in his unpublished diaries (now held in Wisbech Museum) bitterly objected to the new Poor Law.

East Dereham newspaper records that a man committed suicide rather than be sent there.[23]

The workhouses, however, were not the only institutional buildings being constructed in Britain. They were accompanied by a number of others – lunatic asylums (as they were then known), isolation and a variety of civilian and military hospitals – all of which led one of the leading specialists in this field to remark that 'The nineteenth century witnessed the institutionalisation of contemporary English society'.[24] One might have supposed that documentary sources would provide the main clues as to this process of institutionalisation, but archaeology, too, can provide some unexpected insights, most particularly when it comes to the setting of these places within their own, often secure, purpose-built landscapes.[25]

And now for my second topic – landscape. For many people, myself included, the gradual development and laying out of a garden is not just a hobby but a valuable creative experience. This might sound a touch pretentious, but I do seriously believe that many of us are gardeners because we have to be. If I didn't own the land, I would buy a window box, or a growbag. This is because gardening is a cyclical process of renewal and rejuvenation, and not just for the plants but for the gardener, too. That's why the great gardens, the Painshills and Stourheads of this world, still retain evidence of their constant growth and development. Of course, some people lack the confidence (or the foolhardiness) to create their own designs and seek instead the services of a garden designer. But even these people, unless they are excessively rich or stupid, will want to influence their designer's work, to put something of their own into the project. And, of course, we are all, amateurs and professionals alike, subject to the whims and fashions of the time, even if we try to avoid them. Contemporary styles and influences leave their traces in the ground and archaeologists are very good at both detecting and interpreting them.

In Chapter 2 I discussed the country estates and 'polite landscapes' that began to be created in ever-increasing numbers in the later eighteenth and early nineteenth centuries, as general prosperity increased and more people were able to acquire land. Many of these individuals belonged to the social classes that either ran or commissioned the construction of the new institutions of Victorian Britain. If they didn't actually own a small country estate themselves, they would have known people who did. Perhaps more importantly, they would have shared a common belief in the physical and mental benefits of a well-managed landscape, where soothing surroundings would calm disturbed minds and wholesome labour would mend damaged bodies. From this arose the Victorian concept of environmental discipline of the poor in which the workhouses themselves and the grounds in which they sat affected the 'treatment' of their inmates, as much as the regime they had to live by. Similar ideas lay behind the design of the grounds around other institutions, such as asylums, hospitals and orphanages.

The development of estate landscapes was a major feature of Georgian and Victorian times, but it would be a mistake to view these private institutions as physical creations alone. They were about more than roads, houses, farm buildings, woods, hedges and crops. These components of the landscape had to be planned, then constructed, built or planted and, perhaps just as importantly, they then had to be managed and run – and at a profit. This required what today we would describe as a management structure with clearly defined chains of command, which in turn were based around a social structure that was certainly hierarchical but sufficiently flexible to allow the best to rise close to the top – I say 'close to the top' because the position of the man, or more rarely the woman, actually at the top would generally have been hereditary. So estate landscapes in their widest possible sense were seen by most people to work effectively and began to be widely emulated in the sort of public institutions already mentioned, as well as in the growing number of urban cemeteries and parks whose carefully considered layouts reflected both aesthetic and practical considerations, such as ease of maintenance.

I don't want to overdo the similarities between rural estates and their institutional equivalents, but they did have one important symbolic aspect in common with each other. Both the buildings and the grounds in which they sat were expressions of confidence and prestige. In the case of workhouses, the designs were admittedly quite plain as they did not intend to convey opulence of any sort, but the design of the first purpose-built asylum in England, Bethlem (also known as Bedlam) at Moorfields (1674–6), resembles a vast country house set within carefully designed grounds which extend to include, or 'borrow', the landscape of London's first public open space, Moorfields. Later, in 1815, it moved to St George's Fields, just north of Hyde Park. In common with many Victorian asylums, Bethlem included two smaller enclosed 'airing courts' where patients could exercise under close supervision away from the common gaze.

During the nineteenth century lunatic asylums became the largest and most numerous of the institutional estates and, although their layout owed much to Bethlem, The Retreat, a Quaker institution built outside York, in 1792–6, was probably far more influential; here the purpose-built landscape featured enclosed airing courts for its most fragile inmates, but others were encouraged out into its more extensive, but still enclosed, parkland where they could work in orchards, kitchen gardens and fields, but could also take the air in extensive pleasure grounds. The main difference in the layout of The Retreat and of contemporary small villa estates was in the placing of the two airing courts immediately next to the main building, where in private houses one would expect to find formal lawns and gardens.

Many of the features pioneered at The Retreat were further developed at another early nineteenth-century Quaker-built asylum, Brislington House, Bristol. The Retreat sat in 4.5 hectares of grounds, whereas those of Brislington House covered a far more substantial area of 36 hectares. The new asylum was intended for fee-paying patients of high social class. In addition to the main building there were a number of small lodges and cottages where patients could pay for extra privacy. Here the emphasis was on pleasure grounds rather than agricultural or horticultural work, but again six (later rationalised to two) airing courts were placed in the immediate vicinity of Brislington House.

The success of efforts like those of the Quakers led to government action and in 1845 an Act was passed requiring each county to make provision for its 'pauper lunatic population' (politically incorrect language does at least have the merit of brevity). The grounds of these institutions were laid out on common principles of design, which owed much to the earlier projects, but the scale of the operation was to increase rapidly. In 1847, 5,000 pauper patients were housed in twenty-one public asylums and by the time the asylum-building 'boom' came to an end with the outbreak of the First World War, there were no fewer than 109,000 patients in 102 asylums (by way of

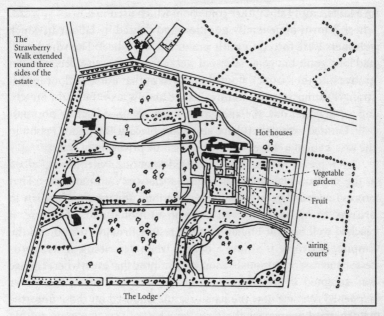

The Strawberry Walk extended round three sides of the estate

Hot houses

Vegetable garden

Fruit

'airing courts'

The Lodge

FIG 24 *A plan of the purpose-built grounds surrounding the Quaker asylum at Brislington House, Bristol (built 1804–6). Immediately right of the house were two enclosed 'airing courts' where patients could exercise under close supervision. At either end of each court were a row of isolation cells for those unfortunates who failed to show restraint while in the open.*

comparison, the 2009 British prison population hovered around 75–85,000[26]). By the end of the nineteenth century the larger asylums resembled institutional towns, sometimes complete with their own branch lines and railway stations, as at the Middlesex Asylum (1900–1905), Napsbury, Hertfordshire, and the Three Counties Asylum (1855–60), Bedfordshire, which featured a tramway off the main line that took goods and visitors to the very heart of this vast complex of buildings.[27]

Unless they do something naughty, most archaeologists rarely find their way into prisons, although excavations and surveys are not unknown there. But I can remember a detailed archaeological survey of the old Oxford Prison where I experienced another of those rather chilling moments which bring the past very vividly to life. I recall being in a large, empty and rather cold room which used to house the tread-wheel, a form of generally pointless and degrading labour in which prisoners were forced to push round a heavy wheel. The wheel itself had long gone, but generations of weary feet had worn a deep circular groove into the wooden floor. As I stared at that horrible floor in that strangely atmospheric building, I could almost hear the heavy breathing as, day after day, the anonymous men strained at their pointless task. Limited excavations have also taken place at Dartmoor Prison in the area known to have housed Napoleonic prisoners of war.[28]

A few paragraphs earlier I discussed what one writer has described as the 'institutionalisation' of English society in Victorian times. That process extended to pre-existing foundations, and most particularly to prisons, to make them even more institutional and, of course, it reached well beyond England, to the rest of Britain, Ireland and the Empire. But there is always a danger when describing general processes, such as institutionalisation, of assuming that everywhere change was accepted in its entirety. In actual fact, of course, this never happened. We saw how the harsh regime imposed on those unfortunate married paupers by the 'new' Poor Law of 1834 was quite quickly modified by the governors of workhouses and we can rest assured that many other people would have been spared its rigours by the generosity of friends, relatives and even strangers.

Governments and career politicians may like to think they can impose harsh or inhumane legislation on a minority of their fellow human beings in the hope that such actions will curry favour with the electorate at large, but when it comes to the administration of these rules, most ordinary, decent people will either refuse to comply or will find means to 'get round' them. The modern example of this is the administration of new and more stringent 'point-based' immigration laws which threaten to expel, among many worthy people, a number of established and well-liked local doctors. For years I have loathed this aspect of Britain's populist democratic system, which seems to encourage the natural ability of many politicians to be hypocritical. By its very nature it becomes extremely difficult to enforce such politically driven legislation, but this is nothing new, as a fascinating excavation in the cells beneath a now disused Edinburgh Court House has recently demonstrated.

The prison system equivalent of the 'new' Poor Law Act of 1834 was published the following year. It consisted of a report by the Parliamentary Select Committee on Gaols and Houses of Correction and it led to a number of separate Acts which were intended to change a system that had grown up piecemeal, was certainly being abused and was in dire need of reform. The two principles at the centre of the new way of running prisons were silence and isolation. It was argued that if prisoners could be prevented from talking they would have the time and tranquillity to ponder their own lives. It was also believed that this process could be helped by church services, Bible reading and preaching. Physical separation removed a prisoner from the 'contaminating influence' of his fellows and many new prisoners spent the initial months of their sentence in solitary confinement.[29] Thereafter there were few opportunities for socialising. These principles seem straightforward enough and they were doubtless well-intentioned, but they were also profoundly inhumane and, as a result, putting them into effect, even half a century later, was another matter altogether.

Now to that case study in Edinburgh. The original Scottish Parliament building was erected between 1632 and 1639 and went out of use after the Act of Union of 1707, at which point it became the home of the highest judicial courts in Scotland. The building that became the subject of excavations between 1998 and 2005 lies within the historic core of Edinburgh (today a UNESCO World Heritage Site), a short distance south-east of James Craig's New Town, which was discussed in the previous chapter. The redevelopment of the Scottish Law Courts involved extensive work on Court Building 3 which became the focus of the archaeological excavation. Like so many of the fine stone buildings in Edinburgh, Court 3 seems to perch rather perilously at the very edge of a steep incline leading down to Cowgate on its south side. Its location was only made possible by a series of thick-walled, small box-like vaulted spaces which provided solid foundation for the court building above. It was soon realised that these cellular spaces could be converted into actual cells in which prisoners awaiting and undergoing trial could be housed.

Before any excavation could begin, the entire building was subject to a detailed and thoroughgoing survey which revealed that one of the spaces in the foundations had never actually been converted to a cell at all. It didn't even have a floor and was described by the archaeologists as 'the Void' (I've capitalised the 'V' for heightened drama). The Void soon began to accumulate debris, which included, among many other things, a nineteenth-century bed frame. At the time of excavation there were fears that the material within the Void could have been contaminated or pilfered during the modern construction works, but close examination revealed that most of the finds were still covered by an intact layer of insect pupae, which had accumulated there over the preceding 130 or so years.

If one reads various prison rule books, and perhaps, more importantly, the contemporary accounts written by supposedly impartial visitors, it would appear that the spirit and the letter of the new laws were successfully implemented in prison, where those incarcerated were kept separated from each other and without any of their personal possessions. Nobody accused of criminal offences could wear their own clothes. Food was also Spartan and, apart from a pint of beer with

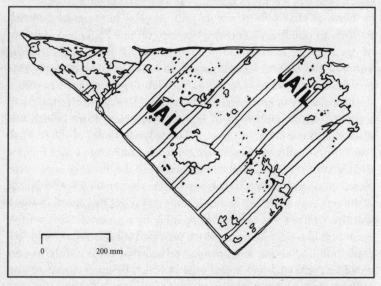

0   200 mm

FIG 25   *Outline drawing of a later nineteenth-century triangular blue cotton neckerchief, worn by male and female prisoners, from a large void beneath Court 3, Parliament House, Edinburgh. Diagonal white stripes were woven in, but the word JAIL was stamped on in red paint.*

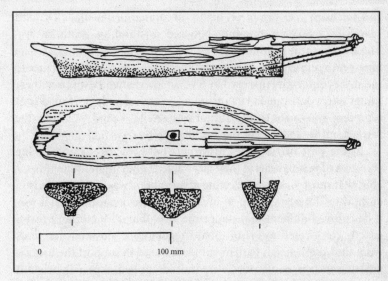

FIG 26   *Hand-carved model boat found in a large void beneath Court 3, Parliament House, Edinburgh. This home-made child's toy was probably carved sometime around the turn of the nineteenth and twentieth centuries.*

a meal, no drink was allowed. Men and women had their heads shaved. This regime was enforced by warders, evidence of whom was provided by the discovery of two door keys in the Void; fragments of a religious tract support the known fact that chaplains played an important role in all prisons. Discoveries of clothing, such as a small triangular scarf, worn by both men and women (Fig. 25), pieces of red-and-white striped women's stockings and scraps of the leather reinforcement found on contemporary warder's trousers, give indications that life in prison was being lived according to the rules. But other finds suggest that this was only a part of the story.

Smoking was strictly forbidden, but the Void revealed several clay pipe stems and a cardboard cigar box. There were fragments of women's clothing, including two parts of a high-necked dress, pieces of brown silk from another dress and silk chiffon from a bodice. There were also fragments of silk from a bonnet and pieces of silk ribbon. Other unusual objects included a child's hand-made model boat (Fig. 26) and an empty Guinness bottle. The finds of pottery were varied and included two complete, highly decorated plates made by John Marshall of Bo'ness sometime between 1855 and his death in 1879. These finds, some of which were quite fancy, all date to the mid- to late nineteenth century and suggest that there was a degree of resistance to the strict conformity imposed by law. An alternative view is that these things were confiscated from prisoners on arrival and therefore do not represent resistance to the authorities at all.* I tend to favour the former, but we should not rule out the latter.

In the past two decades historians have warned against taking accounts of prison visits at their face value.[30] They argue, quite reasonably, that most visits were fleeting affairs and it was not in the prison authorities' interests to appear in any way lax to outsiders. That is why it has proved difficult to dislodge the view that all Victorian prisons strictly conformed to Prison Board regulations. However, the finds from the Void beneath Parliament House tend to support the historians' doubts: yes, some rules were indeed applied, especially when it came to the involvement of the general public in, for example, a court house. But despite such outward compliance, it would appear that a culture developed within prison that made life tolerable for both prisoners and warders, who were grossly underpaid and were able in some instances to double their incomes by supplying prisoners with small luxuries such as stout and tobacco. One could argue, of course, if this was corruption or humanity, or a combination of the two. I don't think we'll ever know, but I would be prepared to wager that the lower- and middle-ranking authorities, if not those at the very top, were aware, and turned a blind eye to what was going on.

It was routine to try children as young as three for crimes and in theory at least they were denied toys when in custody, but surely no normal person would be prepared to enforce such cruel rules? And they didn't, as the model boat, two toy spinning tops and a lead cup from a doll's house tea set, all attest. These little, seemingly unimportant things carry the very important message that we should not rush to judgement. Received stereotypes, such as the moralistic, stern and self-righteous Victorians, are nearly always wrong. In reality, of course, archaeology reveals that, just like us, they were all too human.

---

* I am grateful to my editor, Ben Buchan, who suggested this idea to me.

In the previous chapter I discussed the importance of 'the social dimension' and in this one I have discussed what one might call its institutional expression – how a quite rapidly changing society in post-medieval Britain began to cope with the social problems of industrialisation. Not surprisingly, and unlike the evolution of trade and industry itself, it hasn't proved to be a story of progress in just one direction. It's far more complex – and, indeed, challenging than that.

In the Middle Ages the forces of feudalism provided a degree of coherence in rural areas, if not in the cities. After about 1400 these constraints began to break down and many ordinary people were able to live their lives in greater freedom. In the countryside of the sixteenth to eighteenth centuries, we also see a trend towards the growth of regionally based economies. The Church becomes better adapted towards maintaining local cohesion, and, although far from perfect, the new institutions of Victorian Britain are able to contribute much towards health, welfare and justice.

But other developments, first in roads and canals, then railways, were taking society in a different, more centralised direction. Similarly, national legislation, for example the Poor Laws, was deliberately intended to cut across local and regional boundaries. Although outside the scope of this book, this was also the time when the influence of central government was rapidly increasing. We will be able to examine the results of greater centralised power in the next chapter, when we look at the extraordinary structures left by army and navy, of what by the mid-nineteenth century had become the world's first superpower. But there was another side of the coin. Central authority wasn't always resented. Indeed, far from it, because it also provided the people of Britain with a feeling of security; and, of course, the Royal Navy at sea, and the defences on land, were tangible proof of their unity as a nation.

However, as economic prosperity increased, so too did social inequality. Disaffection, for example, was surprisingly widespread in the nineteenth century. Most people have heard of the Tolpuddle Martyrs (1834), or the Peterloo Massacre (1819), but just round the corner from where I live in the Fens, the Littleport riots of 1816 led to five men being hanged and many transported to Australia.[31] Those particular riots were a part of general rural discontent, following the agricultural recession at the end of the Napoleonic Wars. Moreover, these problems arose despite the existence of institutions such as the Crown and the Church that were then still widely respected. Today, of course, the various institutions of state are more diverse and are probably less respected by the population as a whole. Certainly the better access to democratic local and national government, that started to grow following the passage of Grey's Reform Act in 1832, has contributed to national stability.

But having said all of that, we should never forget that many of the tensions of local versus central authority, which became so evident from the later eighteenth century, are still very much with us today. I believe them to be very deep-rooted. I also think history teaches us that it would be a great mistake to assume that local versus national tensions today are merely about so-called NIMBY ('Not In My Back Yard') issues, such as the construction of wind turbines, although the press often chooses to focus on these as stories that are readily available, and the various single-interest groups understand the workings of modern PR very well. But, no, it seems to me that many of the concerns that fuelled the Peterloo and Littleport riots are still very much with us today: urban and rural poverty, often concentrated and localised, plus a feeling of being effectively disenfranchised: 'my vote doesn't matter' is an opinion one hears frequently expressed. Add to this a belief that central government no longer cares about far-flung communities – and it does not take a seer to anticipate future problems, if, that is, the economy is indeed entering a decade of minimal growth, or worse, of decline.

CHAPTER EIGHT

The First Superpower: Defence and Security

THE ANCIENT AND post-medieval churches we looked at in the last chapter owed their survival quite simply to the persistence of faith. Today even the most redundant of medieval churches remain a presence in the landscape, often isolated and remote but still substantially unaltered. A number of later Nonconformist chapels have indeed been torn down, but a substantial proportion have also been converted to houses, largely, I suspect, because there is a natural reluctance to see such buildings demolished. Sadly, the same cannot be said for the many thousands of pillboxes and other monuments to Britain's defence which can sometimes provide a stark reminder of the nation's previous emergencies. I suppose the conclusion we must draw from this is that faith and hope spring eternal, but enmity is more transient.

Huge numbers of Second World War defensive works were destroyed after the war. The process actually began in the last months of hostilities, but rapidly gathered pace in the 1950s and 1960s when people were keen to escape from wartime austerity and put reminders of the recent conflict behind them. I can't say I blame them. The result was, however, archaeologically disastrous and it took a major research programme, the Defence of Britain project (DoB), involving some six hundred professional and amateur archaeologists, to quantify what had been destroyed over the previous half-century. Only at that point could decisions be made about which monuments ought to be preserved through the statutory Scheduling process.

In the latter 1990s I had the very good fortune to be actively involved with the Council for British Archaeology, the organiser of the DoB, when it was in its final stages. This meant that I was able to get out and visit many of the key sites and areas, one of which happened to be on my doorstep – but more on that later. The DoB ran from April 1995 to March 2002 and recorded some 20,000 twentieth-century military sites – quite an achievement.[1] I have to admit, however, that I hadn't been particularly interested in defensive works before I became a part of the Council for British Archaeology but my conversion was rapid and complete. I suppose it's rather sad for a man in his sixties, but I have to admit that I've become something of a 'concrete anorak' and will happily trek for miles across Fenland fields in search of an example of the rarer Type 24 polygonal pillboxes.[2]

The threat of German invasion in 1940 and 1941 was extremely urgent and as a result much wartime concrete was hastily mixed, and is now actively deteriorating – and there is not much that can be done about it, other than rebuild from scratch using modern materials. So enjoy (if that's the right word) these monuments while they're still around. Earlier post-medieval defences were usually more substantial, although some of the Napoleonic defences, such as the coastal Martello towers that were built to defend England's south-east approaches could be jerry-built, rather like some of the town houses of the period.

While the fortifications of the two world wars and latterly of the Cold War undoubtedly form the majority of Britain's surviving post-medieval defensive works, it would be a great mistake to ignore what had gone before.[3] In particular, some of Britain's finest post-medieval defences date to the Tudor period and include the superb town walls at Berwick-upon-Tweed and many shore forts, such as Hurst Castle, built by Henry VIII on the approaches to Portsmouth and the Solent.[4] Tudor, Jacobean and Georgian military works, rather like prehistoric tin or copper mines, were incorporated within later structures whenever the need to provide enhanced protection arose. The string of coastal Martello towers that were built to protect London and the south-east from Napoleonic attack, for example, were often used as Second World War observation and lookout towers; the more robustly built forts of the Palmerston era of the 1860s, around, for example, Plymouth, Portsmouth and Chatham, were frequently adapted to take anti-aircraft batteries and searchlights some eighty years later.[5]

We tend to think of the great bridges, viaducts and railway stations as the best examples of Victorian civil engineering, but the achievements of their military engineers have for too long remained unsung.

Some of the finest examples can be seen surrounding the great naval base at Portsmouth, both inland and out in the Solent. The line of forts atop Portsdown Hill were intended to protect the Portsmouth basin from attack overland and they feature some of the most massive, brick-faced defensive ditches ever constructed in Britain. Even today they seem completely impenetrable. But I am getting ahead of myself and of the story: if I let my enthusiasm lead me we will never unravel the complexity of post-medieval fortifications. So let's wind the clock right back to the fifteenth and sixteenth centuries.

In the Middle Ages the main fortifications took the form of castles and town walls. These were robustly constructed and were often intended to impress visually, as well – which, of course, is not to say that they were somehow functionally inadequate. But time passed and technology changed. Improved firearms, especially cannons, were more than a match for the castles, as one can see, for example, at Old Wardour Castle in Wiltshire, an impregnable, state-of-the-art building when it was originally constructed in the 1390s, but where an entire wall was blown out in a single strike during the Civil War, in 1644.[6] The change from castles to forts was very rapid indeed, but it would be a mistake to assume that the new structures were entirely built for effectiveness under fire. Some of Henry VIII's forts, for example, are undoubtedly intended to impress both friend and foe alike.

The most important changes in fort design occurred in the seventeenth century when all resemblance to castles was abandoned. Indeed, it was appreciated that massive stonework simply made a good target. So new forts were designed to present a low physical profile, with strange-looking angled walls, known as bastions, which were intended to deflect incoming fire. These places sound horribly efficient and cold-blooded, but in actual fact many of them look much better in plan, on paper, than on the ground. The seventeenth century, especially before the Glorious Revolution of 1688, was a time when many senior officials and high-ranking officers were underpaid and poorly funded. So they did what anyone would do when asked by officialdom to undertake a large or complex operation without the necessary funds: they fiddled the books to make it look as if they had met all their objectives – or targets, to use modern management-speak.

One of the best preserved examples of pre-Victorian fortifications is Landguard Fort, in Suffolk, which was the subject of small-scale excavations in the winter of 2001.[7] In military archaeology a few well-placed small trenches can often reveal big stories and this is precisely what happened at Landguard.

The fort was built in the seventeenth century to protect the port of Harwich from attack, first by the Dutch, then the French. Landguard Point on the south Suffolk coast is a low-lying, flat, windswept and desolate place, usually visible through shrouding mists as one steams into Harwich Haven on the ferry from the Hook of Holland. There is no natural rock to use for building and the ground consists of sand, shingle, mud and clay. So, to keep costs to a minimum, these materials were used to build the seventeenth-century fort; later they added a low wall, or *fausse-braye*, and that, too, was built of bricks made from local clay. Today that early fort has completely vanished and instead one is surrounded by the massive brick and stone walls of the eighteenth-century and Victorian forts that replaced it.

The Crown and government had long appreciated the strategic importance of Harwich and by the late nineteenth century, when the power of France was being surpassed by that of a newly united Germany, its location facing over what some still called the German Ocean was seen to be crucial.[8] By then, too, Harwich had become Britain's fourth largest port. This is almost certainly why the existing fortifications at Landguard are quite so massive. The story of the fort comes to an end in 1901 with the construction of Darrell's Battery whose large guns completely covered all access to the Haven.

The actual process of excavating modern fortifications can be fraught with problems, not least because they were intended to resist bombs and shellfire. Compared with them, picks, spades and shovels are a minor threat. But the excavators at Landguard were not interested in the later brick and stone fort buildings. Their concern was the bastioned fort of the seventeenth century, which a new, specially commissioned survey of the documentary records showed to have been built mostly from clay and turf. As I noted earlier, the documents all seem to suggest that the first Landguard Fort had been built on a shoestring budget and then maintained for even less. Paul Pattison, who carried out the documentary research for the excavations, was

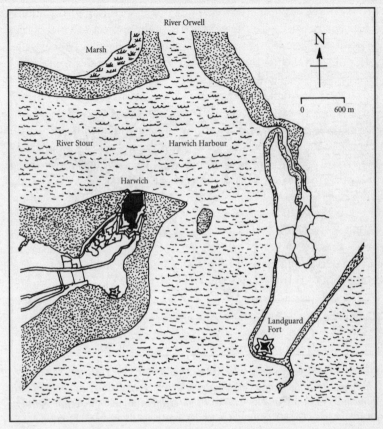

River Orwell

Marsh

N

0   600 m

River Stour   Harwich Harbour

Harwich

Landguard
Fort

FIG 27   *A map of Harwich Basin in the early eighteenth century showing the location of Landguard Fort on the approaches to the Haven from the North Sea.*

able to distinguish some seven phases of work, or neglect, prior to the construction of the new brick fort in 1717.[9] This new fort stands to this day and was used as the basis of the massive Victorian structure around it.

First I'll outline the seven phases and then consider the archaeological evidence for them. The ground plan of the fort features four prominent pointed bastions, one at each corner. Less exaggeratedly bastioned forts first appeared in Britain from the Continent in the second half of the sixteenth century, and the form adapted at

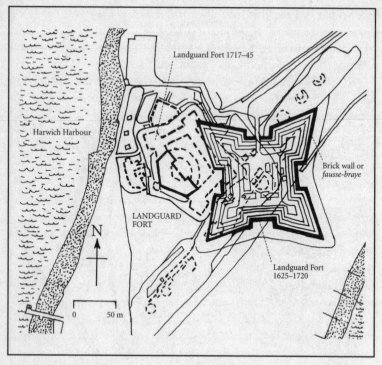

FIG 28   *The defensive landscape at Landguard Fort, near Harwich, Suffolk.*
This plan shows the location of the original seventeenth-century star-shaped fort
immediately behind (and now beneath) the eighteenth- and nineteenth-century
fort to the east. The left and right batteries were constructed in the later
nineteenth century.

Landguard is an almost direct copy of forts developed in Holland
during their war of independence against Spain between 1566 and 1648.
Landguard is a rare complete example in Britain, although similar
developed bastioned forts were constructed in some numbers during
the Civil War (1642–51). Although the actual defences were low and
mostly made from clay and turf, they enclosed some substantial buildings, including a fine Governor's House, which later featured a formal
garden, two large barrack blocks, on either side of a small central
parade ground, a storehouse, guardhouse, powder house and church.
The fort was entered from inland (to the north) via a substantial main

gate which was reached by a drawbridge across the outer defensive ditch, which sometimes flooded at high tide. The building of the fort took place between 1625 and 1628, initially to the designs of a Dutch military engineer, Simon van Cranvelt.

The fort was never fully equipped with the guns it was intended to hold, and money for its maintenance proved hard to come by. An account of 1636 describes how the defences had become so eroded that in some places it was possible to ride through them without dismounting. Despite these problems, Landguard was held for Parliament throughout the Civil War. During this period England's main foreign opponent was Holland and, mindful of its strategic importance in the southern North Sea, the government ordered immediate repairs, including the construction of the substantial *fausse-braye* brick-built wall (in effect a rampart revetment) around the inner face of the outer defensive ditch. The wall was completed in 1667, just in time to repel a Dutch attack. During this year Dutch forces carried out a daring and successful raid on Chatham, then Britain's main naval centre, but their raid on Landguard failed, despite the deployment of some 1,500 men. The raid caused chaos in Harwich, but the three hundred or so defenders of Landguard managed to hold the attackers off, largely due, so contemporary accounts tell us, to the *fausse-braye* wall, which proved one obstacle too many for them.

More repairs were needed between 1672 and 1678, when some of the temporary measures hurriedly adopted in the earlier building campaign began to show their age. Meanwhile, the country was entering another Dutch War, which didn't end until 1678. Despite the renewal of hostilities it would seem that Landguard was not kept in tip-top condition and further repairs were needed in the mid-1680s. Of course, in 1688 the Glorious Revolution, which signalled the end of the Stuart dynasty in England and union with William of Orange, saw the cessation of all hostilities with Holland. This was the cue for renewed tension with the old enemy, France, and one might have supposed that east coast forts, like Landguard, would now cease to be directly relevant. But the government was very suspicious of Catholic France's close links with the Stuarts in Scotland – links which could best be served via the North Sea. Following resumption of hostilities with France in 1702, a new survey of coastal defences recommended that those around Harwich needed greatly to be improved. This led to the complete demolition of the seventeenth-century fort and the construction of a brand new brick-built fort (erected 1717–20); essentially, this was a massive gun battery, which covered the strategically important narrows leading into the Haven.

Those, then, are the main historical events. So what did the dig reveal? The excavators decided to place two trenches directly behind the Georgian and Victorian forts at a spot where they believed they would come down on that crucially important *fausse-braye* brick wall. That was the theory, but when they started work they found they had to hire a large digger to remove about three metres of sand and shingle, most of which had been dumped on top of the seventeenth-century defences. Once the thick overburden had come off, the excavators were faced with a more complex series of deposits than they originally expected. There were a series of sand-filled criss-cross impressions which vaguely resembled plough scratches, but which they soon recognised were in fact filled-in slots left behind by a series of timbers. The main 'background' filling was mostly of sand, but within it were patches of clay, areas of clay lumps and deposits of soot, coal and charcoal. A clean dump of shingle was obviously the original bank's (i.e. the ramparts') core.

When I first saw the drawings made by the excavators of the sections exposed through the various layers in the two trenches, I could hardly believe my eyes. I'd expected to see a series of clean cuts followed by evidence for rebuilding and further modification. Essentially, I suppose, I was expecting something very much simpler than what lay before me, which didn't resemble an example of military engineering so much as a slice through the domestic rubbish deposits of a medieval city. Yes, there were a few clear cuts, but by and large the layers formed an intricate tangle with little obvious shape or form. I'm very glad I didn't have to disentangle them for the first time out there in the field. To take just one example, the main ditch was represented by no fewer than fifteen distinct layers of filling in one trench and twenty-eight in the other – just a few metres distant. Had I been running that dig I'd have been tearing my hair out.

These small accumulations of material reflect the periods when the fort's defences were neglected. This was when flood tides would breach the ditch and winds would blow in fine sands that were never cleared out. But the finds were even more extraordinary. Given the size and depth of the two trenches, there was precious little evidence for what one might term military hardware: no gun fittings or musket balls, just three lumps of iron shot, two lead powder-holder caps and a very rare fragment of a grenade. All the other finds were the sort of thing one might have expected to encounter on, say, a railway navvies' camp or a construction site. Just as we found at Risehill, on the Settle–Carlisle Railway, there were numerous clay tobacco pipe stems, plus fragments of pottery and glass. The large collection of pipe fragments was actually very important because they could be dated quite securely to the 1680s and were probably left behind by the workforce that built the final refurbishments to the defences in 1683–4.

The mention of clay tobacco pipes takes me back to my early days in archaeology, to the early 1970s, when I received the first flakes of the snowstorm of new information that was to threaten to engulf us all for the next two decades. This welter of data was only to subside in the mid-1990s with the arrival of the internet, when paper was gradually replaced by electronics. That initial hint of the storm to come arrived on my doorstep in 1974 in the form of a manila envelope. When I opened it (a report on some very rich Anglo-Saxon burials in Wessex by Tania M. Dickinson[10]) I have to say I was rather disappointed at what my 75p had bought me. It wasn't the quality of the research or the writing, both of which were excellent, so much as the book itself.

In my hand I held a cheap, plain, very non-glossy publication with a suitably no-nonsense title: British Archaeological Reports. The publishers were based in Oxford and I'm glad to say are still very much with us. Among the early BARs were several by Adrian Oswald on the chronology of clay tobacco pipes.[11] Using material from excavations, together with original catalogues, maker's stamps and a mass of other data, Oswald and his colleagues were able to construct an astonishingly accurate chronology for these ubiquitous objects. What makes them so archaeologically important is that they were never retained for long. At most they might have been filled a handful of times before being thrown away. Many have their maker's marks stamped just below the bell, and by referring to the by now huge literature on the subject, one can readily date pipes to within five to ten years, and sometimes even less. And, of course, it's a great deal cheaper than its nearest equivalent, tree-ring dating.

The excavations at Landguard broadly supported the historical interpretation, but more importantly they confirmed that the fort had indeed been very poorly maintained and was in constant need of repair and renewal. With the possible exception of the single brick wall, there was little evidence for major new expense as most of the rebuilding was carried out using material recovered from earlier work. We know that the fort was in existence for almost exactly a century and in comparison with the density of finds we recovered, for example, at Risehill after just seven years of occupation, there were remarkably few finds there. The same can be said for the Napoleonic prisoner-of-war camp we excavated at Norman Cross (below, pp. 255–61). These two examples alone suggest that the garrison at Landguard must have been relatively small – either that or the defences were rarely or spasmodically patrolled. Normally speaking, a great deal of rubbish would accumulate in a century, but not, it would seem, at Landguard.

Finally, what about those sand-filled timber slots? As so often happens, it would seem that they had nothing to do with the life and use of the site being investigated. Rather, they were left behind following the demolition of the original fort to provide a clear field of fire for the new battery, some time shortly after 1717.

It's worth noting here that military structures do not *have* to be ugly, even though their original purpose was sometimes very unpleasant. Defending armies need to move about the landscape unimpeded, which is why, of course, the Roman army bequeathed us the magnificent routes that still form the skeleton of the road network of England, Wales and the Scottish Borders. However, it was a workforce organised by the English army which constructed the main roads of the Scottish Highlands in the mid-eighteenth century, as part of the Crown's effort to bring the turbulent Jacobite Highlanders under its control.[12] Indeed, the parallels with what was happening south of the border in the first century of Roman rule are remarkably close.

The man whose name will always be associated with this work was an Anglo-Irishman, Major General George Wade. I had one of the happiest surprises of my archaeological life when we journeyed north to see the splendid Iron Age reconstructed crannog (a small man-made island), just off the shores of Loch Tay in Perth and Kinross.[13] It was a warm afternoon in late summer and Maisie and I decided to drive along the loch and find something to eat (and perhaps, too, a dram from the distillery there), in the small town of Aberfeldy on the Tay, a short distance to the east. Now I knew that Wade's Roads, as they are still known, also involved the construction of many bridges, the vast majority of which are rather plain but good, functional structures – the sort of thing one would expect a no-nonsense soldier to erect. But I had forgotten about the one at Aberfeldy.

Aberfeldy is an attractive small town with a delightful park down by the river, where we bought sandwiches and decided to eat them in the shade beneath some tall trees we could see close to the water. Also near the river was a fine memorial to the men and the meeting place where, in the eighteenth century, the Black Watch mustered, and this occupied our attention for a few minutes. Then we wandered across to the trees and sat down. Maybe I was still preoccupied with the Black Watch monument, but I didn't look around me for a few moments. Then I did. And promptly dashed back to the car for my camera. Wade's bridge at Aberfeldy was designed by Robert Adam and it has to be one of the most restrained but elegant structures in Britain. The Aberfeldy bridge is illustrated in some history books, but none of the photographs I have seen have attempted to convey anything of its graceful presence. It goes to show that military structures need not be stark and utilitarian, as, indeed, James St George, Edward I's superb architect, understood only too well when he created for his king a Welsh Byzantium at Caernarvon Castle in the later thirteenth century.

As many readers will probably know by now, I spend some time every summer making films for television. In the 1990s I mainly worked on prehistoric sites and mostly as a visiting expert, but ever since 2005, when we filmed at Arkwright's Mill in Manchester (described in Chapter 5), I have been lucky enough to have carved myself a small niche in post-medieval archaeology. That was how, in July 2009, I found myself working on the outskirts of Peterborough, near the A1, on the world's first purpose-built large-scale prisoner-of-war camp. The site was known as Norman Cross, not after the Normans, but the

Norsemen, or Vikings, who soon came to own this part of eastern England.

War had been very much in the news when we began the dig: the British Army had just lost eight men in one day in Afghanistan. Furthermore, on the day (it was a Monday) before the three-day dig, it had also been announced that there was to be a full public inquiry into the death of an Iraqi civilian who died of wounds he sustained after a beating by a soldier. He, like many others, had been influenced by a new, more brutal set of official rules, introduced by the Bush administration, on the 'conditioning' or softening-up of arrested terrorist suspects. One might argue that fighting in anything less than a 100 per cent ruthless fashion is what differentiates human beings from other animals.[14] Indeed, restraint in times of conflict is an important aspect of our humanity and that was one of the reasons why I was so intrigued by the prospect of excavating at Norman Cross, which was originally constructed to keep enemy soldiers alive and living in reasonable comfort.

Up until the construction of the camp, or Depot, at Norman Cross, some time between 1796 and 1797, Napoleonic prisoners were generally housed in old ships, known as hulks, which were moored just offshore, usually in the calmer waters of river estuaries, such as that of the Thames. Confined within these horrible places, prisoners were unable to breathe fresh air or take exercise and consequently the death rate through cholera and other diseases was appalling.

When we recced the site in July, the large field which originally contained the Depot now resembled a country house park, with a background scatter of large old lime trees and a herd of very friendly bullocks that liked to lick and nibble the back of one's shirt and trousers, and there was a covering of long, tussocky grass. I knew this would make the work of our geophysicists almost impossible and it was immediately obvious to me that we'd have to persuade the farmer to mow it. He promised to do so and he was true to his word: the site we eventually arrived at resembled less a park than a madman's playing field with humps and bumps as far as the eye could see.

The various shallow earthworks had been surveyed a few years earlier by the Royal Commission on Historical Monuments which reckoned that there was evidence that the camp had been built and

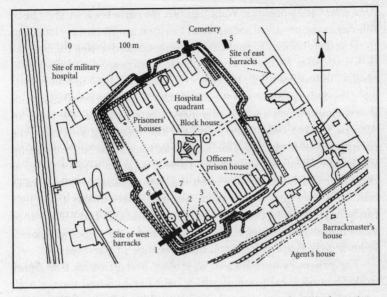

FIG 29   *A composite plan, based on contemporary sources showing the main areas of activity at the Norman Cross (Peterborough) 'Depot', or prisoner-of-war camp, which was in use during the Napoleonic Wars, from 1797 to 1814. The plan also shows the location of archaeological trenches excavated in July 2009.*

then enlarged in two quite distinct phases. These phases could best be seen in the south-west, where there was a series of ditches and banks that seemed to be marking the boundary of the site. Viewed from the air, the Depot was arranged to resemble a fort – it has an uncanny resemblance to Landguard without its spiky bastions – with an octagonal arrangement and four recessed main entrances at the points of the compass. The interior was also arranged in four quadrants separated by two roads and covered by an octagonal low tower or blockhouse at the centre. This tower featured long musket slots, together with small swivel cannons, and would have been guarded by a contingent of British soldiers. Originally all the quadrants were used to house prisoners, but later in its life the north-east one was made over to a large sick bay and hospital, with a permanent house for the doctor in charge.

There is actually quite a lot of documentary material relating to the Depot, but much of it, including at least two books, was written some time after the Napoleonic Wars.[15] In fact the main book we still use to this day as the principal source wasn't written until a century later, and in those days nobody thought about going out and testing the conventional wisdom with a few well-placed trenches. So the story that reached us was essentially this: the camp had been built to house some eight thousand prisoners by the Royal Navy Transport Board in 1796–7. It was closed down and the prisoners repatriated after the Peace of Amiens in 1802 only to be reopened the following year after the resumption of hostilities. This, so the story goes, was when the camp was largely replanned and rebuilt. There was then a mass breakout in 1807, after which the wooden outer wall was replaced by a brick-built one. Two years later a deep ditch was dug – presumably to prevent tunnelling – around the inside of the wall and this had the effect of weakening it, and making it lean inwards. In 1814 the Depot was closed, following the Peace of Paris and the abdication of Napoleon.

The prisoners were housed in sixteen prefabricated, two-storey wooden houses, each one of which held five hundred men, a high proportion of whom were sailors and would have been used to sleeping in hammocks – which explains how so many could be kept in the relatively small barrack blocks. Between each of the barrack blocks was a latrine building – part of the sanitation arrangements needed to avoid disease. Boredom was to prove one of the biggest problems and the prisoners were encouraged to work, both to earn money and to keep themselves occupied. They were not allowed to do anything that might compete with the local economy, such as the weaving of straw hats, which was traditionally done in the area, so they developed their own specialities, one of which was the making of miniatures and models out of finely carved pieces of bone. Peterborough Museum has a large collection of these objects, which include tiny guillotines, highly detailed model ships and spinning wheels, still known in the area as Spinning Jennies. These carvings were sold at markets held in the Depot at regular intervals, to which the public were admitted. One of the early aims of the dig was to see if we could recover any evidence for the manufacture of bone objects which otherwise only survive as complete, finished items in various museums and private collections.

The format of each *Time Team* programme is based around a strict timetable of three days with two additional, unfilmed, days, one at the beginning and one at the end of the shoot; of the two unfilmed days, the final is the most important, as this is when the archaeological team does all the detailed planning and recording before the entire site is carefully backfilled and in this case returfed. After repeatedly walking over the site on the day before and early in the morning of filmed Day 1, we decided to place a long (40-metre plus) trench straight through the various Phase 1 and 2 perimeter earthworks in the south-west corner. It was a very long process, as most of the work had to be done by hand and the ground was dry and very hard. This trench revealed an internal bank, then a wide, flat-bottomed ditch, which we believed to be the Silent Walk, where armed sentries are known to have patrolled. Outside that was a much higher bank which we now know butted up to the outside of the brick wall, and presumably the earlier plank and post-built timber fence that was flattened in one spot by the Great Escape of 1807.

Well beyond the main outer bank was another bank, which an earlier survey by the Royal Commission reckoned belonged to the camp's very first perimeter wall, built in 1796–7. That was the theory, at least. When we came to the excavation we found that this bank had been quite carefully constructed with small drainage ditches along each side and about 6 inches (say 15 centimetres) of gravel as a hard-wearing surface. Plainly, it was a road. And when we examined early plans closely it was clear that it was an access route or track, constructed by navy engineers to service the western garrison buildings from the main Peterborough Road. Even today it entered the field from a gate onto the Peterborough Road – a gate which we then used to drive onto the dig. It was nothing at all to do with an earlier phase of the Depot's perimeter wall.

I mentioned those wonderful bone carvings in Peterborough Museum and I gather from Ben Robinson, the Peterborough City archaeologist, that similar bone models are known from other Napoleonic prisoner-of-war camps in Britain and on the Continent. But we didn't know much about their production and I had only very slight hopes that we'd find a workshop, or something similar, where they were made. I needn't have worried. We laid out the second trench on the morning of Day 1 and it was positioned across one of the prisoners' accommodation blocks. These places must have been very grim.

They measured some 22 x 100 feet and were built of planks fixed to a stout wooden framework which rested on strip foundations made from brick rubble. I had the good fortune to discover one of the very first finds. It immediately caught my eye. In my hand it looked like a perfectly ordinary bone from a joint of beef – a shoulder blade or scapula – but it had two long saw cuts on opposite faces and a deep scratch or incision, which I reckoned had been made to make it easier to break in two. Over the years I've seen tens of thousands of examples of butchery debris from sites of all periods, but nothing remotely like this.

Quite literally two minutes later we came across more sawn bone, some of it very thin and fine, then part of a bone domino and round, ribbed circular pieces, which almost certainly were intended to form parts of those model spinning wheels, or Spinning Jennies. So far as I can recall we found examples of bone-working debris in nearly all the trenches we dug within the Depot, with the exception of the punishment block, or Black Hole, as these places were then generally known, which produced part of a heavy-duty door lock and the hasp of a massive iron padlock. When I first saw that padlock I found it hard not to be reminded of clanking doors, chains and rattling keys. Somehow, I don't think that particular Black Hole would have been at all pleasant.

One of the big mysteries that surrounded the Depot was the location of an apparently lost cemetery, holding some 1,700 graves. That was the number of prisoners who are known to have died in custody at Norman Cross between 1797 and 1814. Many of these would have been victims of typhoid fever, which claimed 1,020 lives in one six-month epidemic between 1800 and 1801. The standard account of the Depot was written just before the First World War and it refers to a large cemetery on the far (western) side of the A1, or Great North Road. A memorial bronze eagle on top of a stone column was erected near that spot in 1915 to commemorate the dead who were believed to lie in the field nearby. Recently the eagle was stolen and money was raised for a replacement which was positioned nearer the Depot on the Peterborough Road. By this time the A1 had been upgraded to motorway status – and nobody could possibly stop near it – so the new site makes much better sense, and, being placed near houses, it ought to be more secure. Even so, local sages have expressed their doubts about the authenticity of the new location.

An archaeological survey in 1990, which was carried out immediately prior to the massive roadworks needed to upgrade the A1 to a motorway, revealed no bodies at the eastern end of the supposed cemetery field. So we took a team to the other, 'low', end by a small stream, which was where the bodies were supposed to have been buried. Our trial trench was about 40 metres long and it failed to reveal so much as a military button, let alone a skeleton. All of this happened on Day 3 when we also decided to open a trench just outside the Depot boundary in what is today a field of hay. Some early accounts describe this as a French cemetery. It was conveniently positioned alongside the northeast quadrant, which we know from several accounts was set aside as the hospital and medical area. As I walked towards the new trench I remember thinking how many nineteenth-century isolation hospitals (sometimes known as 'pesthouses') often had small burial grounds attached. This, of course, made good sense: nobody wants to transport contagious bodies through towns or past houses where diseases could spread.

Geophysics had revealed dozens of possible graves in this area, but some were rather large and frankly ungrave-like. So we put a trench across two of these odd-looking features, and both revealed at least two bodies. It would seem that the large pits had been dug at the time of the 1800–1801 epidemic; bodies were placed in them as soon as possible after death and then they were hastily covered in. None were buried much more than three to four feet (about a metre) below the surface. I can't see any reason why the cemetery near the hospital does not still hold all the 1,700 bodies of men who died at the Depot. If that is so (and I'm quite convinced we're right), the doubters can cease their griping, because the current location of the new bronze eagle is actually very much closer to the men it commemorates than its original position alongside the A1.

I have already mentioned Arkwright's Mill, which was my first exploration of industrial archaeology with *Time Team*, back in 2005; but before we began work there I had spent the previous months filming for a series of three films, also for Channel 4, known as *The Real Dad's*

Army. I had the idea for the series while at the Council for British Archaeology. Some time the following year, 2006, I mentioned what I had been doing over the previous summer to someone in the planning group at *Time Team* who pricked up their ears, because they were then working on the possibility of making a film about the wartime archaeology of Shooters Hill, in south-east London. We actually made the *Time Team* film in October 2007 and it was then, incidentally, that I came across those striking houses that comprise The Paragon, near our hotel on the edge of Blackheath.

I have already discussed how people's natural reaction to the war caused them to erase many daily reminders of it during the 1950s and 1960s. That's doubtless why very few good examples of wartime remains are to be found in Britain's towns and cities. So when I was asked whether I would like to be the archaeological director of the Shooters Hill programme, I did hesitate somewhat. What on earth could have survived for us to dig, I wondered, in this popular and prosperous part of the nation's capital? As it turned out, I needn't have worried. There was more than enough to go around.[16]

It became apparent to everyone that, following the retreat from Dunkirk in early June 1940, Britain was at imminent risk of invasion. The strategy adopted in May 1940 by the commander of British defences, the wonderfully named General Edmund 'Tiny' Ironside, to meet this threat was based on the idea of defences in depth, which were organised in a series of so-called 'stop lines'.[17] The army had learned from the failure of the Maginot Line on the French/German border that a single, all-or-nothing defensive curtain could be bypassed or punctured by a concentrated attack. So the idea was to slow down the advance to allow British forces to be deployed more effectively for a 'last stand', or series of final battles. The outer stop line was known as the coastal crust and consisted of anti-tank cubes, pillboxes and gun emplacements, scaffolding hazards and minefields, most of which were placed along the beach and on the dunes behind. Some of the best preserved of the coastal crust defences can still be seen at Spurn Head on the north shore of the Humber.[18] There's still a wealth of material there: pillboxes, tank traps, even concrete-lined passages beneath the dunes. But a re-examination of wartime aerial photographs has also shown just how extensive the shoreline defences were in less readily defended places, such as the open beaches of Suffolk.[19]

Did they but know it, most people in Britain today probably live quite close to an example of these early wartime defences, such was the extraordinary scale of the work undertaken in 1940 and 1941. I live near the Wash, which was perceived as a major point of weakness until it was realised that the very shallow waters of this vast bay, home to thousands of seals and waders, would have been less welcoming to the many large warships needed to provide covering fire for an invading force. Before it was realised that battleships, cruisers and destroyers would all be grounded, it was proposed to mount a battery of six-inch, shore-based naval guns near King's Lynn and a brick-built tower was hastily constructed to observe the effects of the artillery. Then the penny dropped and the guns were removed to Northumberland, leaving the solitary tower as a forlorn monument to forethought – or its lack of.[20]

Even after it was realised that a major invasion was unlikely to happen across the Wash, its southern shores away from the more extensive marshes were strengthened by a series of gun emplacements and pillboxes which were mounted on the back, or inland, side of the many earthen banks or sea walls that are such a distinctive feature of the area around Holbeach St Matthew in the part of Lincolnshire known as South Holland. The side of the bank facing the North Sea would have been strengthened with trenches, mines and barbed wire. Once they were in position, there was little sense in removing them, as this would weaken the flood defences into which they had been built. So they survive to this day as a remarkably complete example of the way that the separate components of a defensive landscape were so carefully arranged to support and complement each other, while making good use of the natural, or in this case man-made, features of the terrain.[21]

Turning to the defences further inland, there was a single major stop line, known as the GHQ Line, which ran west from the Bristol Channel, rounded London to the south-east, then headed north through East Anglia, crossing the Fens east of Peterborough, then up through Lincolnshire and north to the Humber. It then ran through Yorkshire, the Scottish Borders, to the east of Edinburgh and then north to the foothills of the Highlands, where it stopped.

As its name suggests the GHQ Line was organised by General Headquarters, at a national level, but there were numerous other, usually smaller, stop lines, which were organised by the five Regional Commands: the Scottish, Northern, Southern, Eastern and Western. Some of these were as substantial as the GHQ Line itself, especially those across the flat landscapes of East Anglia, where the perceived threat was greatest. Perhaps rather surprisingly, there were also stop lines organised by Western Command in western England and in Wales, and these are among the most remote and consequently the best preserved. The busy port of Milford Haven, for example, was seen as being under special threat and two parallel stop lines were constructed to help protect it. These had the effect of making the entire Pembroke peninsula a defensive landscape.

We followed the entire course of the Carmarthen stop line for *The Real Dad's Army* and I was astounded by the quality of the archaeological remains along it. Because the landscape here had changed relatively little – unlike in East Anglia, where fields had been amalgamated, hedges rooted out and ditches filled in – it was simpler to discern how the military engineers had made good use of the subtleties of the terrain. Again, the popular image of Britain's anti-invasion measures, as being essentially amateur and rather inept, was clearly very wide of the mark.

I particularly recall a line of concrete tank cubes which ended in a large pillbox at the north end of the line. The pillbox was carefully sited for its fire to cover a steep valley which no tank of the time could possibly have traversed. I was very surprised to see that each of the cubes and the pillbox itself still had its original covering of soil and heather which was intended to conceal them from the air – surely something of a vain hope. However, the most evocative moment for me was not when I saw the earth-covered tank cubes, or even when I managed to get tangled up in rusty wartime barbed wire, but the sight of the beautifully preserved and wonderfully defiant figure of Mickey Mouse and a very Churchillian bulldog painted on the sheltered side of a concrete gun emplacement overlooking the sea at the mouth of the River Tywi. That simple but very confidently executed painting took me straight back to those dark days when a few rather nervous men must have stood by their gun, waiting for something to appear over the horizon.

The stop lines were cleverly positioned to make use of natural features, such as cliffs or rivers and dykes in the Fens. As we have seen, the intention was to stop or delay the German advance, to give the single armoured division that Churchill had so wisely retained in England throughout the early months of the war time to deploy and engage the enemy at a place of its own choosing. That, at least, was the theory. London was ringed by two complete stop lines, the outer of which more or less followed the path of the modern M25. There was also a small semi-circular ring which was confined north of the Thames and was principally intended to protect Westminster and the seat of government from parachute attack. The innermost complete ring was known as Stop Line Central and it passed right through the middle of Shooters Hill. And this is where we return from that brief foray into rural Britain back to the stop lines outside London.

A good deal of research had already taken place when *Time Team* arrived on the scene and a few weeks before I had even taken *The Real Dad's Army* crew there to film the site of a large anti-aircraft rocket battery. The reason for all the wartime activity was simple: Shooters Hill represented the last high ground before the descent to the Thames and London proper. From the top of the Hill one could see the towers of Docklands and Canary Wharf to the north and the Queen Elizabeth Bridge, carrying the M25 across the Thames, far away to the east. Most of our locations were to be around the junction of the dead-straight Roman road to Canterbury, Watling Street (today the A207), and the South Circular (the A205). Before and during the war, just as in Roman times, Watling Street would have been one of the most direct routes into London from the south-east and it was clearly essential to defend it. There simply wasn't time to construct huge concrete walls and, besides, the ease with which the German army had side-stepped the massive defences of the Maginot Line had taught British military planners an important lesson. So they decided on a series of smaller and less obviously visible measures that would have slowed the enemy advance.

When the results of our excavations were combined with the earlier research, the picture that arose was rather chilling – or at least that is how I found it. Most of the fighting was to be done by the Home Guard, many of whom were then recently retired, and seasoned veterans of the

Great War, who would certainly not have been a pushover, despite the somewhat bungling image of them in the *Dad's Army* TV series. The details we and local archaeologists revealed of the defences along the line of Watling Street put one in mind, as Andy Brockman, the leader of the research project, put it, of a potential British Stalingrad. Had the Germans invaded in any numbers, and had they managed to gain air superiority, which they conceded after the Battle of Britain in the summer and autumn of 1940, the battle for London would surely have been a terrible bloodbath.

Before I discuss what we revealed of the defences of Stop Line Central and Watling Street, we also found good evidence of do-it-yourself air-raid and shrapnel shelters. I excavated one myself. It was made from hand-mixed cement, with floorboard shuttering, and was buried beneath an earth mound. It was probably built by Colonel Arthur Bagnold, who owned the large house nearby, for the benefit of his garden staff who would have been exposed to falling anti-aircraft shrapnel from the nearby batteries during air raids. Another, far more elaborate bunker, and still tastefully concealed behind a rockery, featured two underground rooms, electric lighting, double access and two escape shafts. This desirable shelter was built by two neighbouring families, the Griffiths and the Cuffleys, who pooled their resources to do it. This glimpse of a small but relatively well-off part of London illustrates well the extent of the 'privatised' defences of the nation's capital that could have been used for more hostile activities had the need arisen.

The original route and layout of Stop Line Central was surveyed by officers of the Royal Engineers and Royal Artillery, starting in July 1940. Like other stop lines, it made use of natural and man-made obstacles and its precise path was determined by certain important military principles. Gun positions, for example, were always sited below the crest of a hill so that advancing troops and vehicles could be seen against the skyline. It was an extraordinary undertaking and by October 1940 some nine hundred pillboxes had been built in and around London. A large Edwardian pub, the Bull, had been pressed into service and a pillbox, cunningly disguised as an off-licence, was built against its down-slope wall. The top of the hill was essentially a killing zone, covered by fire from the Bull pillbox, another gun emplacement and a road block. Further down the hill we found evidence for a strange flame-throwing device, known as a flame fougasse, which would have shot a five-metre-long flame of burning petrol across the road. Essentially, in modern terms this was an IED, or improvised explosive device, and, like its equivalent in Iraq and Afghanistan, much of its effectiveness depended on its positioning. In this instance the jet of flame would have hit the road at the point where it entered a shallow cutting, thus confining the flames and intensifying the power of its destruction.

The flame fougasse would have been one of the first defensive measures, probably dating to July 1940. One of the later ones was positioned on the western, down-slope, or 'London' side, of Shooters Hill, at the crossroads with the South Circular on Eltham Common. This rather strange looking thing was a stubby, polygonal concrete plinth or pillar fitted with a stainless steel knob or spigot. The so-called spigot mortar was the Blacker Bombard, an anti-tank weapon with a ferocious recoil that had to be attached to a strong pin or spigot mounted on a heavy, usually hexagonal, reinforced concrete pillar.[22] They were serviced and fired by members of the Home Guard who sheltered in a shallow trench often lined with corrugated iron, held in place by angle-iron stakes – all of which we revealed in our excavations. Once the mortar had been fired, the spigot-mortar crew had to run like the devil as there would not have been time for a second shot. These (to everyone) dangerous weapons were installed in the spring of 1942, which was when the last improvements were made to the London stop lines.

Before we move away from the capital I should add that our excavations also revealed the ditch of a later Bronze Age enclosure (say 1000 BC), possibly a form of small hillfort, in Eaglesfield Park, at the very top of Shooters Hill, a short distance from the concrete block anchors of a Second World War barrage balloon. These balloons did indeed serve to keep aircraft from flying too low, but they were also sited at prominent points to help morale and show that the authorities were doing something about the nightly air raids. So, what with the balloons and the Bronze Age hillfort, it would appear that people had considered this particular approach to the London basin as both symbolically and strategically important for at least three millennia.

* * *

The collapse of the Berlin Wall in 1989 and with it the welcome demise of Soviet-style Communism in Eastern and Central Europe signalled a new era of defence across the Western world. From a purely archaeological perspective the cloak of secrecy was lifted and we became better able to see what had been happening on the vast Ministry of Defence estates, which included everything from V-bomber bases, to military ranges and many radar and other early warning sites. Today many of these have either been sold off or 'mothballed', like the American air base at Alconbury or the RAF airfield at Wyton, both in Cambridgeshire.

The events of 1989 led to a proliferation of books about the Cold War, many of which were written with the express intention of avoiding the wholesale and ill-considered destruction of military installations that had happened directly after the Second World War. To my mind, by far the best of these appeared in 2003 and it made truly horrifying reading.[23] I had no idea of the sheer size of the military presence in Britain and of the extent to which successive governments made routine plans for life, such as it would be, after a nuclear holocaust. It put one in mind of Nevil Shute's *On the Beach* (1957), but written within the zone of destruction and with more than a dash of horribly grim reality.

While the strictly military 'empire' within Britain's shores was huge, there were also a large number of essential back-up and infrastructural facilities, such as underground Regional Centres of Government, strategic grain storage silos sited near railway lines and an extraordinary network of microwave communication towers, which were positioned at prominent spots in the landscape as each needed to be in line of sight of each other. The most substantial of these towers were the so-called terminal stations, where the signals were gathered together, and the best known of these is undoubtedly the Post Office Tower (now the BT Tower) in London (which doubtless explains why so prominent a building acquired planning permission so rapidly). Other good examples of terminal towers, also made from concrete, can be seen at Pye Green in Staffordshire and Purdown, in Bristol.[24] Less substantial steel-frame relay towers still pepper the landscape from Land's End to John O'Groats.[25]

What is less well known is the chilling fact that these towers were built as a counter-measure to a deliberate nuclear air burst over the northern North Sea. This would have produced a massive electromagnetic pulse (or EMP) which would simply burn out all above-ground wire-based telecommunications systems.[26] The way round this problem was to avoid wires, by transmitting radio and telephone messages along invisible microwaves that were transmitted and received by the series of towers, all of which had to be within line of sight of each other. Many of these towers have survived because they provide an ideal location for the circular dishes used by mobile phone networks.

Britain's Cold War defensive measures, including the national microwave network, were all linked into a series of wider Western European-, NATO- and government-based radar, reconnaissance and communications systems. In effect this meant that Britain's insularity had become irrelevant, a process that has subsequently been reinforced by the construction of the Channel Tunnel. Whether the population at large likes it or not, Britain has now been effectively reunited with the continental mainland. And this brings me back, full circle, to where I began my story in *Britain BC*, when Palaeolithic hunters were able to leave their bases in South Wales, Sussex or Derbyshire and head out into the great north European plain in search of wild horses, aurochs or reindeer. We've come a long way in 850,000 years,[27] but I wonder who feels the most secure: the hunter in his cave, even with wolves at the door, or a modern family slowly coming to grips with the long-term implications of global population growth, terrorism and climate change? If nothing else, this journey through archaeological time has taught me to treat the word 'progress' with more than a little suspicion.

NOTES

INTRODUCTION — *Archaeology and Modern Times*

1 See W. Foot, *Beaches, fields, streets, and hills … the anti-invasion landscapes of England, 1940*, Council for British Archaeology Research Report No. 144 (York, 2006), p. 6.

2 The issue is addressed in two issues of the *English Heritage Conservation Bulletin*: issues 47 (Winter 2004–5) and 54 (Spring 2007).

3 The Garbage Project was part of an academic approach to the study of modern 'material culture'. See W. L. Rathje, 'Modern Material Culture Studies', in M. B. Schiffer (ed.), *Advances in Archaeological Method and Theory*, Vol. 2 (Academic Press, New York, 1979), pp. 1–37.

4 For a superb collection of essays that illustrate well the breadth of post-medieval archaeology see A. Horning and M. Palmer (eds), *Crossing Paths or Sharing Tracks? Future Directions in the Archaeological Study of Post-1550 Britain and Ireland* (Boydell and Brewer, Woodbridge, Suffolk, 2009).

5 For a useful summary of the potential of science in historical archaeology see Justine Bayley and David Crossley, 'Archaeological Science as an Aid to the Study of Post-Medieval Industrialization', in David Barker and David Cranstone (eds), *The Archaeology of Industrialization* (Maney Publishing, Leeds, 2004), pp. 15–23.

6 Kenneth Hudson, *Industrial Archaeology: An Introduction* (Methuen, London, 1963), p. 11.

7 R. A. Buchanan, *Industrial Archaeology in Britain* (Penguin Books, Harmondsworth, 1972), pp. 23–5.

8 For an excellent summary of the historiography of the subject see Buchanan, op. cit. (1972), pp. 32–49.

9 For an excellent archaeologically based critique of the Industrial Revolution see James Symonds, 'Beyond the Industrial Revolution', *British Archaeology*, No. 72, September 2003, pp. 19–23.

10 Newcomen in turn benefited from detailed design drawings of an engine that was never built, by the Frenchman Denis Papin in 1680. Ibid., p. 20.

11 David Cranstone, 'The Whitehaven Coast 1500–2000 – Post-Medieval, Industrial and Historical Archaeology', in Horning and Palmer, op. cit. (2009), p. 205.

12 For a first-rate textbook of industrial archaeology see Marilyn Palmer and Peter Neaverson, *Industrial Archaeology: Principles and Practice* (Routledge, London, 1998).

13 Palmer and Neaverson, op. cit. (1994).

14 Two notable exceptions spring to mind: J. F. C. Harrison, *The Common People: A History from the Norman Conquest to the Present* (Fontana, London, 1984), and G. M. Trevelyan, *Illustrated English Social History*, Vols 3 and 4 (Penguin Books, Harmondsworth, 1964).

CHAPTER ONE — *Market Forces: Fields, Farming and the Rural Economy*

1 See Francis Pryor, *Britain in the Middle Ages* (HarperCollins, London, 2007), pp. 116–24.

2 Christopher Gerrard with Mick Aston, *The Shapwick Project. Somerset. A Rural Landscape Explored* (Society for Medieval Archaeology, Monograph No. 25, 2007).

3 Ibid., pp. 998–1010.

4 For a superbly illustrated exposition of the concept see B. K. Roberts and S. Wrathmell, *An Atlas of Rural Settlement in England* (English Heritage, London, 2000). I have redrawn their map in *Britain in the Middle Ages*, fig. 35, p. 225.

5 Oliver Rackham was one of the first to draw the distinction between 'planned' and 'ancient' landscapes: *The History of the Countryside* (J. M. Dent, London, 1986).

6 Roberts and Wrathmell, op. cit. (2000), figs 24–5.

7 I discuss 'champion', or Open Field farming, in *Britain in the Middle Ages*, pp. 223–56.

8 The long-term Whittlewood Project is one of the most important recent case studies to investigate the origins and development of an English medieval village: Richard Jones and Mark Page, *Medieval Villages in an English Landscape: Beginnings and Ends* (Windgather Press, Macclesfield, 2006).

9 See Paul Stamper, 'Landscapes of the Middle Ages: Rural Settlement and Manors', in J. Hunter and I. Ralston (eds), *The Archaeology of Britain: An Introduction from the Upper Palaeolithic to the Industrial Revolution* (Routledge, London, 1999), pp. 247–63. For more on the different social effects see Colin Platt, *King Death: The Black Death and its Aftermath in Late-medieval England* (University of Toronto Press, 1997).

10 See, for example, papers by Gaimster and Finch in David Gaimster and Roberta Gilchrist (eds), *The Archaeology of Reformation 1480–1580* (Maney Publishing, Leeds, 2003).

11 I discuss Laxton at some length in *The Making of the British Landscape*, chapter 8. See also C. Delano Smith (ed.), 'The Open Field Village of Laxton', papers published as *The East Midland Geographer*, Vol. 7, Part 6, No. 54, December 1980.

12 I discuss Fen drainage at some length in *The Making of the British Landscape*, chapter 12. See also Susanna Wade Martins, *Farms and Fields* (B. T. Batsford, London, 1995), pp. 124–32.

13 The maps shown here are taken from Joan Thirsk, *England's Agricultural Regions and Agrarian History, 1500–1750*, Studies in Economic and Social History, Maps II and III (Macmillan Education, London, 1987).

14 Climate seems to have played a significant role in many of these long-term changes. For an excellent account, with full references, see Brian Fagan, *The Little Ice Age: How Climate Made History, 1300–1850* (Basic Books, New York, 2000), pp. 106–10. See also Susanna Wade Martins, *Farmers, Landlords and Landscapes: Rural Britain, 1720 to 1870* (Windgather Press, Macclesfield, 2004), p. 5.

15 Susanna Wade Martins and Tom Williamson, *Roots of Change: Farming and the Landscape in East Anglia, c. 1700–1870*, British Agricultural History Society Supplementary Series, No. 2, 1999, pp. 99–119.

16 I refer to the Moretonhampstead region of Devon in *The Making of the British Landscape*, chapter 10. See also James Bond, 'Dynamics and Demography', p. 111, and 'A Kaleidoscope of Regions', pp. 118 and 121, both in Barry Cunliffe (ed.), *England's Landscape: The West* (English Heritage and Collins, London, 2006).

17 A process clearly illustrated by David Hall, *Medieval Fields* (Shire Books, Princes Risborough, 1982), pp. 5–9.

18 P. S. Barnwell and Colum Giles, *English Farmsteads, 1750–1914* (Royal Commission on the Historical Monuments of England, Swindon, 1997), p. 153.

19 Wade Martins, op. cit. (1995), p. 82.

20 See Ian Whyte, 'Taming the Fells: Parliamentary Enclosure and the Landscape in Northern England',

Landscapes, Vol. 6, No. 1, 2005, pp. 46–61.

21 Quoted from Richard Muir, *Landscape Encyclopaedia* (Windgather Press, Macclesfield, 2004), p. 38; Barnwell and Giles, op. cit. (1997), p. 4.

22 Robert Sylvester, 'Landscapes of the Poor: Encroachment in Wales in the Post-Medieval Centuries', in P. S. Barnwell and Marilyn Palmer (eds), *Post-Medieval Landscapes: Landscape History after Hoskins* (Windgather Press, Macclesfield, 2007), pp. 55–67.

23 Ibid., p. 55.

24 Encroachment has also been recorded from south-western England; see Sam Turner, 'The Changing Landscape: South-west England c.1700–1900', *Landscapes*, Vol. 5, No. 1, 2004, p. 30.

25 Sylvester, op. cit., p. 59.

26 Under-drainage is discussed extensively in Wade Martins, op. cit. (2004).

27 For an excellent recent account see Hadrian Cook and Tom Williamson, *Water Meadows: History, Ecology and Conservation* (Windgather Press, Macclesfield, 2007).

28 Ibid., pp. 113–16.

29 Wade Martins, op. cit. (2004), p. 4.

30 The title of the standard modern account of the period says it all: Mark Overton, *Agricultural Revolution in England: The Transformation of the Agrarian Economy 1500–1850* (Cambridge University Press, Cambridge, 1996).

31 The wholesale importation of guano from islands off the coast of Peru had an adverse effect on their ecology and ultimately impoverished the soils of farms where it was used or overused, much as recent excessive use of artificial fertilisers has degraded most of the arable soils of Britain.

32 Pat Stanley, *Robert Bakewell and the Longhorn Breed of Cattle* (Farming Press, Ipswich, 1995). A very important breed of the time (and recently re-created) was the Norfolk Horn from which came the now almost ubiquitous Suffolk. See Peter Wade Martins, *Black Faces: A History of East Anglian Sheep Breeds* (Norfolk Museums Service, 1993).

33 Quoted from Susanna Wade Martins, *Farmers, Landlords and Landscapes: Rural Britain, 1720 to 1870* (Windgather Press, Macclesfield, 2004), p. 8.

34 Francis Pryor, *Farmers in Prehistoric Britain*, 2nd edn (Tempus Books, Stroud, 2006), p. 18.

35 Wade Martins, op. cit. (2004), p. 2.

36 R. C. Allen, *Enclosure and the Open Farmer* (Oxford, 1992), p. 310, quoted in ibid., p. 4.

37 Cynthia Brown, 'Drovers, Cattle and Dung: The Long Trail from Scotland to London', *Proceedings of the Suffolk Institute for Archaeology and History*, Vol. 38, 1996, pp. 428–41.

38 Wade Martins, op. cit. (2004), p. 13.

39 Jones and Page, op. cit. (2006), pp. 201–21.

40 I have considered medieval aspects of the survey in *Britain in the Middle Ages*, pp. 242–5. For a clear interim statement see Chris Dyer, 'Whittlewood: Revealing a Medieval Landscape', *Current Archaeology*, No. 182, 2002, pp. 59–63.

41 Jones and Page, op. cit., pp. 203–11.

42 M. W. Barley, *The English Farmhouse and Cottage* (Routledge & Kegan Paul, London, 1961; reprinted (and cited here) by Alan Sutton Publishing, Gloucester, 1987).

43 Ibid., pp. 90–91.

44 Ibid., pp. 238–9.

45 A huge amount has been written about the Holkham estate. See, for example, Wade Martins, op. cit. (1995); Wade Martins and Williamson, op. cit. (1999), and for the operation of the estate and its buildings later in the nineteenth century: Susanna Wade Martins and Tom Williamson, *The Countryside of East Anglia, Changing Landscapes, 1870–1950* (Boydell Press, Woodbridge, 2008).

46 Barnwell and Giles, op. cit. (1997), p. 4.

47 For an excellent review of recent trends in the study of vernacular architecture see Sarah Pearson and Bob Meeson (eds), *Vernacular Buildings in a Changing World: Understanding, Recording and Conservation*, Council for British Archaeology Research, Report No. 126 (York, 2001).

48 Antony Walsh, 'A prefabricated temporary building at Cranford Primary School, Kettering, Northamptonshire', *Northamptonshire Archaeology*, Vol. 35, 2008, pp. 277–86. Shaun Richardson, 'Welcome to the Cheap Seats: Cinemas, Sex and Landscape', *Industrial Archaeology Review*, Vol. 27, 2005, pp. 145–52.

49 Alexander Fenton and Bruce Walker, *The Rural Architecture of Scotland* (John Donald, Edinburgh, 1981); Barley, op. cit. (1961).

50 Gerry Barnes and Tom Williamson, *Hedgerow History: Ecology, History and Landscape Character* (Windgather Press, Macclesfield, 2006).

51 Tom Williamson, *The Transformation of Rural England: Farming and the Landscape 1700–1870* (University of Exeter Press, Exeter, 2002), p. 110; J. Caird, *English Agriculture in 1851*, published in London, 1852.

52 English Heritage, *Conservation Bulletin: Modern Times*, ed. John Schofield, 56 (2007), p. 15.

53 There is a huge literature on the damage caused to buried archaeological remains by agriculture, but for a detailed report written at the height of the crisis in the mid-1970s see: George Lambrick, *Archaeology and Agriculture* (Oxford Archaeological Unit, 1977).

54 I cover the process in chapter 3 of *Britain in the Middle Ages*.

55 I discuss the adoption of farming in chapter 6 of *Britain BC* and the development of Bronze Age fields in chapter 10.

56 I discuss late Roman and early Saxon Britain in chapters 5 and 6 of *Britain AD*.

57 B. Short, C. Watkins and J. Martin (eds), *The Front Line of Freedom: British Farming in the Second World War* (British Agricultural History Society, Exeter, 2007).

CHAPTER TWO — *'Polite Landscapes': Prestige, Control and Authority in Rural Britain*

1 Many great country houses and their parks have been open to visitors for generations. Adrian Tinniswood, *A History of Country House Visiting* (National Trust/Blackwell, Oxford, 1989). For a superb contemporary account see Christopher Morris (ed.), *The Illustrated Journeys of Celia Fiennes c. 1682–c. 1712* (Webb and Bower, Exeter, 1982).

2 For a superb discussion, written with archaeology in mind, see Tom Williamson, *Polite Landscapes: Gardens and Society in Eighteenth-Century England* (Johns Hopkins University Press, Baltimore, 1995).

3 The specialist journal is *Garden History*, published by the Garden History Society.

4 Sir Roy Strong is also a first-rate gardener, a fact that comes through clearly in his book *The Spirit of Britain: A Narrative History of the Arts* (Pimlico, London, 2000). Chapter 27 (pp. 415–31) discusses landscape gardens.

5 For both sites see the anniversary issue of *Current Archaeology*, No. 200, 2005, pp. 426–8, also Brian Dix, 'Garden Archaeology at Kirby Hall and Hampton Court', *Current Archaeology*, No. 140, 1994, pp. 292–9.

6 Barry Cunliffe, *Fishbourne: A Roman Palace and Its Garden* (Thames & Hudson, London, 1971). Colour plate II shows the bedding trenches, probably for box plants, of an elaborate formal garden of the second half of the first century AD.

7 The best and most accessible account is by Chris Gaffney and John Gater, *Revealing the Buried Past: Geophysics*

for Archaeologists (Tempus Books, Stroud, 2003).

8 Sir Geoffrey and Susan Jellicoe, Patrick Goode and Michael Lancaster (eds), *The Oxford Companion to Gardens* (Oxford University Press, London, 1986), pp. 418–19.

9 Chris Catling, 'Kenilworth Castle: The Wooing of a Virgin Queen', *Current Archaeology*, No. 232, July 2009, pp. 34–41.

10 Tom Williamson, 'Designed Landscapes: The Regional Dimension', *Landscapes*, Vol. 5, No. 2, 2004, pp. 16–25.

11 Ibid., p. 23.

12 Tom Williamson, ibid., p 24, quotes the example of two Herefordshire landowners of the 1790s who deliberately set about creating a landscape style that celebrated local character, as a reaction to the then widespread adoption of 'Capability' Brown-style parks.

13 I discuss castle approaches in *Britain in the Middle Ages*, pp. 275–9. For landscaped parks see Oliver H. Creighton, *Designs upon the Land: Elite Landscapes of the Middle Ages* (Boydell Press, Woodbridge, Suffolk, 2009).

14 I discuss Castle Acre, with a map of the diversion, in *The Making of the British Landscape*, pp. 272–6.

15 See also P. S. Barnwell, 'Farm Buildings and the Industrial Age', *Industrial Archaeology Review*, Vol. 27, No. 1, 2005, pp. 113–20.

16 The archaeology of rural estates is now recognised as an increasingly important field of research. For an excellent theoretical overview see Tom Williamson, 'Archaeological Perspectives on Landed Estates: Research Agendas', in Jonathan Finch and Kate Giles (eds), *Estate Landscapes: Design, Improvement and Power in the Post-Medieval Landscape*, Society for Post-Medieval Archaeology Monograph No. 4 (Boydell and Brewer, Woodbridge, Suffolk, 2007), pp. 1–16.

17 Susanna Wade Martins, *The English Model Farm: Building the Agricultural Ideal, 1700–1914* (Windgather Press and English Heritage, Macclesfield, 2002), p. 207.

18 For a first-rate collection of essays on the archaeology of rural estates see Finch and Giles, op. cit. (2007).

19 Barnwell and Giles, op. cit. (1997); these paragraphs draw heavily on Wade Martins, op. cit. (2002).

20 For example, ibid., pp. 52–3, 63.

21 Ibid., fig. 29 (p. 63).

22 Summarised by Susanna Wade Martins, ibid., pp. 203–23.

23 The plans and their captions appear in ibid., pp. 6–7.

24 To find out more about visiting Aston Hall go to www.bmag.org.uk/ aston-hall

25 The following discussion of Aston Hall excavations is based on Leonie Driver, Malcolm Hislop, Stephen Litherland and Eleanor Ramsey, 'The North Service Range, Aston Hall, Birmingham: Excavations and Recording, 2004', *Post-Medieval Archaeology*, Vol. 42, Part 1, 2008, pp. 104–29.

26 Alan Davidson, *The Oxford Companion to Food*, 2nd edn (Oxford University Press, Oxford, 2006), p. 393.

27 Marilyn Palmer, 'The Country House: Technology and Society', *Industrial Archaeology Review*, Vol. 27, No. 1, pp. 97–103.

28 Ibid., p. 98. The quotation is by Mark Girouard from *Life in the English Country House* (Yale University Press, London, 1978), p. 263.

29 Ibid., p. 101. Bramah patented the modern-style water closet, but the flush-through water closet was probably first invented by Sir John Harrington in 1596.

30 Brian K. Roberts, *The Making of the English Village* (Longman, London, 1987).

31 This following discussion relies heavily on Lorna J. Philip, 'Planned Villages in South-West Scotland, 1730–1855:

Analysing Functional Characteristics', *Landscapes*, Vol. 6, No. 1, 2005, pp. 83–107.

32 A. J. Durie, *Scotland for the Holidays: A History of Tourism in Scotland, 1780–1939* (Tuckwell Press, East Linton, East Lothian, 2003).

33 I discuss fermtouns at greater length in *The Making of the British Landscape*, pp. 309–12.

34 Ibid., pp. 483–6, with references.

CHAPTER THREE — *The Rise of the Civil Engineer: Roads, Canals and Railways*

1 Stephen R. Martin, 'The Long Meadow: An Historical Ecology of Roadsides in Britain', *Landscapes*, Vol. 4, No. 2, 2003, pp. 90–110. 'The Long Meadow' is a term coined in Ireland (ibid., p. 99).

2 Gerry Barnes and Tom Williamson, *Hedgerow History: Ecology, History and Landscape Character* (Windgather Press, Macclesfield, 2006).

3 Quoted in Martin, op. cit. (2003), pp. 95–6.

4 Cynthia Brown, 'Drovers, Cattle and Dung: The Long Trail from Scotland to London', *Proceedings of the Suffolk Institute for Archaeology and History*, Vol. 38, 1996, pp. 428–41.

5 Martin, op. cit. (2003), p. 100.

6 The following section draws heavily on A. R. B. Haldane, *The Drove Roads of Scotland*, reprinted 2008 (Birlinn, Edinburgh). This superb book is the standard work, unlikely ever to be wholly replaced.

7 Ibid., pp. 168–86.

8 Road classification was one of the first achievements of the new Ministry of Transport, created in 1919. Initially routes were graded into Classes 1 and 2. See Trevor Rowley, *The English Landscape in the Twentieth Century* (Hambledon Continuum, London, 2006), p. 20.

9 For an excellent introduction to the complex archaeology of turnpikes see Geoffrey N. Wright, *Turnpike Roads* (first published 1992), reprinted 2008 (Shire Publications, Botley, Oxford).

10 At Maesol Farm and Cae'r-llo Farm. Jamie Quartermaine, Barrie Trinder and Rick Turner, *Thomas Telford's Holyhead Road: The A5 in North Wales*, Council for British Archaeology, Report No. 135, pp. 67–8 (York, 2003).

11 Christopher Taylor, *The Cambridgeshire Landscape* (Hodder & Stoughton, London, 1973), p. 227.

12 The archaeological monuments along the road have been superbly described and assessed by Quartermaine, Trinder and Turner, op. cit. (2003).

13 Ibid., pp. 71–2.

14 Ibid., p. 77.

15 R. A. Buchanan, *Industrial Archaeology in Britain* (Penguin Books, Harmondsworth, 1972), p. 296.

16 R. Hayman, *Ironmaking: The History and Archaeology of the Iron Industry* (Tempus Books, Stroud, 2005), pp. 60–62.

17 For a good summary of early canals see Buchanan, op. cit. (1972), pp. 292–303.

18 Marilyn Palmer and Peter Neaverson, *Industry in the Landscape, 1700–1900* (Routledge, London, 1994), pp. 173–4; David Blagrove, *The Canal at Stoke Bruerne* (The Canal Museum, Stoke Bruerne, 1971).

19 D. M. MacRaild and A. W. Purdue, 'The North East: Modern Period', in Fred Aalen (ed.), *England's Landscape: The North East* (English Heritage and HarperCollins, London, 2006), p. 94.

20 Stephen Grenter, 'The Bersham Ironworks', *Current Archaeology*, No. 141, December 1995, pp. 332–5.

21 David Jenkinson, *Rails in the Fells: A Railway Case Study*, 2nd edn (Peco Publications, Beer Seaton, Devon, 1980).

22 See G. Tyler, *The Railway Years in Chapel le Dale 1870–77* (Friends of St Leonard's Church, Chapel-le-Dale, North Yorkshire, 2001).

23 *Risehill Tunnel Navvy Camp, Cumbria: Archaeological Evaluation and*

Assessment of Results. Wessex Archaeology Report 68737 (Salisbury, Wiltshire, December 2008).

24 M. Morris, 'Towards an Archaeology of Navvy Huts and Settlements of the Industrial Revolution', *Antiquity*, Vol. 68, 1994, pp. 573–84.

25 Information kindly provided by Roderick Luis.

26 D. Brooke, 'Railway Navvies on the Pennines, 1841–71', *Journal of Transport History*, New Series, Vol. 3, No. 1, February 1975, pp. 41–53.

27 The following paragraph draws heavily on Tyler, op. cit. (2001), pp. 84–94.

28 Patrolling volunteers sell passengers an excellent booklet on the line: David Toothill and Marian Armstrong, *The Settle Carlisle Railway* (Settle–Carlisle Railway Development Company, 2008). The recent upsurge in freight traffic is discussed on pp. 16–17.

29 My thoughts on motorways owe much to Trevor Rowley, op. cit. (2006), pp. 11–52.

30 This anecdote is based on a story in *Current Archaeology*, No. 228, March 2009, p. 8.

CHAPTER FOUR — *Rapid Expansion: The Growth of Towns and Cities*

1 I discuss recent trends in urban archaeology further in *Britain in the Middle Ages*, pp. 188–9.

2 Ibid., pp. 266–70.

3 Brian Short, *England's Landscape: The South East* (Collins and English Heritage, London, 2006).

4 Caron Newman and Richard Newman, 'Housing the Workforce in 19th-century East Lancashire: Past Processes, Enduring Perceptions and Contemporary Meanings', *Post-Medieval Archaeology*, Vol. 42, No. 1, 2008, pp. 181–200.

5 *Britain in the Middle Ages*, pp. 165–71.

6 Alan died in February 2009. Obituary: *The Archaeologist*, No. 71, Spring 2009, p. 52.

7 Roger M. Thomas, 'Mapping the Towns: English Heritage's Urban Survey and Characterisation Programme', *Landscapes*, Vol. 7, No. 1, 2006, pp. 68–92.

8 The best and most accessible introduction to HLC is one entire volume of English Heritage's *Conservation Bulletin*, Issue 47, Winter 2004–5.

9 Thomas, op. cit. (2006), p. 68.

10 Ibid., p. 75.

11 David Crossley, 'Water Power in the Landscape: The Rivers of the Sheffield Area', in Barker and Cranstone, *The Archaeology of Industrialization* (2004), pp. 79–88.

12 Thomas, op. cit. (2006), p. 87.

13 Nicholas Barton, *The Lost Rivers of London* (Leicester University Press, 1962, republished 1992 by Historical Publications Ltd, London).

14 Greater London in post-medieval times has been comprehensively discussed by John Schofield, 'Post-Medieval London: The Expanding Metropolis', in Monica Kendall (ed.), *The Archaeology of Greater London: An Assessment of Archaeological Evidence for Human Presence in the Area Now Covered by Greater London* (Museum of London, 2000), pp. 255–82. For a more recent overview see Short, op. cit. (2006), pp. 161–96.

15 Nixon and Sloane, in Kendall, op. cit. (2000), p. xi.

16 The following paragraphs rely heavily on Schofield, op. cit. (2000).

17 *Britain in the Middle Ages*, p. 219.

18 Jo Lyon. '"This wooden O". The Rediscovery of Shakespeare's First Theatre', *Current Archaeology*, No. 225, December 2008, p. 15.

19 The discovery of the Rose was first revealed in *Current Archaeology*, No. 115, June 1989, pp. 243–4. My main source of information on both the Rose and the Globe has been Hedley Swain et al., 'Shakespeare's Theatres', *Current Archaeology*, No. 124, May 1991, pp. 185–9.

20 Lyon, op. cit. (2008).

21 Rosemary Sweet, *Antiquaries: The Discovery of the Past in Eighteenth-Century Britain* (Hambledon and London, 2004), pp. 114–15.

22 Neil Rhind, *Blackheath Village and Environs 1790–1970* (Bookshop Blackheath Ltd, London, 1983), pp. 43–52.

23 Domesday mentions there is land for four ploughs, four acres of meadow and woodland for fifteen pigs. Ann Williams and G. H. Martin (eds), *Domesday Book* (Penguin Books, London, 2002), p. 16.

24 Quoted from Rhind, op. cit. (1983), p. 45.

25 I discuss the situation in London at the time in *Britain in the Middle Ages*, pp. 165–7.

26 O. Owen, 'Sound Foundations: Archaeology in Scotland's Towns and Cities and the Role of the Scottish Burgh Survey', *Antiquity*, Vol. 76, 2002, pp. 802–7.

27 Ibid., p. 802.

28 E. P. Dennison and R. Coleman, *Historic North Queensferry and Peninsula*, the Scottish Burgh Survey (Historic Scotland, Edinburgh, 2000).

29 W. G. Hoskins quotes an example in Nottingham: *The Making of the English Landscape* (Penguin Books, Harmondsworth, 1955), p. 285.

30 I discuss both in chapter 13 of *The Making of the British Landscape*.

31 The railway town and the engineering works at Swindon have been discussed in a beautifully illustrated report by John Cattell and Keith Falconer, *Swindon, Legacy of a Railway Town* (English Heritage, Swindon, 1995).

32 The Booth maps are held at the London School of Economics and can be visited at http://booth.lse.ac.uk

33 The following paragraphs are based on The Hungate Special Issue, *Yorkshire Archaeology Today*, No. 12, Spring 2007 (York Archaeological Trust).

34 For a comparable excavation of an impoverished nineteenth-century urban area see 'Excavating the Slums of Belfast', *Current Archaeology*, No. 229, November 2009, pp. 32–9.

CHAPTER FIVE — *Dynamic, but Diverse: The Development of Industrial Britain*

1 Paul Belford, 'Rethinking Industrial Origins', *British Archaeology*, No. 107, July/August 2009, p. 25.

2 This account draws heavily upon N. Cossons and B. Trinder, *The Iron Bridge: Symbol of the Industrial Revolution*, 2nd edn (Phillimore, Chichester, 2002).

3 The discussion of excavations at Wednesbury and Upper Forge, Ironbridge, is based on Belford, op. cit. (2009), pp. 30–35.

4 For other famous ironmasters see Richard Hayman, *Ironmaking: The History and Archaeology of the Iron Industry* (Tempus Books, Stroud, 2005), pp. 94–103.

5 British history can be a perplexing topic. *The Oxford Dictionary of British History* only mentions Abraham Darby I and deals with his achievements in ten lines. By way of contrast, the various Earls of Derby are together given approximately one hundred lines.

6 For more on workers in the iron industry see Hayman, op. cit. (2005), pp. 104–15.

7 For an excellent account of the cotton process and its effect on the form and shape of mills: I. Miller and C. Wild, *A & G Murray and the Cotton Mills of Ancoats*, Lancaster Imprints 13 (Oxford Archaeology North, Lancaster, 2007).

8 Ian Mellor, 'Space, Society and the Textile Mill', *Industrial Archaeology Review*, Vol. 27, No. 1, 2005, pp. 49–56.

9 For some good examples of enabling development see *IMPACT*, the annual report of the Historic Environment Enabling Programme, Special Edition, 2004–6 (English Heritage Commissions, London). Their website: www.english-heritage.org.uk/HEEP

10 The best account of Owen and New Lanark is by Ian Donnachie and George Hewitt, *Historic New Lanark* (Edinburgh University Press, 1993).

11 Ibid., pp. 65–6.

12 *The Story of New Lanark* (New Lanark Trust, undated).

13 There is a display on the Mepal Colony in the Octavia Hill Birthplace Museum, 1 South Brink Place, Wisbech, PE13 1JE. See also the Welney website: www.welney.org.uk/Manea_colony.htm

14 David Crossley, 'English Woodlands and the Supply of Fuel for Industry', *Industrial Archaeology Review*, Vol. 27, No. 1, pp. 105–12.

15 And Darby was not the first man to use coke for smelting. He was the first to do so in a commercially viable way. See Hayman, op. cit., pp. 34–45.

16 Ibid., p. 23.

17 Francis Pryor and David Collison, *Now Then: Digging up the Past* (Batsford Books, London, 1993), pp. 44–6.

18 Adult miners were self-employed and were only paid for what they produced, but the mining company would issue them with a 15/- (62½p) weekly advance. Ian Forbes, 'Whar a candel will not burn': The Story of Park Level Mine (Durham County Council, 1996), p. 27.

19 Ian Forbes, *Spar Boxes: Secret Worlds of the North Pennines* (Killhope Lead Mining Museum, undated).

20 D. Cranstone, 'The Archaeology of Washing Floors: Problems, Potentials and Priorities', *Industrial Archaeology Review*, Vol. 12, No. 1, pp. 40–49.

21 For the surface features at Killhope see Ian Forbes, *Lead and Life at Killhope* (Durham County Council, 1987), and for the Park Level Mine itself, Forbes, op. cit. (1996).

22 Ian Forbes, Brian Young, Clive Crossley and Lesley Hehir, *Lead Mining Landscapes of the North Pennines Area of Outstanding Natural Beauty* (Durham County Council, 2003).

23 The following paragraphs draw extensively on Alan Blackburn, 'From Pick to Powder – Phases of Change in a North Pennine Landscape', in Barker and Cranstone, *The Archaeology of Industrialization* (2004), pp. 103–17.

24 Martin Roe, 'Lead Mining Archaeology in the Yorkshire Dales', *Landscapes*, Vol. 4, No. 1, 2003, pp. 65–78.

25 The Peak District Mines Historical Society maintains an excellent website: www.tidza.demon.co.uk

26 Palmer and Neaverson, *Industrial Archaeology: Principles and Practice* (1998), pp. 30–31.

27 David Hey and John Rodwell, 'Wombwell: The Landscape History of a South Yorkshire Coalfield Township', *Landscapes*, Vol. 7, No. 2, Autumn 2006, pp. 24–47.

28 Ibid., pp. 42–4.

29 Ibid., pp. 44–5.

30 The quotation forms the title of an excellent edition of historical accounts of life in and around Coalbrookdale, by Barrie Trinder, *'The Most Extraordinary District in the World': Ironbridge and Coalbrookdale* (Phillimore, Chichester, 2005).

31 Hudson, *Industrial Archaeology: An Introduction* (1963), pp. 69–70.

32 Effie Photos-Jones, Chris Dalglish, Scott Coulter, Allan J. Hall, Rocio Ruiz-Nieto and Lyn Wilson, 'Between Archives and the Site: The 19th-Century Iron and Steel Industry in the Monklands, Central Scotland', *Post-Medieval Archaeology*, Vol. 42, Part 1, pp. 157–80.

CHAPTER SIX — *Capitalism Triumphant: Markets, Trade and Consumers*

1 For a recent overview see Alasdair Brooks, 'The View from Afar: International Perspectives on the Analysis of post-1750 Ceramics in Britain and Ireland', in Horning and Palmer (eds), *Crossing Paths or Sharing Tracks? Future Directions in the Archaeological Study of Post-1550 Britain and Ireland* (2008), pp. 287–300.

2 The best book on the manufacture, decoration and use of pottery is by Anna O. Shepard, *Ceramics for the Archaeologist*, Publication 609, Carnegie Institution of Washington (Washington DC, 1971).

3 I have decided to avoid discussing the rise of market economies that are truly free – very few were. Instead, I suggest readers refer to my *Britain in the Middle Ages* (pp. 41–54) where I discuss the *wics* (trading communities) of Middle Saxon England.

4 Nigel Woodcock and Rob Strachan, *Geological History of Britain and Ireland* (Blackwell, Oxford, 2000), p. 334.

5 Richard Hillier, *Clay That Burns: A History of the Fletton Brick Industry* (London Brick Company, London, 1981).

6 Palmer and Neaverson, *Industry in the Landscape, 1700–1900* (1994), pp. 129–33.

7 As we saw earlier, this scarcity may have been more apparent than real. David Crossley, 'English Woodlands and the Supply of Fuel for Industry', *Industrial Archaeology Review*, Vol. 27, No. 1, pp. 105–12.

8 David Dawson and Oliver Kent, 'The Development of the Bottle Kiln in Pottery Manufacture in Britain', *Post-Medieval Archaeology*, Vol. 42, Part 1, pp. 201–26.

9 Ibid., pp. 212–22.

10 Ibid., pp. 221–2.

11 I discuss Ipswich Ware in *Britain in the Middle Ages*, pp. 57–67.

12 Paul Courtney, 'Pathways to Change: Towards a Long-term Analysis of the Ceramic Industry', in Barker and Cranstone (eds), *The Archaeology of Industrialization* (Maney Publishing, Leeds, 2004), pp. 181–201.

13 '… a truly revolutionary transformation', ibid., p. 191. I have drawn extensively on two main sources: David Barker, 'The Industrialization of the Staffordshire Potteries', in Barker and Cranstone, op. cit. (2004), pp. 203–21, and Alasdair Brooks, 'The View from Afar: International Perspectives on the Analysis of post-1750 Ceramics in Britain and Ireland', in Horning and Palmer, op. cit. (2008), pp. 287–300.

14 Courtney, 'Pathways to Change', in Barker and Cranstone, op. cit. (2004), p. 191.

15 Barker, op. cit. (2004), p. 210.

16 Ibid, pp. 212–13.

17 Ibid., p. 214.

18 www.thepotteries.org

19 For a superb overview of the archaeology of craft workshops see P. S. Barnwell, Marilyn Palmer and Malcolm Airs, *The Vernacular Workshop: From Craft to Industry, 1400–1900*, Council for British Archaeology Research Report 140 (York, 2004). Sometimes small workshops come to light during the excavation of other buildings; see, for example, Simon Cox, 'Excavation of a Tannery, Quaker Meeting House and Methodist Tabernacle at Broadmead, Bristol', *Post-Medieval Archaeology*, Vol. 42, Part 2, 2008, pp. 333–7.

20 N. McKendrick, J. Brewer and J. Plumb, *The Birth of a Consumer Society: The Commercialisation of 18th Century England* (Europa, London), 1982.

21 These paragraphs draw heavily on Ross J. Wilson, 'The Mystical Value of Commodities': The Consumer Society in 18th-century England', *Post-Medieval Archaeology*, Vol. 42, Part 1, 2008, pp. 144–56. For a further summary of recent critiques of the eighteenth-century 'consumer society', see Barker, op. cit. (2004), p. 203.

22 This bias towards our own time and culture is termed 'ethnocentricity' and I discuss it further in *Britain BC*, p. 270.

23 The paper is about the role of familiar constellations in promoting relations between the native population and colonists in the Virginia colony. Kathryn Sikes, 'Stars as Social Space? Contextualising 17th-century Chesapeake Star-motif Pipes', *Post-Medieval Archaeology*, Vol. 42, Part 1, pp. 75–103.

24 Wilson, op. cit. (2008), pp. 147–51.

25 Ibid., p. 147.

26 Ibid.

27 Ibid., p. 148.

28 By this period nationality is becoming irrelevant. For two informative studies of the early days of modern consumerism see papers by Liv Ramskjaer (on mid-twentieth-century Norway) and Louise Trottier (Canada, 1920–90), in Marilyn Palmer and Peter Neaverson (eds), *From Industrial Revolution to Consumer Revolution* (The Association for Industrial Archaeology, 2001), pp. 111–18 and 119–27.

29 J. G. Coad, 'A Major Industry before the Industrial Revolution: Great Britain's Royal Dockyards', in Palmer and Neaverson (2001), pp. 23–9.

30 Two first-rate naval histories by N. A. M. Rodger: *The Safeguard of the Sea: A Naval History of Britain, 660–1649* (Penguin, London, 1997) and *The Command of the Ocean: A Naval History of Britain, 1649–1815* (Penguin, London, 2004).

31 J. G. Coad, *The Royal Dockyards 1690–1850* (Scolar Press, Aldershot, 1989).

32 Ibid. (2001), p. 29.

33 Rodger, op. cit. (1997), p. 63.

34 The following paragraphs draw heavily on Coad, op. cit. (2001).

35 Coad, op. cit., p. 24.

36 Cranstone, op. cit. (2009).

37 Angus Winchester, 'Moving Through the Landscape', in Angus Winchester (ed.), *England's Landscape: The North West* (English Heritage/Collins, London, 2006), pp. 63–4.

38 Here I am thinking most particularly of the series of excellent studies of early industrialisation by Mike Nevell and his colleagues in Tameside, Greater Manchester. See, for example, Michael Nevell with Brian Grimsditch and Carolanne King, *Carrbrook: A Textile Village and its Valley. A Study in the Industrialisation of the Pennine Uplands* (Tameside MBC, 2006); Michael Nevell and John Walker, 'Industrialization in the Countryside: The Roles of the Lord, Freeholder and Tenant in the Manchester Area, 1600–1900', in Barker and Cranstone, op. cit. (2004), pp. 53–77.

39 For an excellently illustrated account see Colum Giles and Bob Hawkins, *Storehouses of Empire: Liverpool's Historic Warehouses* (English Heritage, London, 2004).

40 I have reproduced this in *The Making of the British Landscape*, p. 529.

41 M. W. Barley, *A Guide to British Topographical Collections* (Council for British Archaeology, London, 1974).

42 One of my most cherished possessions: Ralph Hyde, *A Prospect of Britain: The Town Plans of Samuel and Nathaniel Buck* (Pavilion Books, London, 1994).

43 Ibid., p. 10.

44 Giles and Hawkins, op. cit. (2004), p. 7.

45 Ibid., p. 5.

46 I discuss (with references) Birkenhead and other urban parks in chapter 13 of *The Making of the British Landscape*.

47 Ibid., pp. 425–7.

48 A. G. Crosby, 'The Quest for Utopia', in Winchester, op. cit. (2006), pp. 184–5.

49 James Schmiechen and Kenneth Carls, *The British Market Hall: A Social and Architectural History* (Yale University Press, New Haven and London, 1999), pp. 3–29.

CHAPTER SEVEN — *The Big Society: Faith, Justice and Charity*

1 All the Pevsner guides have excellent illustrated glossaries of architectural terms such as these.

2 My attention was drawn to the extraordinary tombs at Bottesford by Candida Lycett Green's 'Unwrecked Britain' column in *The Oldie*, May 2009, pp. 56–7. Visit www.theoldie. co.uk

3 Nikolaus Pevsner and Elizabeth Williamson, *The Buildings of England: Leicestershire and Rutland*, 2nd edn (Yale University Press, New Haven and London, 1984), pp. 105–7.

4 Edward A. Shipman, *Gleanings About the Church of St. Mary the Virgin, Bottesford* (Parochial Church Council of St Mary the Virgin, Bottesford, Leicestershire, 1995).

5 Readers of my *Seahenge* (HarperCollins, London, 2001) might like to know that the timbers have been conserved and are now permanently displayed in a splendid new gallery at King's Lynn Museum.

6 This account is based on *Little Gidding: An Illustrated History and Guide*, 2nd edn (Friends of Little Gidding, Huntingdon, 2006) and Nikolaus Pevsner, *The Buildings of England: Bedfordshire, Huntingdon and Peterborough* (Yale University Press, New Haven and London, 1968), pp. 284–6.

7 Pryor, *Seahenge*, p. 34.

8 Sarah Tarlow has made a special study of the archaeology of graveyards and has written a number of fine papers. Here I have used two: 'Reformation and Transformation: What Happened to Catholic Things in a Protestant World', in Gaimster and Gilchrist (eds), *The Archaeology of Reformation 1480–1580* (2003), pp. 108–21, and 'Death and Commemoration', *Industrial Archaeology Review*, Vol. 27, No. 1, 2005, pp. 163–9.

9 Tarlow, op cit. (2005), p. 166.

10 *Nonconformist Chapels and Meeting-houses of Central England* (1986); *South-West England* (1991); *North of England* (1994); and *Eastern England* (2002). Today they are published by English Heritage (Kemble Drive, Swindon).

11 J. Prentice, 'The Tin Tabernacle, Havelock Street, Desborough', *Northamptonshire Archaeology*, Vol. 35, 2008, pp. 271–6.

12 Essential reading: Gordon Thorburn, *Men and Sheds* (New Holland, London, 2002).

13 Sharman Kadish, 'Jewish Heritage UK: New Research and Recording', English Heritage, *Conservation Bulletin*, Issue 46, Autumn 2004, pp. 29–31.

14 Sarah Brown, 'The Shah Jehan Mosque, Woking', English Heritage, *Conservation Bulletin*, Issue 46, Autumn 2004, pp. 32–4.

15 For the Caxton gibbet see Enid Porter, *Cambridgeshire Customs and Folklore* (Routledge, London, 1969), pp. 184–5.

16 Nicola Whyte, 'The Deviant Dead in the Norfolk Landscape', *Landscapes*, Vol. 4, No. 1, 2003, pp. 24–39.

17 For various Gallow or Gallows Hills – gallows on top of Bronze Age barrows – in Norfolk, see Andrew Lawson, Edward Martin and Deborah Priddy, 'The Barrows of East Anglia', *East Anglian Archaeology*, Vol. 12 (Norwich, 1981), p. 12.

18 Whyte, op. cit. (2003), p. 36.

19 Ibid., p. 37.

20 Ibid.

21 Andy Reid, *Gressenhall Workhouse: An Historical Introduction*, 2nd edn, Norfolk Museums and Archaeology Service (Gressenhall, Norfolk, 2002).

22 The two paragraphs on the Poor Laws are based on J. Cannon (ed.), *The Oxford Dictionary of British History* (Oxford University Press, 2001), pp. 517–18.

23 Reid, op. cit. (2002), p. 5.

24 Sarah Rutherford, 'Victorian and Edwardian Institutional Landscapes in England', *Landscapes*, Vol. 5, No. 2, 2004, p. 25.

25 The following discussion is based on Rutherford, op. cit., pp. 25–41.

26 Source: www.timesonline.co.uk, August 2009.

27 Rutherford, op. cit. (2004), p. 33.

28 Chamberlain, *Hell Upon Water: Prisoners of War in Britain 1793–1815* (2008), pp. 93–6.

29 The following paragraphs rely heavily on Victoria Oleksy, 'Conformity and Resistance in the Victorian Penal System: Archaeological Excavations at Parliament House, Edinburgh', *Post-Medieval Archaeology*, Vol. 42, Part 2, 2008, pp. 276–303.

30 Ibid., p. 298.

31 For a first-rate account go to: www. cambridgeshirehistory.com/People/ riots/littleportriot.html

CHAPTER EIGHT — *The First Superpower: Defence and Security*

1 The DoB database is now housed at the Archaeology Data Service. Go to: http://ads.ahds.ac.uk

2 Ian J. Sanders, *Pillboxes: Images of an Unfought Battle* (Pillbox Study Group: ISBN 1-4116-2651-6). For a useful summary of the principal twentieth-century defensive monuments and their classification, see Bernard Lowry (ed.), *20th Century Defences in Britain: An Introductory Guide*, Council for British Archaeology Practical Handbooks in Archaeology, No. 12 (York, 1996).

3 For an excellent introduction to post-medieval defensive works, see Bernard Lowry, *Discovering Fortifications from the Tudors to the Cold War* (Shire Books, Princes Risborough, 2006).

4 I discuss Hurst Castle in chapter 13 of *The Making of the British Landscape*.

5 I discuss Palmerston forts in ibid., pp. 567–71.

6 Ibid., chapter 10.

7 The following account of Landguard Fort is based on Jezz Meredith, 'Excavation at Landguard Fort: An Investigation of the 17th-century Defences', *Post-Medieval Archaeology*, Vol. 42, Part 2 (2008), pp. 229–72.

8 Lowry, op. cit. (2006), pp. 92–5.

9 Paul Pattison, 'Documentary Evidence' in ibid., pp. 231–42.

10 Cuddesdon and Dorchester-on-Thames, Oxfordshire: two early Saxon 'princely' sites in Wessex, British Archaeological Reports, No. 1 (Oxford, 1974).

11 In addition to numerous more specialised works, Oswald also wrote an excellent introduction to the subject: A. Oswald, *Clay Pipes for the Archaeologist*, British Archaeological Reports, British Series, No. 14.

12 I discuss the formation of the Scottish Highland road system in *The Making of the British Landscape*, chapter 10.

13 See *Britain BC*, pp. 399–400.

14 I argue in the closing passages of *Britain in the Middle Ages* (pp. 307–9) that the perceived chasm separating the Muslim East from the secular or Christian West is not as deep as some would have us think.

15 The standard account of the Norman Cross Depot is by T. J. Walker, *The Depot for Prisoners of War at Norman Cross, Huntingdonshire, 1796 to 1816* (Constable, London, 1915). For an excellent discussion of Napoleonic prisoners of war in Britain see Paul Chamberlain, *Hell Upon Water: Prisoners of War in Britain 1793–1815* (The History Press, Stroud, 2008).

16 The *Time Team* dig formed the basis of an excellent article by Andy Brockman, 'Digging up Dad's Army: The Archaeology of World War II on Shooters Hill', *Current Archaeology*, No. 228, March 2009, pp. 35–42.

17 For more on stop lines and the subsequent story, see Mike Osborne, *Defending Britain: Twentieth-century Military Structures in the Landscape* (Tempus Books, Stroud, 2004).

18 Ibid., pp. 13, 225.

19 Sarah Newsome, 'The Coastal Landscapes of Suffolk during the Second World War', *Landscapes*, Vol. 4, No. 2, 2003, pp. 42–58.

20 Osborne, op. cit. (2004), p. 24.

21 Foot, *Beaches, fields, streets, and hills … the anti-invasion landscapes of England, 1940* (2006), pp. 151–6.

22 Ibid., pp. 79–80.

23 Wayne D. Cocroft and Roger J. C. Thomas, *Cold War: Building for Nuclear Confrontation 1946–1989* (English Heritage, London, 2003).

24 Ibid., pp. 225–7.

25 I illustrate a good example, at Newton, Cambridgeshire, in *The Making of the British Landscape*, p. 586.

26 Bob Clarke, *Four-Minute Warning: Britain's Cold War* (Tempus Books, Stroud, 2005), pp. 200–206.

27 When I finished writing *Britain BC* early in 2003 the earliest site in Britain, at Happisburgh on the Norfolk coast, was then dated to 600,000 years ago. More recent dates (based on the magnetic polarity of the archaeological sediments) reliably suggest that the date should be pushed back a further quarter of a million years. See Simon Parfitt, Nick Ashton and Simon Lewis, 'Happisburgh', *British Archaeology*, No. 114, Sept./Oct. 2010, pp. 14–23.

INDEX